T0301636

Deregulation and its Discontents

Deregulation and its Discontents

Rewriting the Rules in Asia

Edited by

M. Ramesh

National University of Singapore

Michael Howlett

Simon Fraser University, Canada

Edward Elgar

Cheltenham, UK • Northampton, MA, USA

Published by
Edward Elgar Publishing Limited
Glensanda House
Montpellier Parade
Cheltenham
Glos GL50 1UA
UK

Edward Elgar Publishing, Inc.
136 West Street
Suite 202
Northampton
Massachusetts 01060
USA

A catalogue record for this book
is available from the British Library

Library of Congress Cataloguing in Publication Data

Deregulation and its discontents : rewriting the rules in Asia / edited by
M. Ramesh, Michael Howlett.
        p. cm.
    Includes bibliographical references and index.
    1. Deregulation—Asia. I. Ramesh, M., 1960– II. Howlett, Michael, 1955–
        HD3616.A773D47 2006
        338.95—dc22

                                                                        2006044015

ISBN 978 1 84542 877 8

Printed and bound by CPI Group (UK) Ltd, Croydon, CR0 4YY

Contents

v

Figures

Tables

Contributors

Mukul G. Asher

Mukul G. Asher is Professor at the Lee Kuan Yew School of Public Policy, National University of Singapore. He specializes in social security reforms in Asia, public finances in developing countries, and India's economic relations with the rest of Asia. He has published extensively in international journals, and has authored or edited more than ten books. He has been a consultant to multilateral organizations on tax reforms and pension issues in several countries. He is on the editorial advisory board of the International Social Security Review, and Consulting Editor for an online journal eSocialSciences. He has addressed many academic, professional and business gatherings around the world.

Sudeshna G. Banerjee

Sudeshna G. Banerjee is an economist in the Africa Finance, Private Sector, and Infrastructure Unit at the World Bank.

Jane Ebinger

Jane Ebinger is an energy specialist in the Eastern Europe and Central Asia Energy and Infrastructure Unit at the World Bank.

Ashima Goyal

Ashima Goyal is a professor at the Indira Gandhi Institute of Development Research, Mumbai, India. She has been a faculty member in the Delhi School of Economics and Gokhale Institute of Politics and Economics, India, a visiting fellow at the Economic Growth Centre, Yale University, USA, and a Fulbright Senior Research Fellow at Claremont Graduate University, USA. Her research interests are in institutional macroeconomics, the open economy, international finance, development and governance. She is the author of numerous international and national publications, and a book on Developing Economy Macroeconomics. Her research has received national and international awards. She is also active in the Indian policy debate.

Neil Gunningham

Neil Gunningham is an interdisciplinary social scientist specializing in environmental law, policy and regulation. He is currently Professor in the

Regulatory Institutions Network, Research School of Social Sciences, and in the School of Resources Environment and Society at the Australian National University. From 1991–2001 he was Foundation Director of the Australian Centre for Environmental Law also at the ANU. His recent books include: *Shades of Green: Business, Regulation and Environment* (with Robert Kagan and Dorothy Thornton), 2003; and *Leaders and Laggards: Reconfiguring Environmental Regulation* (with Darren Sinclair), 2002.

Anil Hira

Anil Hira is Associate Professor of Political Science and Latin American Studies at Simon Fraser University, Canada. He also has over ten years of policy-related experience. His main interests are international political economy, development, and industrial and technology policy. He has written two books, *Ideas and Economic Policy in Latin America* (1998), and *Political Economy of the Southern Cone* (2003), and co-authored two others, *Development Projects for a New Millenium* (2004, with Trevor Parfitt) and *Outsourcing America* (2005, with Ron Hira). Other recent publications include: 'The FTAA as a Three Level Bargaining Game', 'Participation and Regulation: An International Survey', 'Regulatory Games States Play: Managing Globalization Through Sectoral Policy', 'Measuring International Electricity Integration: A Comparative Study of the power systems under the Nordic Countries, MERCOSUR, and NAFTA', 'The Distributional Politics of Dollarization: the Latin American Case', 'The Brave New World of International Education', and 'Does Energy Integrate?'. Hira has recently completed a manuscript comparing industrial policy in East Asia and Latin America.

Michael Howlett

Michael Howlett is the Professor and Burnaby Mountain Chair in the Department of Political Science at the Simon Fraser University, Canada. He specializes in public policy analysis, Canadian political economy, and Canadian resource and environmental policy. He is co-author of *Studying Public Policy* (2003, 1995), *In Search of Sustainability* (2001), T*he Political Economy of Canada* (1999, 1992) and *Canadian Natural Resource and Environmental Policy* (1997, 2005). He has edited *Canadian Forest Policy* (2001) and coedited *Executive Styles in Canada* (2005); *Designing Government* (2005); *The Real Worlds of Canadian Politics* (2004); *The Provincial State In Canada* (1992 & 2000); *Innovation Systems in a Global Context* (1998); *Policy Studies in Canada* (1996), and *The Puzzles of Power* (1994, 1998). His articles have been published in numerous professional journals in Canada, the United States, Europe, Brazil, New Zealand and Australia. Dr Howlett is currently English Language Co-editor of the

Canadian Journal of Political Science (2002–2006) and *Encounters: Political Science in Translation*, Book Review Editor of the *Journal of Comparative Policy Analysis*.

Irina Klytchnikova

Irina Klytchnikova is an economist in the Latin America and Caribbean Infrastructure Unit at the World Bank.

Julian A. Lampietti

Julian A. Lampietti is a Senior Economist working for the World Bank. He has written extensively on the poverty and social impacts of power sector reform in Europe and Central Asia. His research interests are in modelling household behaviour in response to policy conditionalities. Mr Lampietti has a Masters degree in environmental economics from Duke University and a PhD in Public Policy from the University of North Carolina at Chapel Hill.

Amarendu Nandy

Amarendu Nandy is completing his Doctorate in Economics at the National University of Singapore. His core research interests are in issues relating to international migration, and social security reforms. He has published articles and book reviews in journals such as *International Social Security Review, Policy and Society*, *ASEAN Economic Bulletin*, and *South Asia Economic Journal*. He has also contributed chapters to several edited books.

Jon M. Peha

Jon M. Peha is Associate Director of the Center for Wireless and Broadband Networking at Carnegie Mellon University, and Professor of Electrical Engineering and Public Policy. He leads research on technical and policy issues of information and communications technology (ICT), including Internet, telephone, wireless, and e-commerce systems. Dr Peha actively consults for companies and government agencies around the world. He has previously launched a US Government programme to assist developing countries with their information infrastructure, and been Chief Technical Officer for several ICT companies. Dr Peha has also served on legislative staff in the US Congress, where he specialized in telecommunications and electronic commerce.

M. Ramesh

M. Ramesh is Associate Professor at the Lee Kuan Yew School of Public Policy, National University of Singapore. He is a leading expert on social policies in East and Southeast Asia. He is the author or co-author of *Social Policies in East and Southeast Asia*, *Welfare Capitalism in Southeast Asia*,

Studying Public Policy and *Canadian Political Economy*. He has also published widely in senior refereed journals and is the Editor of the journal *Policy and Society*. His current research is on comparative political economy of the People's Republic of China, India, and Korea. Ramesh has held teaching or visiting appointments in Australia, Canada, Hong Kong, New Zealand, Norway and the USA. He currently teaches business and government, globalization and public policy and social policy.

Gevorg Sargsyan

Gevorg Sargsyan is Senior Infrastructure Specialist in the Eastern Europe and Central Asia Energy and Infrastructure Unit at the World Bank.

Maria Shkaratan

Maria Shkaratan is a consultant in the Eastern Europe and Central Asia Environmentally and Socially Sustainable Development Unit at the World Bank.

Lucas A. Skoufa

Lucas A. Skoufa has been with the University of Queensland Business School, Australia, since 1999. His area of research interest is concerned with the strategic behaviours of electricity generation firms in reformed electricity supply industries. Lucas's specific research interest is concerned with how generation firms can use generation technologies to create and maintain a competitive advantage. Lucas has undergraduate qualifications in mechanical engineering and business and was a Naval Officer and Power Station Engineer before doing the PhD. He is currently in the process of preparing his doctoral dissertation for publication as a book.

Priyambudi Sulistiyanto

Priyambudi Sulistiyanto is Assistant Professor at the Southeast Asian Studies Programme at the National University of Singapore. He is a political scientist and currently teaching Southeast Asia politics, religion and politics in Southeast Asia and Southeast Asian studies. His current research looks at the politics of reconciliation and forgiveness in post-Suharto Indonesia, local politics in Indonesia and the power sector reforms in Southeast Asia. His publications includes *Thailand, Indonesia and Burma in Comparative Perspective* (2002) and *Regionalism in Post-Suharto Indonesia* (with Maribeth Erb and Carole Faucher, 2005). His articles have also appeared in journals published in both English and *Bahasa Indonesia*.

Jessie L. Todoc

Jessie L. Todoc is a researcher and consultant in energy-environment policy, regulation, planning, and markets with ten years of international research and project management experience based in Thailand and four years of Philippine government experience. He has developed, managed, and researched on national and regional projects sponsored by the Asian Development Bank (ADB), Asia Pacific Economic Cooperation (APEC), various energy and environment programmes of the European Commission (EC), Food and Agricultural Organization (FAO), International Atomic Energy Agency (IAEA), International Energy Agency (IEA), New Energy and Industrial Development Organization (NEDO), United Nations Economic and Social Commission for Asia and the Pacific (UNESCAP), and the World Bank. In the Philippines, he held responsible positions with the Energy Regulatory Board (ERB) and Department of Energy (DOE). His specific areas of project experience, research and publications are in power sector privatization, deregulation, and restructuring; regional and international co-operation on energy and environment; energy and sustainable development; coal and natural gas; power tariffs and pricing; and macroeconomic analysis and modelling. Mr Todoc has a bachelor's degree in electrical engineering, an International MBA, and attended graduate studies in industrial economics.

Katelijn Van den Berg
Katelijn Van den Berg is an environmental economist in the Eastern Europe and Central Asia Environmentally and Socially Sustainable Development Unit at the World Bank.

Xun Wu
Xun Wu is Assistant Professor at the Lee Kuan Yew School of Public Policy, National University of Singapore. His research focuses on the political economy of public policy reforms in developing countries. He has published in academic journals such as *Governance*, *Energy Policy*, *Energy Economics*, and *Water Policy*, as well as in edited volumes. His current research interests include electricity sector restructuring in Southeast Asia, corporate governance and corruption, health policy reforms in Asia, and conflict resolution in international river basins. He has consulted for various international organizations such as the World Bank and the International Vaccine Institute. He teaches environmental policy, natural resource management, policy research methods, policy evaluation, and cost-benefit analysis.

Acknowledgements

Most chapters in this volume were presented at the Regulation, Deregulation and Reregulation in Globalizing Asia conference held in Singapore on 22–24 March 2004. The conference was organised and funded by the Master of Public Policy Program (subsequently re-launched as the Lee Kuan Yew School of Public Policy) at the National University of Singapore. The support provided by the Program Director, faculty, and especially staff in hosting the conference is gratefully acknowledged.

1. Preface: the evolution of de/reregulation

Michael Howlett and M. Ramesh

The evolution of regulation as a key policy instrument in the toolbox of modern government is a well known story. From the development of the principle of delegated legislation in the early years of the evolution of the modern state (Gilardi 2002; Page 2001; Thatcher and Stone Sweet 2003) to the first creation of specialized quasi-judicial independent regulatory commissions in the United States after the civil war (Huntington 1952; Eisner 1994a and 1994b), the gradual development of bureaucratic expertise and capacity in the social and economic realms has been oft-told and is a defining characteristic of the predominant policy style found in modern governments (Howlett and Ramesh 2002; Howlett 2004).

Debate about the merits of this development continues in many areas, for example, whether or not regulations are in the public or private interest (Stigler 1975; Posner 1974) and whether or not they contribute to economic efficiency by correcting market failures or instead create new government failures (Le Grand 1991; Wolf 1979, 1987; Zerbe and McCurdy 1999). The discussion has generated a plethora of studies about the merits of particular types of regulation over others (Ringquist *et al.* 2003; Williams 2000), and the difficulties of legislative and judicial oversight of regulatory activities (McCubbins and Lupia 1994; McCubbins and Schwartz 1984; Angus 1974; de Smith 1973), among many other topics.

Much less known is the reversal of regulations – deregulation – and even less about its twin: reregulation. Studies are very limited with respect to clarifying the general historical process through which deregulation has occurred and answering associated questions relating to whose interest it serves or detailing the specific aspects of the administrative difficulties associated with it. Some early studies of deregulation initiatives in North America and Europe exist (Beesley 1992; Collier 1998; Gayle and Goodrich 1990; Richardson 1990; Rubsamen 1989; Swann 1988), as do some theoretical works attempting to explain the origins of the deregulatory initiative (Crew and Rowley 1986; Derthick and Quirk 1985; Daugbjerg 1997; Hammond and Knott 1988; Lazer and Mayer-Schonberger 2002), but these are limited and suggestive, rather than definitive in nature.

Only a few works exist that examine the third phase in the regulatory–deregulation cycle, that of reregulation (for examples, see Steven Vogel 1996, David Vogel 2005 and Hira *et al.* 2005). Just as public interest, capture, and lifecycle theories of regulation (Stigler 1975; Posner 1974; Bernstein 1955) have great difficulty explaining deregulation, so do most existing theories of deregulation as the inevitable result of globalized 'race-to-the-bottom' encounter problems in explaining the reregulatory initiative (Crew and Rowley 1986). This book attempts to go some way to filling this void by addressing these two under-examined phases of the 'regulatory cycle' in the context of recent developments in the Asia-Pacific region.

REGULATION: BACKGROUND AND THEORY

There are numerous definitions of regulation, but most tend to be quite restrictive in focus (Mitnick 1978). A good general one is offered by Michael Reagan, who defines it as 'a process or activity in which government requires or proscribes certain activities or behaviour on the part of individuals and institutions, mostly private but sometimes public, and does so through a continuing administrative process, generally through specially designated regulatory agencies' (Reagan 1987). Thus, regulation is a prescription by the government which must be complied with by the intended targets; failure to do so usually involves a penalty. This type of policy instrument is often referred to as 'command and control' regulation.

Some regulations, like ones dealing with criminal behaviour, are laws and involve the police and judicial system in their enforcement. Most regulations, however, are administrative edicts created under the terms of enabling legislation and administered on a continuing basis by a government department or a specialized, quasi-judicial government agency (called an independent regulatory commission in the USA) which is more or less autonomous of government control in its day-to-day operations. Regulations take various forms and include rules, standards, permits, prohibition, laws and executive orders among others. Although not always apparent they govern for instance the price and standards of a wide variety of goods and services we consume, including the quality of the water we drink and the air we breathe.

The nature of regulations varies somewhat depending on whether they are targeted towards the economic or social spheres of human activity. Economic regulations control aspects of the production processes specific to particular goods and services, such as the prices and volumes of production, or return on investment, or the entry into or exit of firms from an industry. Their objective is often to correct perceived imbalances or inequities in economic relationships that may emerge as a result of the operation of market forces. Economic regulations have been the traditional form of regulation; their social counterparts are of more recent origin (Salamon 2002).

Social regulations refer to controls in matters of health, safety and social practices such as the protection of civil rights and the prevention of discrimination of various sorts. They have more to do with our physical and moral well-being than with our pocket-books (Reagan 1987). Examples of social regulation include rules regarding liquor consumption and sales, gambling, consumer product safety, occupational hazards, water-related hazards, air pollution, noise pollution, discrimination on the basis of religion, race, gender or ethnicity, and the control of pornography, among other vices (Padberg 1992). Many areas of regulation, like environmental protection, exist as hybrids between pure economic and pure social regulation, because, while the problems may have economic origins, their adverse effects are mostly social. While there is a great deal of overlap between the two, social regulations tend to be more general than economic ones and do not focus on particular industries (for example, banks or telecommunications) as do economic regulations, but on broader problems or functions such as pollution, safety or morality (May 2002). This has important implications for their administration and enforcement as social regulation tends to cut across several industries and come under the jurisdiction of several government agencies.

There are several advantages to governments of using regulation as a policy instrument (Mitnick 1980). First, the information needed to establish regulation is less than with many other tools because a government need not know in advance the subject's preferences, as is necessary in the case of other instruments. It can just establish a standard, for example, a permitted pollution level, and expect compliance. This is also unlike the situation with financial incentives which will not elicit a favourable response from regulatees unless their intended subjects have a preference for them. Second, where a concerned activity is deemed entirely undesirable, such as is the case with films and videos depicting paedophilia, prohibiting the possession of such products is preferable to other options such as devising ways of encouraging the production and distribution of other types of more benign goods or services. Third, regulations allow for better co-ordination of government efforts and planning because of the greater predictability they entail with respect to target behaviour. Fourth, this predictability makes them a more suitable instrument at certain times, such as crises, when an immediate government response to a problem is needed. Fifth, regulations may be less costly than other instruments such as subsidies or tax incentives. Finally, regulations may also be politically appealing if the public or policy sub-system desires quick and definite action on the part of the government.

The disadvantages of regulation are equally telling. First, regulations quite often distort voluntary or private sector activities and can promote economic inefficiencies. Price regulations and direct allocation restrict the operation of the forces of demand and supply and affect the price mechanism, thus causing sometimes unpredictable economic distortions in the market. Restrictions on entry to and exit from industrial sectors, for example, can reduce competition and thus have a negative impact on prices. Second, regulations can, at times, inhibit innovation and technological progress because of the market security they afford existing firms and the limited opportunities for experimentation they permit. Third, regulations are often inflexible and do not permit the consideration of individual circumstances, resulting in decisions and outcomes not intended by the regulation (Dyerson and Mueller 1993). Social regulations are particularly problematic. It is almost impossible to specify in many instances exactly what is acceptable under regulation. The use of phrases such as 'safe and effective' drugs, for instance, allows for too much uncertainty. If the regulation specifies specific standards, however, then it can become irrelevant in new circumstances (Bardach 1989). Fourth, in terms of administration, it may simply not be possible to set regulations for every undesired activity. For example, there are millions of pollutants; a special regulatory would be required for each if this instrument were chosen for policy purposes. Finally, the cost of enforcement by regulatory commissions may be high because the costs of information, investigation and prosecution in regulating enforcement may make policy-making unnecessarily legalistic, adversarial, time-consuming and expensive.

The early 1980s saw a turn in the debate on regulations as the idea that regulations were conceived and executed solely in the public interest came under heavy attack from a range of critics. Much of this criticism relied heavily on works by authors of the Chicago and Virginia schools of political economy who showed how regulations could be inefficient as well as inequitable (for examples of the former, see Becker 1983; Peltzman 1976; Stigler 1971. For the latter, see Buchanan and Tollison 1984; Landes and Posner 1975; Posner 1974; Tollison 1991). Politicians like Ronald Reagan and Margaret Thatcher further fanned popular sentiments against regulations and put deregulation at the centre of economic policy reform agendas right around the world.

As a part of broader efforts to roll back the size and scope of government, governments began to experiment with less intrusive regulations, including delegated regulation and self-regulation. Unlike the situation with command and control regulation, in these instances governments allow non-governmental actors to regulate themselves. Delegated regulations can be explicit and direct, such as when governments allow professions such as doctors, lawyers or teachers to regulate themselves through the grant of a licensing monopoly to a bar association or a College of Physicians and Surgeons, or a Teacher's College (Sinclair 1997; Tuohy and Wolfson 1978). However, they can also be much less visible, such as occurs in situations where manufacturing companies develop standards for products or where independent certification firms or associations certify that certain standards have been met in various kinds of private practices (Andrews 1998; Gunningham and Rees 1997; Iannuzzi 2001). While many standards are invoked by government command and control regulation, others can be developed in the private sphere. As long as these are not replaced by government enforced standards, they represent the acquiescence of a government to the private rules, a form of delegated regulation. (Haufler 2000 and 2001; Knill 2001). These kinds of self-regulation, however, are often portrayed as being more 'voluntary' than is actually the case. That is, while non-governmental entities may, in effect, regulate themselves, they typically do so with the implicit or explicit permission of governments, which consciously refrain from regulating activities in a more directly coercive fashion as long as private and public sector goals remain congruent (Ronit 2001; Gibson, 1999).

A major advantage often cited for the use of voluntary standard-setting is cost, since governments do not have to pay for the creation, administration, and renewal of such standards, as would be the case with traditional command and control regulation. This is especially the case in areas such as professional regulation, where information asymmetries between regulatees and regulators mean public administration of standards would be especially expensive and time-consuming. Such programmes can also be effective in international settings, where establishment of effective governmental regimes can be especially difficult (Elliott and Schlaepfer 2001; Schlager 1999). However, again, possible savings in administrative costs must be balanced against additional costs to society which might result from ineffective or inefficient administration of voluntary standards, especially those related to non-compliance (Gibson 1999; Karamanos 2001). The 2002 Enron scandal in the US involving the energy giant's accounting firm Arthur Anderson, for example, undermined confidence in the profession's ability or even willingness to police itself and led to a crisis in confidence in many aspects of business self-regulation (Vogel 2005).

THE PLAN OF THE BOOK

While the different phases of regulatory activities are little studied, the linkages between the phases are even less understood. Bernstein (1955) postulated the existence of a regulatory 'life cycle' moving from birth to senescence and regulatory decline, but his notion of a regulatory cycle did not anticipate either deregulation or reregulation. While it is very possible that these latter two phases might emerge in the twilight of an established regulatory order, it is an empirical questions whether this is the case. Other hypotheses, however, are equally plausible: for example, that deregulation occurs as a separate process from regulation and 'imposes itself' on an existing regulatory regime; or that reregulation emerges at the end of a regulatory cycle, not deregulation. Again, these questions are all empirical ones and it is the aim of this volume to shed light on these and other issues through the detailed study of cases of regulatory, deregulatory and reregulatory activity in the Asia-Pacific region, seen in comparative context.

More specifically this book addresses several key issues associated with the evolution of regulatory regimes in the region. It highlights two important contemporary developments (a) the movement towards deregulation in certain sectors and (b) the seemingly associated movement towards reregulation in those same sectors.

In the first part of the book, Hira examines the twin movements of deregulation and reregulation in the Asia-Pacific region, providing an overview of these developments and a comparative study of these trends *vis à vis* those apparent in other developing areas, notably Latin America. He specifically addresses the question of whether efforts to de/reregulate the economy necessarily involve abandonment of the 'Development State' strategy characteristic of East Asia, and finds the answer to be negative. Ramesh then discusses the two global dynamics often observed about regulatory behaviour, the 'Delaware effect' in which regulatory regimes converge towards the lowest common denominator and the 'California effect' in which regulatory behaviour can adopt a more virtuous form and develop a 'race to the top' rather than a 'race to the bottom' (Greenwood 2005; Berry *et al.* 2003). He shows that both trends can and do occur simultaneously, reflecting the contradictory economic and political pressures, both international and domestic, that shape regulations.

In the second part of the book, authors examine actual cases of regulatory reform in recent years. In Chapter 4, Lampietti and his co-authors offer a comparative study of electricity reforms in Central Asia and Eastern Europe, both regions that have undergone an unusually high degree of economic transformation in the last decade. Using copious primary data, they show a variety of intended and unintended consequences of regulatory reform which have led to some results not anticipated by policy-makers, suggesting the need for delicate fine-tuning of reforms in a way that maximizes benefits of market-based reforms while minimizing the adverse side-effects. In the following chapter, Skoufa studies the electricity generation industry in Australia in comparison to its British counterpart within a 'Governance-Strategic Choice' framework. His study cautions against reliance on neo-classical economics to guide regulations and proposes that policy-makers take strategic choice of firms into account. The following two chapters are also on the electricity sector. In Chapter 7, Todoc compares the short and long-term environmental impacts of power deregulation in the Philippines and Thailand. He finds that while the short-term impacts have been largely satisfactory, he is less sanguine about their long-term prospects and suggests additional regulatory efforts to promote sustainable energy use. Chapter 8 by Asher and Nandy addresses the issue of regulating pension funds in Asia and points to numerous lacunae. Their analysis leads to the conclusion that pension funds require a tight regulatory framework while allowing flexibility and competition for managers. The following chapter by Goyal is in a similar vein, but focuses on regulation of capital markets in India. She finds the mixture of deregulation and reregulation of capital markets in recent years a significant improvement on previous arrangements but shortcomings remain which require a tough but flexible regulatory environment for the capital markets in India to expand and function effectively.

In the third part, Neil Gunningham and Jon M. Peha take up the issue of the 'optimal' design of regulatory measures in contemporary circumstances. 'Smart' or appropriate regulation in this era, they argue, requires the use of a variety of instruments beyond typical 'command and control' regulation, combining elements of traditional regulatory and deregulated regimes into a new mix of regulatory tools.

Finally, in the conclusion, the editors look at the general pattern of regulatory change highlighted by the sectoral and national case studies set out in the book and extract the elements of a common model of de/reregulatory cycles. Focusing on the two dynamics of policy learning and 'spill-over' effects, they argue that a parsimonious model of regulatory behaviour can be developed to cover regulatory developments in these and other instances.

REFERENCES

Andrews, Richard (1998) 'Environmental Regulation and Business "Self-Regulation" ', *Policy Sciences*, **31**, 177–97.
Angus, William H. (1974) 'Judicial Review: Do We Need It?', in D. J. Baum (eds), *The Individual and the Bureaucracy*, Toronto: Carswell, pp. 101–35.
Bardach, Eugene (1989) 'Social Regulation as a Generic Policy Instrument', in L. M. Salamon (ed.), *Beyond Privatization: The Tools of Government Action*, Washington, DC: Urban Institute, pp. 197–229.
Becker, G. S. (1983) 'A Theory of Competition Among Pressure Groups for Political Influence', *Quarterly Journal of Economics*, **98** (August), 371–400.
Beesley, M. E. (1992) *Privatization, Regulation and Deregulation*, New York: Routledge.

Bernstein, Marver H. (1955) *Regulating Business by Independent Commission*, Princeton: Princeton University Press.

Berry, William D., Richard C. Fording and Russell L. Hanson (2003) 'Reassessing the "Race to the Bottom" in State Welfare Policy', *The Journal of Politics*, **65**(2), 327–49.

Buchanan, James M. and Robert D. Tollison (1984) (eds) *The Theory of Public Choice – II*, Ann Arbor: University of Michigan Press.

Collier, Ute (1998) *Deregulation in the European Union: Environmental Perspectives*, London: Routledge.

Crew, Michael A. and Charles K. Rowley (1986) 'Deregulation as an instrument in industrial policy', *Journal of Institutional and Theoretical Economics*, **142**, 52–70.

Daugbjerg, Carsten (1997) 'Policy Networks and Agricultural Policy Reforms: Explaining Deregulation in Sweden and Re-regulation in the European Community', *Governance*, **10**(2), 123–42.

de Smith, S. A. (1973) *Judicial Review of Administrative Action*, London: Stevens and Son.

Derthick, Martha and Paul J. Quirk (1985) *The Politics of Deregulation*, Washington DC: Brookings Institute.

Dyerson, Romano and Frank Mueller (1993) 'Intervention by Outsiders: A Strategic Perspective on Government Industrial Policy', *Journal of Public Policy*, **13**(1), 69–88.

Eisner, Marc Allen (1994a) 'Discovering Patterns in Regulatory History: Continuity, Change and Regulatory Regimes', *Journal of Policy History*, **6**(2), 157–87.

Eisner, Marc Allen (1994b) 'Economic Regulatory Policies: Regulation and Deregulation in Historical Context', in D. H. Rosenbloom and R. D. Schwartz (eds), *Handbook of Regulation and Administrative Law*, New York: Marcel Dekker, pp. 91–116.

Elliott, Chris and Rodolphe Schlaepfer (2001) 'The Advocacy Coalition Framework: Application to the Policy Process for the Development of Forest Certification in Sweden', *Journal of European Public Policy*, **8**(4), 642–61.

Gayle, Dennis J. and Jonathan N. Goodrich (eds) (1990) *Privatization and Deregulation in Global Perspective*, Westport, CT: Quorum Books.

Gibson, Robert B. (ed.) (1999) *Voluntary Initiatives: The New Politics of Corporate Greening*, Peterborough: Broadview Press.

Gilardi, Fabrizio (2002) 'Policy Credibility and Delegation to Independent Regulatory Agencies: A Comparative Empirical Analysis', *Journal of European Public Policy*, **9**(6), 873–93.

Greenwood, Daniel J. J. (2005) 'Democracy and Delaware: The Mysterious Race to the Bottom/Top', *Yale Law and Policy Review*, **23**(2), 402–25.

Gunningham, Neil and Joseph Rees (1997) 'Industry Self-Regulation: An Institutional Perspective', *Law and Policy*, **19**(4), 363–414.

Hammond, Thomas H. and Jack H. Knott (1988) 'The Deregulatory Snowball: Explaining Deregulation in the Financial Industry', *Journal of Politics*, **50**(1), 3–30.

Haufler, Virginia (2000) 'Private Sector International Regimes', in R. A. Higgott, G. R. D. Underhill and A. Bieler (eds), *Non-state Actors and Authority in the Global System*, London: Routledge, pp. 121–37.

Haufler, Virginia (2001) *A Public Role for the Private Sector*, Berkeley, CA: Carnegie Endowment for International Peace.

Hira, Anil, David Huxtable and Alexandre Leger (2005) 'Deregulation and Participation: An International Survey of Participation in Electricity Regulation',

Governance, **18**(1), 53–88.

Howlett, Michael and M. Ramesh (2002) 'The Policy Effects of Internationalization: A Subsystem Adjustment Analysis of Policy Change', *Journal of Comparative Policy Analysis*, **4**(3), 31–50.

Howlett, Michael (2004) 'Administrative Styles and the Limits of Administrative Reform: A Neo-Institutional Analysis of Administrative Culture', *Canadian Public Administration*, **46**(4), 471–94.

Huntington, Samuel P. (1952) 'The Marasmus of the ICC: The Commissions, the Railroads and the Public Interest', *Yale Law Review*, **61**(4), 467–509.

Iannuzzi, Alphonse (2001) *Industry Self-Regulation and Voluntary Environmental Compliance*, Boca Raton: Lewis Publishers.

Karamanos, Panagiotis (2001) 'Voluntary Environmental Agreements: Evolution and Definition of a New Environmental Policy Approach', *Journal of Environmental Planning and Management*, **44**(1), 67–84.

Knill, Christoph (2001) 'Private Governance Across Multiple Arenas: European Interest Associations as Interface Actors', *Journal of European Public Policy*, **8**(2), 227–46.

Landes, W. M. and Posner, R. A. (1975) 'The Independent Judiciary in an Interest Group Perspective', *Journal of Law and Economics*, **18** (December), 875–901.

Lazer, David and Viktor Mayer-Schonberger (2002) 'Governing Networks: Telecommunication Deregulation in Europe and the United States', *Brooklyn Journal of International Law*, **3**, 820–51.

Levi-Faur, D. and S. Gilad (2005) 'The Rise of the British Regulatory State – Transcending the Privatization Debate', *Comparative Politics*, **37**(1), 105–24.

May, Peter J. (2002), 'Social Regulation', in L. M. Salamon (ed.) *The Tools of Government: A Guide to the New Governance*, New York: Oxford University Press, pp. 156–85.

McCubbins, Mathew D. and Arthur Lupia (1994) 'Learning from Oversight: Fire Alarms and Policy Patrols Reconstructed', *Journal of Law, Economics and Organization*, **10**(1), 96–125.

McCubbins, Mathew D. and Thomas Schwartz (1984) 'Congressional Oversight Overlooked: Policy Patrols Versus Fire Alarms', *American Journal of Political Science*, **28**(1), 165–79.

Minogue, M. (2002) 'Governance-Based Analysis of Regulation', *Annals of Public and Cooperative Economics*, **73**(4), 649–66.

Mitnick, Barry M. (1978) 'The Concept of Regulation', *Bulletin of Business Research*, **53**(5), 1–20.

Mitnick, Barry M. (1980) *The Political Economy of Regulation: Creating, Designing and Removing Regulatory Forms*, New York: Columbia University Press, 401–4.

Padberg, D. I. (1992) 'Nutritional Labeling as a Policy Instrument', *American Journal of Agricultural Economics*, **74**(5), 1208–13.

Page, Edward C. (2001) *Governing by Numbers: Delegated Legislation and Everyday Policy-Making*, Portland: Hart Publishing.

Peltzman, S. (1976) 'Toward a More General Theory of Regulation', *Journal of Law and Economics*, **19**(2), 211–40.

Posner, R. A. (1974) 'Theories of Economic Regulation', *Bell Journal of Economics and Management Science*, **5** (Autumn), 355–8.

Posner, Richard A (1974) 'Theories of Economic Regulation', *Bell Journal of Economics and Management Science*, **5**(2), 335–58.

Reagan, Michael D. (1987) *Regulation: The Politics of Policy*, Boston: Little Brown.

Richardson, J.J. (ed.) (1990) *Privatisation and Deregulation in Canada and Britain*, Aldershot, UK: Dartmouth Publishing Company.

Ringquist, Evan J., Jeff Worsham, and Marc Allen Eisner (2003) 'Salience, Complexity and the Legislative Direction of Regulatory Bureaucracies', *Journal of Public Administration Research and Theory*, **13**(2), 141–65.

Ronit, Karsten (2001) 'Institutions of Private Authority in Global Governance: Linking Territorial Forms of Self-regulation', *Administration and Society*, **33**(5), 555–78.

Rubsamen, Valerie (1989) 'Deregulation and the State in Comparative Perspective: The Case of Telecommunications', *Comparative Politics*, **22**(1), 105–20.

Salamon, Lester A. (2002) 'Economic Regulation', in L. M. Salamon (ed.), *The Tools of Government: A Guide to the New Governance*, New York: Oxford University Press, pp. 117–55.

Schlager, Edella (1999) 'A Comparison of Frameworks, Theories, and Models of Policy Processes', in P. A. Sabatier (ed.), *Theories of the Policy Process*, Boulder: Westview Press, 233–60.

Sinclair, Darren (1997) 'Self-Regulation Versus Command and Control? Beyond False Dichotomies', *Law and Policy*, **19**(4), 529–59

Stigler, G. J. (1971) 'Theory of Economic Regulation', *Bell Journal of Economics and Management Science*, **2**(1), 3–21.

Stigler, George (1975) 'The Theory of Economic Regulation', in G. Stigler (ed.), *The Citizen and the State*, Chicago: University of Chicago Press, pp. 114–41.

Swann, Dennis (1988) *The Retreat of the State: Deregulation and Privatisation in the UK and US*, Hemel Hempstead, Hertfordshire: Harvester Wheatsheaf.

Thatcher, Mark and Alec Stone Sweet (ed.) (2003), *The Politics of Delegation*, London: Frank Cass.

Tollison, R. D. (1991) 'Regulation and Interest Groups', in Jack High (ed.), *Regulation: Economic Theory and History*, Ann Arbor: University of Michigan Press, pp. 59–76.

Tuohy, C. J. and A. D. Wolfson (1978) 'Self-Regulation: Who Qualifies?', in P. Slayton and M. J. Trebilcock (eds), *The Professions and Public Policy*, Toronto: University of Toronto Press, pp. 111–22.

Vogel, David (2005) *The Market for Virtue: The Potential and Limits of Corporate Social Responsibility*, Washington, DC: Brookings Institute.

Vogel, David and Robert A. Kagan (eds) (2002) *Dynamics of Regulatory Change: How Globalization Affects National Regulatory Policies*, Berkeley: University of California Press.

Vogel, Steven K. (1996), *Freer Markets, More Rules: Regulatory Reform in Advanced Industrial Countries*, Ithaca: Cornell University Press.

Williams, Juliet A. (2000) 'The Delegation Dilemma: Negotiated Rulemaking in Perspective', *Policy Studies Review*, **17**(1), 125–46.

Wolf Jr., Charles (1979) 'A Theory of Nonmarket Failure: Framework for Implementation Analysis', *Journal of Law and Economics*, **22**(1), 107–39.

Wolf Jr., Charles (1987) 'Markets and Non-Market Failures: Comparison and Assessment', *Journal of Public Policy*, **7**(1), 43–70.

Zerbe, Richard O. and Howard E. McCurdy (1999) 'The Failure of Market Failure', *Journal of Policy Analysis and Management*, **18**(4), 558–78.

PART I

Introduction: governance and globalization

2. Governance crisis in Asia: developing a responsive regulation

Anil Hira

During the post-World War II years, developmental states in East Asia used regulation as an important tool for increasing national competitiveness. In line with increasing success and globalizing pressures, East Asia in the 1990s began to deregulate, signaling what some analysts see as the end of heavy state intervention in the region's economies. The Asian Financial Crisis (AFC) beginning in 1997 has raised alarm bells about the process of deregulation, leading to reforms now known as 'reregulation'. This chapter argues first that globalization pressures for reregulation do not require an abandonment of the developmentalist state. Rather, reregulation can be modified in order to maintain the basic formula that led to growth with equity in East Asia. Second, this chapter argues that nonetheless in East Asia greater adjustments are needed to developmentalist-oriented reregulation adjustments to increase the participation of society in order to avoid future regulatory crises.

GLOBALIZATION AND PRESSURES FOR DEREGULATION AND THEN REREGULATION

Pressures on the East Asian developmental state for first deregulation and now reregulation can be traced in good part to historical changes in the Western conception of regulation. As Karl Polanyi pointed out in his seminal study of the rise of the welfare state, *The Great Transformation*, all economic markets are embedded in social and political structures (Polanyi 1957). Regulation refers to the rules, procedures, and norms that govern all economic transactions in the broadest sense. Therefore, regulation may be the most underestimated aspect of economic life. In its more common usage, regulation means the specific rules that states set to guide markets.

The evolution and usage of this more specific meaning of regulation change over time and space. Regulation at the turn of the twentieth century referred primarily to attempts in the West to change the increasingly apparent negative social effects of the Industrial Revolution. These changes went hand-in-hand with the rising political strength of labor movements as a result of the increasing need for skilled labor in factories as well as concerted efforts by activists. For North America and Europe, the key changes were proscriptions on certain natural outcomes of the market, created by uneven bargaining power among parties. The main changes included child labor and worker safety regulations; union, strike, and other legislation, and anti-trust commissions to break up robber baron monopolies. From the late 1960s, both a booming economy and a host of social movements for change again spilled over, redefining regulation. This period is marked by the addition of environmental, affirmative action (anti-discrimination), and pro-active social welfare regulations, such as requiring employers to grant a certain level of maternity leave. Therefore, we can see that regulation has not only been a vehicle for market rules, but also an instrument of evolving social policy.

The period of the late 1970s saw the rise of neoliberal thinking about the economy, which has had obvious effects on regulation. The now well-known thinking of Milton Friedman and the Chicago School of Economics had profound effects in dismantling the newly activist elements of state regulation in the West by asserting not just the optimality of markets over states but also the inefficiencies and problems of state interventions. These were not new ideas; in fact they had been argued by Friedrich Von Hayek in *The Road to Serfdom* dating back to 1944. Rather the timing of the deregulation movement and the disappearance of Keynesian Economics had as much to do with the international inflationary and growth crises of the 1970s as it did with the at the time extreme observations of a group of economists. With the Reagan and Thatcher revolutions claiming the government was 'not the solution, but part of the problem', the 1980s saw the rise of deregulation as the new mantra for reclaiming economic growth in the West. The seeming rejuvenation of the US and European economies by the mid-1980s reinforced this revolution in ideas and practices of regulation. With the initial economic success, the 'return to market' paradigm spread even further in scope, leading, for example, to the 'new public management', a school of thought that suggests that when privatization is not possible, market-like competition and incentive structures should still be brought into the public bureaucracies and state contracts (Hira 2004). Married with the idea that democracy attains some of the decision-making efficiencies of markets, the new perspective became known as neoliberalism; its supposed triumph reinforced by the fall of Communism throughout the world beginning with the Soviet Union in 1989. Through financial and external pressures wrought by Western-dominated international financial and trade institutions and governments, partly in response to growing East Asian export success, global pressures for deregulation as part of a package of neoliberalism led to changes in East Asia in the late 1980s (MacIntyre and Jayasuriya 1992).

Yet, by the 1990s, a new wave of economic thinking signaled that the idea of moving toward deregulation might have some flaws, and paved the way for the present paradigm of 'reregulation'. The work of Douglas North, George Akerlof and a number of other economists became well-accepted by the early 1990s (Akerlof 1970; North 1990; and Hira and Hira 2000). New institutionalist and transactions costs economists point out that markets left alone do not always yield optimal results. The work of these new institutionalist and transactions costs economists pointed out that markets left alone might not always yield optimal results. North's work on institutions ushered in a gush of work on the importance of property rights and contract enforcement. Akerlof's work on the dysfunctionality of markets where complete information is not present or is unevenly shared, such as his famous example of the market for used cars, brought about a whole new school of thought about potential market failures in the absence of a strong regulator. These ideas about the need for states to facilitate the effective functioning of markets are now accepted virtually without question by most economists and figure prominently in the writings of every international institution, including the World Bank.

This latest wave of theorizing has brought to light the fact that from the 1980s, states that moved to privatize companies, reduce 'red tape', and use market-like incentive systems both within the bureaucracy and in public infrastructure and social welfare contracting, were not really deregulating, but 'reregulating'. This term, popularized by Steven Vogel, among others, refers in an emerging literature to the changing nature of state interventions to reduce the institutional and transactions costs of facilitating private markets (Vogel 1996). The World Bank has pushed reregulation as a means of stabilizing and facilitating markets in the developing world under the label 'governance'. Moreover, as integration increases, analysts point to the increasing development of international and regional regulatory architecture (Jayasuriya 2003 and 2004). A simple example of reregulation is where a state-owned electricity company previously worked as an arm of the government to make decisions political leaders deemed optimal in terms of electricity rates, size of workforce, and investment in long-term generation infrastructure, a newly privatized market may lead to a wide variety of results depending on institutional arrangements. The government will need to write a new set of regulations to avoid creating a private monopoly; price gouging of customers with little bargaining power; environmental safety; and ensuring investment in long-term power generation. In the 1980s, the early deregulation of the airline industry in the US led to major decreases in fares, though the market continues to be plagued by instability and poor quality service. The celebrated example of the failure of the rules of the 'deregulated' California power system beginning in 2001 brought on a host of doubts and opposition about the shift in state-market relations. In Canada, there is grave concern that the national health care system will be forced to open itself up to competition due to pressures from US companies via the WTO. These examples demonstrate the deep questioning presently occurring as to whether deregulation of newly freed markets is really leading to better results in terms of economic efficiency, that is a return to greater state intervention is once again needed. In this sense, the anti-trust case against Microsoft and the recent changes in corporate accounting rules in the wake of the Enron debacle encapsulate a movement toward 'reregulation'. In fact, reregulation is the creation of new rules to deal with the negative and generally unexpected problems resulting from deregulation. However, it is very important to point out that the new wave of reregulation is not akin to recreating the state monopolies or strong welfare components of the post-World War II North American and European societies. For example, welfare reform has swept throughout the West, with new incentive structures designed to guide recipients back to the labor market. Of course, it remains to be seen how effective these adjustments of the neoliberal model will be. Nonetheless, as throughout the century, we see that there is a clear embeddedness of regulation in social ideas as well as an interaction between regulation and social needs and demands.

The reregulation literature still does not go far enough, in my opinion, in explaining the new role of regulation in state economies and internationally. Nor is there any developed literature on regulation in the international political economy or development literatures. Regulation is used on the international level to in a few oblique senses. 'The Regulation School' runs parallel to world systems theory, in suggesting that an exploitative global commodity chain of production has arisen with the development of mass production (Boyer 1990). Regulation on an international level sometimes also appears in discussions of international regime theory, with applications to international trade law and norms (Emadi-Coffin 2002). Yet, there is no literature on how domestic regulation is affected by, and attempts to deal with, international factors. We can begin to address this lacuna by looking at the East Asian developmental state, and how its regulatory features have been transformed by global forces, as highlighted with the Asian Financial Crisis.

ASIAN FINANCIAL CRISIS – WHY REREGULATION DOES NOT REQUIRE ABANDONING DEVELOPMENTALISM

Globalizing Pressures for Liberalization on the Developmental State in East Asia

The idea of a developmental state in East Asia has strong elements of regulatory guidance as well as other aspects of state intervention in markets.

A number of analysts have noted the astute use of regulations in East Asia to promote competitiveness. A foundational literature on East Asia's remarkable economic growth after World War II coined the term developmental state to capture this unique style of state-market relations geared toward international competitiveness (Johnson 1982; Amsden 1989; Wade 1990). The idea behind the developmental state is that the government pro-actively supports national champions into new higher-value added and technologically-sophisticated industries over time, using a variety of mechanisms for targeting and promotion. The goal is to increase exports in competitive international markets, and this provides a discipline upon national companies receiving state help. A 'pilot' agency, such as MITI, guides this process, creating changing incentives and goal posts that companies receiving help need to meet over time. As industries become successful, they are weaned off state aid, and the export revenues they produce help to subsidize a new generation of industries. Jayasuriya points out that the developmental state really required intensive regulation of a dualistic economy – an internationally-competitive export sector, and a protected, weak domestic non-tradable sector (Jayasuriya 2001), for example Mitsubishi and protected Japanese rice farmers.

Since the introduction of its conception, the developmentalist state idea has been under heavy fire. The World Bank fired the heaviest salvo with its publication of *The East Asian Miracle* report (1993). The report acknowledged some benefits from state targeting, but also stated that the successes were peppered with many failures and accompanying economic efficiency. The overall flavor of the report was that East Asia's growth was in spite of develop-mentalist intervention, not because of it. Success was based on the neoliberal formula of macroeconomic stability and upon high levels of human capital, rather than state intervention. This seems to be the widespread sentiment shared by mainstream economists on the subject (Stiglitz and Shahid 2001; Quibria 2002). Indeed, a survey of conventional economic statistics indicates that government intervention (as measured by government spending/GDP) is lower and degree of liberalization (as measured by openness, or exports+imports/GDP) is greater than in other regions (Hira, forthcoming).

The developmentalist state response could best be characterized by Robert Wade's concept that the East Asian state 'governs the market'. Wade (1990), using a detailed study of Taiwan as evidence, suggests that East Asian state-market relations are somewhere between free markets and state-controlled markets. Rather than determining market outcomes, states 'guide' markets toward certain outcomes. According to Wade, these types of state interventions are 'market-conforming', and so not easy to detect using macro-level economic indicators. For example, a market-conforming exchange rate intervention would not be the inefficient one of providing differential exchange rates or restricting foreign exchange, but merely holding one's exchange rate at a devalued rate compared to one's export market, as is the case with the Chinese currency (renminbi) *vis-à-vis* the US dollar. As another example, Wade suggests that the Taiwanese Government promoted foreign investment in industries for which Taiwan seemed to have export potential. The government also fostered national industries over time that could compete with these same foreign companies, using the learning and know-how gleaned from foreign factories to start building national ones. Wade's conception of the East Asian state thus fits perfectly within our exploration later in this chapter of regulatory policy as a vehicle for industrial and competitiveness policy (Hira 2003a and 2003b).

Certainly, there are important differences in national styles of developmentalist state (Wade 1990; Jomo 1997; Hira, forthcoming). The early adaptation of the Japanese blueprint had to consider national realities, from the more decentralized factories of Taiwan to the *chaebols* of South Korea. In the last two decades, the model as been adapted to the 'flying geese' aspects of Southeast Asian dependence on Japanese and US capital, as well as the importance of Chinese business networks. The most recent adaptation in China toward strong military and Communist Party ownership has its own idiosyncratic aspects. Nonetheless, we can recognize the basic parameters of the developmentalist state and importance of regulation in each case.

The Asian Financial Crisis Spearheads the Move from De- to reregulation in East Asia

It is well beyond the scope of this chapter to analyze in any detail the Asian financial crisis (AFC) beginning in 1997. However, we should note the implications of the AFC for the regulatory aspects of the Asian developmental state. Diagnoses of the AFC predictably vary from mainstream to institutional perspectives, though clearly these are all post hoc explanations, given in the aftermath of the shocking sudden financial disintegration of the fastest growing economies in the world. Indeed, the flood of external capital pouring into Southeast Asia in the early 1990s should, in hindsight, have brought warning signs before the meltdown. Mainstream institutions, such as the International Monetary Fund (IMF), point primarily to a lack of attention to macroeconomic fundamentals (Berg 1999). These include an overvaluation of the exchange rate (which many states pegged to the dollar to ensure investors) and an accompanying weakening current account; high levels of external debt; inadequate reserves, and similar problems. These accounts also seize upon the weakness of Asian financial systems, such as inadequate reserve requirements, and (as is now known) huge numbers of questionable loans to non-productive sectors, such as real estate. More institutionally-based perspectives support the idea of a financial 'bubble' including soft investments, an upsurge in capital inflows, and weak financial systems (Krugman 1997). Some economists, notably Stiglitz and Sachs, suggest that the weakness lies not just on the domestic, but also on the international level, reflecting the idea that the 'herd' aspects of financial volatility and lender responsibility, suggesting need further regulation of financial flows on the international level (Stiglitz 1998; Radelet and Sachs, no date). These same critics turned their ire toward the IMF for worsening the crisis through its stagnating policies of adjustment in the aftermath of the crisis.

What would a developmentalist explanation of the AFC be? Robert Wade's work gives us a good starting point (Wade, no date). Wade points out that the mainstream and institutionalist arguments alone are inadequate to explain the timing of the crisis. In particular, they fail to explain why the crisis did not happen sooner, since the conditions of weak financial sectors, international financial panics, and external capital flows had occurred in previous periods. While not dismissing new elements such as emerging weaknesses in Japanese finance and large increases in investment flows, Wade suggests that the real key was the movement away from the developmentalist state model of the state guiding resources into national industry through close control of national finance. Wade points to external (IMF and US Government) as well as internal pressures for liberalization on developmental states (Wade 2001). For example, he notes that Korea began to liberalize the *chaebol* system in 1993, with the ascension of a new democratic government suspicious of old patronage ties and eager to join the OECD. Radical financial liberalization occurred in the same period in Indonesia and Thailand. Indeed, we can see that the financial bubble of poor investment reflects the ceding of control over domestic finance by East Asian states. In other words, in the transition to a more market-based financial system, an upsurge in external investment exposed the weaknesses of a financial system set up for developmental purposes. It is interesting to note in this vein that Malaysia, which kept developmentalist capital controls, weathered the crisis much better than its neighbours. Certainly, the crisis has opened up questions about the future parameters of the developmentalist state in East Asia (Beeson 2002).

Those questions centre around the idea that the developmental state, and the paternalistic, informal networks behind it, is rife with corruption and cronyism (Arvis and Berenbeim 2003; Tay and Seda 2003; Menkhoff and Gerke 2002). Moreover, the idea of a unique Asian set of cultural values including most importantly pragmatism, that allows the developmental state to succeed, seems to be in question following the AFC (Sung-Joo 1999; Richter and Mar 2004). The cases against the Suharto family and allegations at all levels in China seem to point to a serious problem. Transparency, accountability and participation are the new mantra of the international push for governance reform. International lenders and institutions have created what Jayasuriya and

Rosser call a 'new Washington consensus', with an agenda of reregulation, maintaining markets but also focusing on questions of governance and social capital (Jayasuriya and Rosser 2001). While the latter remain fuzzy concepts in practice, these institutions have demanded financial liberalization, including privatization of the banking sector and opening it up to foreign ownership. They also include the reregulation of the financial sector to include greater government control over reserve requirements and a revamping of auditing and accounting practices. As well, foreign governments continue to push for greater import and investment liberalization. Calls for reform of corporate governance abound, on the premise that corruption and inefficiency are fueled by state favoritism and coddling of local companies in which they have a financial interest (Zhuan *et al.* 2000). These pressures have reduced the previously strong ties between the state and national champions, which supposedly led to bad loans and inefficient investments, exacerbating the financial crisis. In the case of Korea, foreign companies have become partners in some of the *chaebols*, with large multinationals such as General Motors now having a stake (Daewoo). Given the financial crisis, and the desperate need for capital, such reforms seem to be a natural response to a heightened vulnerability to external global pressures, though the effectiveness of such governance reforms can be questioned (Hira 2004).

Do these changes signal the inevitable end of the developmental state in East Asia and a movement to liberalized, Western-style markets? (Antons 2003).

In fact, as we might expect, empirical studies of post-AFC Asia, as has been the case in India, indicate more of a limited set of reforms, varying by country and sector, depending on the local nature of the crisis and context (Cheung and Scott 2003). This is not surprising to regional specialists, who have long noted the close informal ties between domestic business and politics, ties which remain central to decision-making, regardless of the regulatory arrangements, or even the transition to democracy (Dittmer *et al.* 2000). Besides dismissing East Asian state intervention as either irrelevant or costly to economic growth, mainstream critics of the developmentalist approach more recently have also claimed that interventions à la Wade are no longer possible under global (WTO) free trade rules, claims that are reinforced by the heightened external pressures of the Asian Financial Crisis, as discussed. However, more recent studies of the acquisition of new industries in the region point to the ongoing and obvious active efforts of the East Asian state to attract new industries, the most prominent examples being in the information technology industry (Hong 1997) . For example, the movement of the software industry to South India can be directly traced to pro-active government efforts (Hira 2005). Indeed, in the sense that direct interventions, such as export requirements, become circumscribed by international trade rules, we would expect that regulatory mechanisms of industrial policy being more indirect and less openly egregious of the norms of free trade, become all the more important.

Indeed, in my work 'Regulatory Games States Play' (Hira 2003a), I develop a theory of how state regulatory autonomy and capacity are affected by the international political economy, such factor endowments and size of domestic market. I have also suggested a number of mechanisms by which states do use regulation to further national interests (Hira 2003a and 2003b). The fact is that, despite the constant rhetoric about free trade and private markets, states are as entrenched in markets as ever before, just in a different way. World agricultural markets are characterized by a strong level of protection and subsidization in Europe, North America and Japan, the largest world consumer markets. Industrial markets are subject to a host of direct and indirect interventions. In direct terms, the US has not shied away from using countervailing duties and anti-dumping procedures to reduce foreign competition with recent actions against Brazilian steel and Chinese textiles. Similarly, European governments have invested heavily into strategic industries, with Airbus being one prominent example. In indirect terms, all countries have available important tools that allow them to avoid the appearance of contravening international trade agreements and norms. For example, the West heavily subsidizes research and development through defense expenditures and academic grants. These expenditures directly fuel technological developments, such as the US DARPA agency's development of the Internet, and indirect subsidization of Boeing aerospace through defense contracts. Taxation and anti-trust policies can also have a direct effect on national competitiveness. In sum, governments on every level use regulation to favor certain market outcomes, from zoning on the local level to restrictions on entry into banking on the national level.

Therefore, given East Asia's and currently China's amazing record in achieving equitable growth, what is needed is not an abandonment of the developmentalist state, but a movement from direct intervention toward the more indirect methods of sectoral promotion. Copying from the West, Asian states can, for example, continue to develop their strong research and development possibilities through targeted funding of national innovations systems; offer strong tax and cultural incentives to continue high savings rates; and continue to favor national producers through government assistance, including financing, in capturing market share in emerging exports. They would be committing no greater sins than the US in its defense contracts or the EU in its protection of agriculture. However, these logical adjustments of the developmental state model in regard to economic regulation would still not be enough. Regardless of the exact contours of this adjustment of reregulation for developmental interests, there can be no doubting that regulation will be adapted to the local context, institutions, interests, and cultural values (Jayasuriya 1999).

REGULATORY CRISES IN ASIA DEMONSTRATE THE NEED FOR FURTHER REGULATORY EVOLUTION

While the East Asian state continues its strong track record in developing new industries and services, a number of crises in the region suggest the need for greater consideration of the social consequences of regulatory decision-making. Not only the AFC, but other recent crises have brought to the forefront global pressures for the need for greater transparency and participation in regulatory decision-making. As is the case elsewhere, the most prominent regulatory crises in Asia have involved environmental consequences of regulatory decision-making. However, more recently, additional crises involving deregulation of key industries, labour conditions, and other associated inequalities and problems of economic development bring the need for a further evolution of regulation to our attention.

Environmental Crises of Regulation: The Case of Three Gorges Dam

Environmental controversies remain the most important source of regulatory contention, attracting the attention of a coalition of domestic activists and foreign non-governmental organizations. In Asia, a number of environmental questions have arisen in regard to state management of resources, including clear-cutting of tropical forests in Indonesia and Malaysia; hazardous levels of pollution around large Asian cities; and continual questions of wildlife extinction. Some of the most celebrated examples include major controversies surrounding large dam projects in India and China. These projects, designed to provide hydroelectricity for growing energy needs, almost inevitably raise questions about habitat destruction from flooding, resettlement of local groups, and whether there are less destructive alternatives. The celebrated case of the Three Gorges Dam project is one recent example of the failure of governments to adequately consider the reactions of civil society activists. The project created a firestorm of controversy over the resettlement of an estimated 700 000; the changing of rich local eco-systems; and questions about corruption and political grandstanding in the project's administration. The controversy seemed to take the Chinese government by surprise, and led to the denial of World Bank and US Export-Import Bank support (Anonymous 2003; Jackson and Sleigh 2001; Quing and Sullivan 1999; Kearins and O'Malley 1999).

The Enron Debacle in India

In 1999, the State of Maharashtra in India, desperate for new investment to feed power-hungry Bombay, signed a deal with the now infamous Enron company for the construction of a new power plant.[1] The $2.9 billion Dabhol power project was massive, designed to produce 2200 MW of power in two phases of constructing natural-gas fired generation. The Dabhol contract was under fire from the beginning of construction, supposedly for giving away too lucrative a deal to Enron and for not ensuring low rates for the poor. A strong coalition of Indian activists, spearheaded by the coalition 'National Alliance of People's Movements' put enormous political pressure on the state and federal governments to halt the project, which it saw as exploitative and corrupt in terms of bribery, displacing local population and charging unfair rates.[2] Moreover, the state government began to dispute the value of the contract, falling behind on its payments to Enron, refusing payment on the basis that the rates charged were unfair (Wilke 2002). Under this pressure, the state government rescinded the contract, creating a huge problem with the US government and investors. With minor stakeholders GE and Bechtel taking over Enron's stake as that company disintegrated, the first phase of the project is now 90 per cent complete. However, the second phase remains halted amidst a legal quagmire, and foreign investors have shied away from further projects in India as a result of the debacle and similar disputes across India.[3]

Labour Regulations

A third example of problems of regulation can be found in the growing disputes over labour regulations (or lack thereof) in Asia. A strong coalition of human rights activists, and foreign labour and non-governmental organizations have successfully brought enormous pressure upon Asian governments to consider treatment of factory workers. An ongoing controversy surrounds the supposed use of prisoners and other forms of forced labor in China for factory (export) production.[4] Efforts by activists have had surprising success in US shame campaigns against major US companies supposedly exploiting the local Asian workforce. Campaigns against Nike, the Gap, Liz Claiborne, and Kathy Lee Gifford's line of shoe and textile production have led to major changes in industry practices (Dhume and Tkacik 2002; Zachary and Marshall 1997; Merrick 2004; Mason 2000; Lee and Bernstein 2000; Greathead 2002).

CONCLUSION: BALANCING STATE-SOCIETY NEEDS IN DEVELOPMENTAL AND PARTICIPATORY REGULATION

Our review of recent regulatory crises in Asia underscores the framework for our analysis. In each case, there was an inter-play between external (international) forces, domestic regulators and domestic civil society. External forces would like regulation to favor their long-term returns on investment. States attempt to use regulation in developmentalist fashion to 'leapfrog' different modes of production to higher value-added ones that will raise the population's standard of living. Domestic civil society, external to the process of regulatory decision-making, uses extraordinary means, such as protest and shaming campaigns, to pressure the state for responsiveness to the costs of regulation.

The power balance among external corporate and government interests, the Asian state, and a transnational coalition of external and internal social movements varies by case. In the case of the Three Gorges Dam, the Chinese developmentalist state showed it had the upper hand. In Dhabol, the domestic state saw its own financial and political interests threatened by a foreign company and so rescinded its own contract. In the case of exploitative labor practices, social movements, primarily with the help of external non-governmental organizations, have made an impact on investment decisions and factory conditions in the region. The AFC demonstrates the deep complex interactions of different international and domestic forces at work in the evolution of domestic regulation in Asia.

However, it is vital to note that regardless of the particularities, each crisis demonstrates an unresolved conflict among powerful actors. These unresolved conflicts suggest the need for further development of regulatory practices both in Asia and elsewhere. While the developmental state model has led to great improvements in overall standards of living in East Asia, the stresses and crises of development, including regional differentiation and other forms of inequality, environmental degradation, and differential impacts on distinct populations, particularly acute in China and Indonesia, call for an adjustment of regulatory practices. Just as the developmental state in East Asia transitioned in a macro-political sense into democracies, regulatory practices can follow suit by opening up for greater participation from civil society. This would help the developmental state to consider the different costs of development choices in regulatory decision-making and avoid the acute crises of neglect noted in the examples above.

How exactly to create a more participatory form of regulation is another question that meets a theoretical abyss. In a recent article exploring modes of participation in electricity regulation in Europe, North America and Latin America, I found a surprisingly low consideration of civil society input in regulation globally (Hira *et al.* 2005). Institutional arrangements ranged from virtually nil communication of regulation with the population in some cases to a few exceptional cases of direct citizen input in Denmark and the Netherlands. There are a number of experiments as well, principally in the environmental arena, such as conducting surveys, developing citizen committees for key issues, and public outreach campaigns by regulatory commissions. Evidently, the form and type of institutional arrangement will have to vary by context.

This brings us to our most important question – can the adjusted developmental state approach as suggested above be reconciled with a more participatory regulation. While the developmental state has been strongly associated with centralized decision-making, including sectoral targeting, there could be room for modification both in terms of timing and type of decision-making. At base value, there seems to be widespread consensus within the region about the success of the developmental state within Asia. As with the relatively smooth transition to democracy in the region, the success of the developmental state can now be institutionalized on the micro level with a gradual opening toward direct civil participation. In each of the crises we reviewed, prior consultation with civil society would have diminished, if not altered, the negative impacts of regulatory decision-making. From the state's point of view, with a clear show of majority political support and some concessions to groups that do not fundamentally alter the developmental purposes of decisions taken, much political and economic grief could be avoided. By engaging activists more directly, the sense of conspiracy and outrage at a lack of transparency and consultation could be avoided. Similarly, greater transparency and participation in decision-making could show that the majority of the population stand behind the state's decision. In both cases, activists' ability to use the domestic and foreign media to shame the state (in the absence of hard information, such claims can be exaggerated) would be circumscribed. Thus, activist groups could become more integral to the political system, with their claims legitimately heard and considered. Such an evolution in regulation brings us ultimately back to the need to recognize on all sides the social embeddedness and profound consequences of regulatory decisions for society. The solution will have to be found in a new and distinctly Asian form of regulatory evolution.

ACKNOWLEDGEMENTS

I would like to thank the editor for substantial help in improving this piece. I would like to dedicate this chapter to my colleague, Mike Howlett, for his steadfast support and encouragement.

NOTES

1. Enron was a 65 per cent stakeholder, while GE and Bechtel held 10 per cent each.
2. 'Against globalization – and for power to the people', *Multinational Monitor*, **18**(11), 18–22, 1997.
3. Joanna Slater (2003), 'Another Dispute Is Brewing Between India and US Energy Companies', *Wall Street Journal*, 19 August, A7. See updated information on Dabhol at US

Energy Information Agency, http://www.eia.doe.gov/emeu/cabs/india.html, accessed 7 January 2005.
4.   'A jail by another name; China', *The Economist*, **365**(8304), 86, 2002; Bruce Gilley (2001), 'Toil and trouble', *Far Eastern Economic Review*, **164**, 50.

REFERENCES

Akerlof, George (1970) 'The Market for Lemons: Quality Uncertainty and the Market Mechanism', *Quarterly Journal of Economics*, **84**, 488–500.
Amsden, Alice (1989) *Asia's Next Giant: South Korea and Late Industrialization*, New York: Oxford University Press.
Anonymous (2003) 'Water Rising On The Yangtze', *Environment*, **45**(7), 927–32.
Antons, Christoph (ed.) (2003) *Law and Development in East and Southeast Asia*, New York: RoutledgeCurzon.
Arvis, Jean-Francois and Ronald E. Berenbeim (2003) *Fighting Corruption in East Asia: Solutions from the Private Sector*, Washington, DC: The World Bank.
Beeson, Mark (ed.) (2002) *Reconfiguring East Asia: Regional Institutions and Organisations After the Crisis*, New York: RoutledgeCurzon.
Berg, A. (1999) 'The Asia Crisis: Causes, Policy Responses, and Outcomes', Working Paper WP/99/138, Washington, DC: IMF, October.
Boyer, Robert (1990) *The Regulation School: A Critical Introduction*, New York: Columbia University Press.
Cheung, Anthony B. L. and Ian Scott (eds) (2003) *Governance and Public Sector Reform in Asia: Paradigm shifts or business as usual?*, New York: RoutledgeCurzon.
Dhume, Sadanand, and Maureen Tkacik (2002) 'Footwear Is Fleeing Indonesia – Output Drop by Nike, Others Has Implications for Key Export Model', *Wall Street Journal*, 9 September, A.12.
Dittmer, Lowell, Haruhiro Fukui and Peter N. S. Lee (eds) (2000) *Informal Politics in East Asia*, New York: Cambridge University Press.
Emadi-Coffin, Barbara (2002) *Rethinking International Organization: Deregulation and Global Governance*, New York: Routledge.
Greathead, Scott (2002) 'Making it Right', *Chain Store Age*, **78**(5), (May), 42–4.
Hira, Anil (2003a) 'Regulatory Games States Play', in Marjorie Griffin Cohen and Stephen McBride (eds), *Global Turbulence: Social Activists' and State Responses to Globalization*, Burlington, VT: Ashgate, pp. 41–58.
Hira, Anil (2003b) *Political Economy of Energy in the Southern Cone*, Westport, CT: Praeger.
Hira, Anil (2004) 'Can Development Organizations be Reinvented', in Avril Hira and Trevor Parfitt, *Development Projects for a New Millenium*, Westport, CT: Praeger, pp. 91–102.
Hira, Anil (2005), 'How Developing Countries Attract American Jobs', in Anil Hira and Ron Hira, *Outsourcing America*, New York: Amacom, pp. 147–2.
Hira, Anil (forthcoming) *The New Path: How Industrial Policy Succeeded in East Asia and Can Work in Latin America* (working title), manuscript under review.
Hira, Anil and Ron Hira (2000) 'The New Institutionalism's Contradictory Notions of Change', *The American Journal of Economics and Sociology*, (April), 267–82.
Hira, Anil, David Huxtable and Alexandre Leger (2005) 'Deregulation and Participation: An International Survey of Participation in Electricity Regulation',

Governance, **18**(1), 53–88.

Hong, Sung Gul (1997) *The Political Economy of Industrial Policy in East Asia: The Semiconductor Industry in Taiwan and South Korea*, Northampton, MA, USA and Cheltenham, UK: Edward Elgar.

Jackson, Sukhan, and Adrian C. Sleigh (2001) 'The Political Economy and Socio-Economic Impact of China's Three Gorges Dam', *Asian Studies Review*, **25**(1), 57–73.

Jayasuriya, Kanishka (ed.) (1999) *Law, Capitalism and Power in Asia: The Rule of Law and Legal Institutions*, New York: Routledge.

Jayasuriya, Kanishka (2001) 'Southeast Asia's Embedded Mercantilism in Crisis: International Strategies and Domestic Coalitions', Working Paper no. 3, April.

Jayasuriya, Kanishka (ed.) (2003) 'Governing the Asia-Pacific – Beyond the "New Regionalism"', special edition of *Third World Quarterly*, **24**, 2.

Jayasuriya, Kanishka (ed.) (2004) *Asian Regional Governance: Crisis and Change*, New York: RoutledgeCurzon.

Jayasuriya, Kanishka, and Andrew Rosser (2001) 'Economic Orthodoxy and the East Asian Crisis', *Third World Quarterly*, **22**(3), 381–96.

Johnson, Chalmers (1982) *MITI and the Japanese Miracle: The Growth of Industrial Policy, 1925–75*, Palo Alto, CA: Stanford University Press.

Jomo, K. S., C. Y. Chung, B. C. Folk, I. ul Haque, P. Pongpaichit, B. Simatupang and M. Tateshi (1997) *Southeast Asia's Misunderstood Miracle: Industrial Policy and Economic Development in Thailand, Malaysia and Indonesia*, Boulder, CO: Westview.

Kearins, Kate, and Greg O'Malley (1999) 'International Financial Institutions and the Three Gorges Hydroelectric Power Scheme', *Greener Management International*, **27**, 85-97.

Krugman, Paul (1997) 'Currency Crises', http://web.mit.edu/krugman/www/crises.html.

Lee, Louise and Aaron Bernstein (2000) 'Who Says Student Protests Don't Matter?', *Business Week*, 12 June, 94.

MacIntyre, Andrew J. and Kanishka Jayasuriya (eds) (1992) *The Dynamics of Economic Policy Reform in South-east Asia and the South-west Pacific*, New York: Oxford University Press.

Mason, Tania (2000) 'Nike axes "sweatshop" after BBC investigation', *Marketing*, 19 October, **5**.

Menkhoff, Thomas and Solvay Gerke (eds) (2002) *Chinese Entrepreneurship and Asian Business Networks*, New York: RoutledgeCurzon.

Merrick, A. (2004) 'Gap Offers Unusual Look at Factory Conditions; Fighting "Sweatshop" Tag, Retailer Details Problems Among Thousands of Plants', *Wall Street Journal*, 12 May, A.1.

North, Douglass C. (1990) *Institutions, Institutional Change and Economic Performance*, New York: Cambridge University Press.

OECD (2001) *Corporate Governance in Asia: A Comparative Perspective*, Paris: OECD.

Polanyi, Karl (1957) *The Great Transformation*, Boston, MA: Beacon Press.

Quibria, M. G. (2002) *Growth and Poverty: Lessons from the East Asian Miracle Revisited*, ADB Institute Research Paper 33, Tokyo: Asian Development Bank Institute, February.

Quing, Dai and Lawrence R. Sullivan (1999) 'The Three Gorges Dam and China's Energy Dilemma', *Journal of International Affairs*, **53**(1), 53–72.

Radelet, Steven and Jeffrey Sachs (no date) 'The East Asian Financial Crisis: Diagnoses, Remedies, Prospects', Discussion Paper No. 29, http://www.cid.harvard.edu/caer2/htm/content/papers/bns/dp29bn.htm

Richter, Frank-Jurgen, and Pamela C. M. Mar (eds) (2004) *Asia's New Crisis: Renewal Through Total Ethical Management*, Singapore: John Wiley & Sons.

Stiglitz, Joseph E. (1998), "Bad Private Sector Decisions," *The Wall Street Journal*, 4 February.

Stiglitz, Joseph E. and Shahid Yusuf (eds) (2001) *Rethinking the East Asian Miracle*, Washington, DC: World Bank and New York: Oxford University Press.

Sung-Joo, Han (ed) (1999) *Changing Values in Asia: Their Impact on Governance and Development*, Tokyo: Japan Center for International Exchange.

Tay, Simon C. and Maria Seda (eds) (2003) *The Enemy Within: Combating Corruption in Asia*, Singapore: Eastern Universities Press.

Vogel, Stephen K. (1996) *Freer Markets, More Rules: Regulatory Reform in Advanced Industrial Countries*, Ithaca, NY: Cornell University Press.

Von Hayek, Friedrich A. (1944) *The Road to Serfdom*, Chicago: University of Chicago Press.

Wade, Robert (1990) *Governing the Market: Economic Theory and the Role o Government in East Asian Industrialization*, Princeton, NJ: Princeton University Press.

Wade, Robert (2001) 'The US role in the long Asian crisis of 1990–2000', in Arvid John Lukauskas and Francisco L. Rivera-Batiz (eds), *The Political Economy of the East Asian Crisis and its Aftermath: Tigers in Distress*, Northampton, MA, USA and Cheltenham, UK: Edward Elgar, pp. 195–226.

Wade, Robert (no date) 'From Miracle to Meltdown: Vulnerabilities, Moral Hazard, Panic, and Debt Deflation in the Asian Crisis', working paper found at http://www.ids.ac.uk/ids/global/conf/pdfs/wade.pdf.

Wilke, John R. (2002) 'Enron Criminal Probe Focuses On Alleged Corruption Abroad', *Wall Street Journal*, 5 August, A.1.

World Bank (1993) T*he East Asian Miracle: Economic Growth and Public Policy*, Washington, DC: The World Bank.

Zachary, G. Pascal and Samantha Marshall (1997) 'Nike tries to quell exploitation charges', *Wall Street Journal*, 25 June, A.16.

Zhuan, Juzhong, David Edwards and Ma. Virginita A. Capulong (eds) (2000), *Corporate Governance and Finance in East Asia: A Study of Indonesia, Republic of Korea, Malaysia, Philippines, and Thailand*, Manila: Asian Development Bank.

3. Globalisation and national regulations: race to the bottom, top, and middle

M. Ramesh

The need for public management reforms to adjust to and accommodate forces unleashed by globalisation has been a major preoccupation for policy makers and commentators in recent years. International organisations, think tanks, and researchers have produced numerous reports highlighting the need for reform in the face of globalisation and proposing the mix of policy instruments they would prefer to be used. The main thrust of much of the effort is to eliminate or at least reduce the burden that regulations and other command and control policy tools supposedly impose on the economy. Notwithstanding the broad support the position enjoys in policy circles, the empirical and intellectual case for it remains under-explored.

The purpose of this chapter is to assess the forces that shape the use of regulations in the context of globalisation. Much of the existing literature on the subject treats globalisation as an omnipotent homogenising force leading governments to engage in a race to the bottom or top of the stringency ladder. The chapter will show that this is a wrong way to approach the subject because racing to the bottom or top are not the only options open to governments, as regulations may be tightened and loosened at the same time. Moreover, focus on globalisation alone underestimates the critical role that domestic factors continue to play in shaping regulations. What we have in the area of regulations is imperatives to increase competition in both public and private sectors which requires deregulation as well as reregulation. Societies' concern for cheaper goods and services is counterbalanced by their wish for higher standards of safety, equity, and accountability which, again, requires both deregulation and reregulation. Overall, there is no evidence of overwhelming global pressures promoting a race to the bottom or top, but rather a conjunction of global and domestic factors fostering something more akin to a race to the middle.

GLOBALISATION AND REGULATIONS

The debates on both globalisation and regulations are highly polarised. The debate centres on what the phenomena entail, the extent to which they have occurred, and the effects they have had on the domestic sphere. Unsurprisingly, discussions on the link between the two is rancorous and not particularly enlightening. It is not the place here to comprehensively survey the debate, but a brief sketch is unavoidable.

Much of the literature on globalisation is cast in terms of images of the state that portray the latter either as a victim or one that continues to be resilient and strong. The former – 'decline of the state' view – tends to highlight the overwhelming constraints imposed by the structure of global capitalism, whereas the opposing view – 'strong state' view – asserts the continued vitality and centrality of the sovereign state. The 'decline of the state' thesis rests on the assumption that the capitalist world economy forms a global structure which requires states to adapt to its constraining logic. (Examples of hard-line position include Ohmae 1990; Reich 1991; Falk 1997; Friedman 1999 and 2005.) For a more moderate position see Cerny (1990); Cox (1996); Palan and Abbott (1996); Strange (1996); Hoogvelt (1997) and Scholte (1997). Conversely, the 'strong state' thesis shows that the decline of the state is a 'myth', evident in the deep differences in policies and the instruments by which they are implemented across nations (Kapstein, 1994; Helleiner 1995; Evans 1997; Rodrik 1997 and 1998; Armstrong 1998; Weiss 1998).

Recently, many commentators have pointed out the shortcomings of these polar positions on the relationship between states and globalisation (see Hobson and Ramesh 2002; Bernhagen 2003). It is hard to deny that states are very much alive and are as active today in both domestic and international spheres as they have ever been. At the same time, states cannot do whatever they wish if they are to participate in the international system. The circumstances leading up to the 9/11 attack and the tough security measures that followed across the globe are as much an evidence of the globalised world as it is of the states' continuing centrality in the international arena. The recognition of the pervasive impact of globalisation coexisting with continued vitality of the state has generated a burgeoning *third way* which seeks to overcome the restrictive parameters of the conventional state/globalisation debate (see Palan and Abbott 1996; Clark 1998; Weiss 1999; Hobson and Ramesh 2002; Bernhagen 2003). But this latest trend is yet to be fully reflected in the globalisation literature dealing with national regulations, as we will see shortly in this chapter.

Debates on regulations have a longer history but continue to be just as contentious. In the first half of the twentieth century, the scope of regulations and the arguments in its support expanded greatly despite staunch opposition from many quarters, especially mainstream economists. The post-war decades saw the continuation of the momentum for expansion of regulations, reinforced by the popularity of Keynesianism which approved of state intervention in market processes. The dominance of Keynesianism at the policy level did not, however, silence detractors who saw it as fundamentally misguided, promoting economic inefficiency and even political servitude (Hayek 1944).

The critics of expansion of regulatory activities moved from the periphery to the centre of the debate amidst the economic turmoil of the 1970s and the subsequent election of conservative politicians and parties running on anti-government platforms in the UK and USA. By the mid-1980s, most Western governments had launched varying levels of efforts to deregulate the economy and privatise public enterprises with the purpose of expanding choice and competition and, assumedly, economic efficiency. The measures generated its own detractors, who described deregulation and privatisation as surrender to powerful capitalist interests and an assault on political and economic arrangements on which post-war prosperity was built and had served so well for almost three decades. Old arguments about the merits of free markets versus regulated markets were revived and regurgitated in intellectual and political debates.

The intellectual case for regulations, developed over nearly a century, is strong. It can correct many types of market failures, including public goods, monopoly industries and asymmetrical information. Economic regulations are often rooted in a desire to promote the supply of desirable public goods or introduce competition in monopoly industries whereas social regulations are more likely to have arisen to address problems of information asymmetry and social injustice.

The case against regulation and, as a corollary, the case for deregulation is no less convincing. Regulations are alleged to erode economic efficiency by muting competition and generally distorting market processes. Political objections to it are raised on the grounds that regulations foster a revolving door among the regulators and the regulated and pandering to powerful sectional interests at the expense of consumers. On practical grounds, it is argued that even when regulations may be justifiable on technical grounds, they are hard to employ effectively due to government failures in the form of incomplete information, institutional fragmentation and pressures from powerful social groups.

The spread of globalisation is argued to have enhanced the case for deregulation, especially in the economic sphere. It is argued that to the extent globalisation has expanded the scope and intensity of market processes, firms need to be free to respond to it as they deem fit or is wiped out by competition.

There are others, however, who remain unconvinced that regulations are, or have become, as dysfunctional and unnecessary as alleged and have a counter-argument for every claim in favour of deregulation. Some retort that economic efficiency based on market competition is a mirage because of the dominance of international oligopolies promoted by globalisation. Furthermore, corruption and pork-barrelling are not particular to regulated economies: indeed governments vulnerable to them would find it no easier to maintain competitive markets. And so the debate between those in favour of regulation and those against goes on.

GLOBALISATION'S EFFECTS ON REGULATIONS

Discussion on globalisation's effects on regulation reflect and extend the controversies surrounding each. But one point over which most of the contending protagonists agree is that globalisation is promoting regulatory convergence across nations. However, this is where the agreement ends. For some, the convergence is towards laxity whereas for others it is towards greater stringency. The two lines of argument are metaphorically summarised as Race to the Bottom (RTB) and Race to the Top (RTT). There are further divisions within the RTB camp: for some it is a race away from over-regulation, and hence desirable, while for others it a destructive beggar-thy-neighbour competition in abnegation of governmental responsibility (Kahler 2004: 5).

Despite diametrically opposite conclusions, a similar starting point and logic underlies the contending views. Based on the assumption that market forces unleashed by globalisation reign supreme in the modern world, both sides argue that states have no choice but to conform to the homogenising imperatives of globalisation. The global imperatives to deregulate the economy and society in the face of globalisation are accepted as a *fait accompli* by both sides. Where they differ is their different conceptualisation of how globalisation interacts with national governments.

Beneath the technical niceties of the debate lie the protagonists' personal predilections and ideologies. Those who prefer market to state celebrate globalisation and its deregulatory effects and call for more of it, whereas the sceptics take the opposite position.

Underlying the support for deregulation lays preference for the efficiency and choice that market competition involves and the freedom it upholds. In globalisation they find yet another reason for calling for further deregulation (Evans 1997). The superior economic performance of the UK, USA and Australia during the 1990s is attributed to their governments' enthusiastic deregulation and privatization efforts. Problems at Enron, Andersen and Long

Term Capital Management are shrugged off as anomalies and indeed excessive rather than insufficient regulations (Dowd 1999; Kiesling 2001).

Those in favour of extensive use of regulations tend to be suspicious of the market and see the state as an essential component of efforts to curb its ill-effects. The accentuation of market competition under globalisation only highlights the case for stricter competition. They also argue that the basic purpose of any government is to protect its citizens from uncertainties, including those generated by globalisation, through regulations and other means. Similarly, the emphasis on profits in globalised firms is said to expand the scope for negative externalities which accentuates rather than undermine the case for regulation of business.

The images of governments engaged in a race to the bottom to cope with imperatives of globalisation occupy a central position in popular as well as academic debates. The notion of RTB has its origins in studies of competition among American states for firms to incorporate in their territory. In this understanding, each state government feels pressured to at least match Delaware's relaxed chartering requirements. The concept of the 'Delaware Effect', as it is popularly known, was later extended to the international arena whereby national governments compete for foreign investments by lowering their regulations and taxes. The perception was further reinforced by high profile privatisation and deregulation in transportation, telecommunication and financial industries in many countries in the 1980s and 1990s, rationalised by governments as an unavoidable response to globalisation. The New Public Management (NPM) initiative further reinforced the image of retreating states in the face of globalisation (see OECD 1995; Peters 2000; McCourt and Minogue 2001). But anecdotes do not make evidence.

The global economy offers unprecedented opportunities for firms to locate in jurisdictions with lower costs in terms of not only lower wages but also regulations and taxes (Cerny 1996). In this view, in the words of Myles Kahler (2004: 4), 'Governments that do not participate in the race to the bottom risk isolation on a high-cost mountaintop, eroding the competitiveness of their economies.' Import competing firms when faced with enhanced competition they find difficult to cope with interpret it as a result of regulatory laxity in the exporting economy, requiring parallel deregulation at home (Kahler 2004: 11–12). 'Process-related' regulations[1] are particularly vulnerable to 'Delaware effect' due to producers' demand for it on the belief that the restrictions impose an unnecessary cost on them and the consumers' lack of concern for how products are made (Scharpf 1998).

The rise of tiger economies (Hong Kong, Korea, Singapore, Taiwan) in the 1980s, and cubs (Malaysia and Thailand) and dragon (China) in the 1990s as major players in export markets further galvanised the debate. Their lower wages combined with lesser regulation and taxes, the argument goes, make it impossible for Western producers to compete with them. Their home governments' support in the form of lower regulations and taxes, it was claimed, was essential for them to be able to compete. The industrialised countries that have deregulated and privatised – particularly the Anglo-American countries – are cited as reaping the benefits of higher economic growth while the reform laggards in continental Europe continue to struggle.

The global economic competition exerts pressures not only on the developed but also the developing countries. The latter, even when they do adopt tough regulations, are reluctant to enforce them due to fears that doing so would render their economies less competitive in comparison with other developing countries (Porter 1999: 138). The competition is thus '"dragging down" the regulatory standards not of rich countries but of other poor ones' (Vogel and Kagan 2002: 5).

The preoccupation with RTB and the widespread fear of it is not supported by empirical evidence, however (Wheeler 2000; Drezner 2001). Kahler (2004: 20) in his survey of empirical findings on globalisation finds little evidence of RTB in regulations: 'Even in regulatory domains where the effect of regulation on firm costs is substantial and transparent, such as taxation and financial regulation (e.g., reserve requirements or interest rate ceilings) and the barriers to mobility are relatively low, a race to the 'bottom' has not occurred. If a RTB had been completed, no tax havens, offshore banking or Delaware effect would remain: the 'bottom' would have been reached.' Nor have process-related regulations, which are supposedly more vulnerable, been rolled back despite producers' demands (Scharpf 1998). Even in instances when there has been significant deregulation, often they have been offset by institution of other regulations. For example, in banking, which is one of the most globalised sectors, deregulation and reregulation has proceeded simul-taneously (Busch 2002).

It is arguable that the lack of empirical evidence in support of RTB does not matter because in politics it is the perception that matters more than the reality. And the perception is that nations are locked in internecine competition for trade and investment which leads them to do whatever will please international business, including reduction of regulations. Swire acknow-ledges that the 'perception of a prisoner's dilemma may well be more important than whether one really exists', while Steven Vogel argues that 'market pressures are most constraining when leaders believe them to be all-powerful ...' (cited in Kahler 2004: 27).

Kahler (2004: 34) sums up the situation well: 'Evidence is slender for a "race" rather than a more benign competitive process that produces regulatory diversity without persistent downward pressure on regulatory standards in the large, rich economies. The political bases for RTB claims, however, remain sturdy, and that produces a central policy dilemma (but not an unprecedented one): dealing with a "threat" that is more a set of beliefs or perceptions than an established empirical reality.'

Not only is there no evidence of overall deregulation, much less a race to the bottom, it is arguable that the movement is in the opposite direction as regulations have increased rather than declined during the heightened period of globalisation. Levi-Faur and Gillard (2005) note the following recent trends in the field of regulations. First, there has been an increase in the number and power of autonomous regulatory agencies and separate 'next step' delivery agencies. Second, there has been conscious increase in 'formalisation of rules and codification of responsibilities in both public and private spheres'. Third, there has been a 'Proliferation of [new] technologies of regulation, most notably self-regulation, meta-regulation, and enforced self-regulation'. The new instruments are administered not just by governmental regulators but also social groups and professional bodies. Observation of expansion of regulations has led some to conclude that we now live in an era of 'regulatory state' (Majone 1997; Jayasuriya 2001).

While governments were claiming to be engaged in deregulation, they were actually strengthening regulatory bodies with expanded authority and greater analytical and policing resources. In the UK, Levi-Faur and Gillard (2005) note, total personnel in regulatory bodies nearly doubled between the mid-1970 and 1990s at the same time as the numbers declined by one-quarter in the overall civil service. By the end of 2002, at least 120 countries had established new regulatory authorities in the telecoms industry and 70 in electricity, compared with only 11 and 5 respectively in 1989 (Levi-Faur and Gillard 2005). Many of the new regulations were intended to compensate for privatisation of public monopolies which required separate regulations for what used to be done directly as a function of ownership. Heightened concerns about the environment, product safety, and working conditions also led to expansion and tightening of regulations in these areas.

Some commentators, among whom Vogel (1995) is the most prominent, take the argument yet further and argue that in the area of regulations, there is a 'race' to tighten regulations. Genschel and Plumper (1997 cited in Vogel and Kagan 2002: 8) point to the standardisation of capital adequacy requirements in international banking and agreement on a common withholding tax on interest payments present as examples of regulatory standards inching upwards. Similarly, Wheeler (2000) finds air quality in major urban areas in both developed and developing countries – China, Brazil, Mexico and the US – to have improved significantly during periods of accelerated globalisation.

Globalisation, in the race to the bottom perspective is said to have strengthened both product and process-related regulations. Consumers' preference for safe products leads firms to try to provide them, while governments find it politically expedient to prescribe it. What is more remarkable is that even in the area of process standards, which do not directly concern consumers and thus allow governments to succumb to producers' demand for lower standards, there is an upward rather than downward movement. Measures to protect workers, women and the environment in most countries have been strengthened rather than weakened in recent decades, at least partly due to the demands of cross-national environmentalist and human rights groups that have emerged in recent years.

To argue whether there is a race to the top or the bottom with respect to regulations may be the wrong way to address the issue, however, because it assumes that shifts can only be in one direction. In reality, deregulation and reregulation in any policy sector may be going on at the same time as governments loosen some regulations and tighten others. The complex interplay between global and national forces mediated by national governments and civil society preclude the emergence of predictable trajectories. In the environment sector, for instance, some prescriptive regulations have been substituted with charge or tradeable quota based systems at the same time as regulations are being applied to areas which were previously left alone. Labour standards is yet another example of seemingly contradictory regulatory developments. Some regulations regarding hiring and firing have been eased while others related to discrimination and workplace safety have been increased. This would appear contradictory only if one starts from the simple assumption that globalisation fosters unlinear shifts in policies.

The more sophisticated writings on the subject have begun to recognise that both regulation and deregulation can and do occur at the same time (Levi-Faur 2005; Vogel 1996). In many respects deregulation and reregulation are two sides of the same coin. Indeed it is arguable that some degree of reregulation is essential for deregulation and privatisation to proceed. Successful liberalisation of financial markets, for instance, requires enhanced supervision and regulation, a point proven painfully by the Asian economic crisis of 1997–98. The awareness is sharpened by the increasing realisation, notwithstanding the dogmatism of many protagonists in the debate, that regulations are inherently neither good nor bad: their impact rather depends on the context and the purpose for which they are used (see Howlett, this volume; Gunningham, this volume).

THE IMPERATIVES FOR DEREGULATION AND REREGULATION

Two seemingly contradictory trends are evident in the area of contemporary regulations: governments are deregulating at the same time as they are reregulating. While governments express commitment to reducing their control over the economy and society and have taken measures to put it into practice, they have also been increasing the scope and intensity of regulations. There is more than hypocrisy underlying the contradiction between what governments say and do. As mentioned earlier, deregulation and reregulation are not separate phenomenon but different aspects of the same one. Many of the factors that precipitated and promoted deregulation have also shaped, though not in the same ways or to the same degree, reregulation. The literatures on deregulation and Race to the Bottom on the one hand and on reregulation and Race to the Top on the other are so disconnected from each other that their proponents fail to see the common grounds between them. The point will become clearer in the following discussion.

The factors shaping deregulation and reregulation may be usefully categorised as global and domestic.

Global Factors

Multinational corporations (MNCs) are the key vehicles of economic globalisation and their priorities are believed to have had a decisive impact on what governments do. Their extreme cost consciousness and the global scope of their activities is said to afford them both the motive and ability to move to sites with lowest costs, threatening production sites elsewhere with higher regulatory, labour, and other costs. Faced with such powerful and mobile corporations, governments are left with no option but to establish conditions that would both dissuade them from leaving their territory and, preferably, attract new ones to invest. Since governments can only indirectly affect costs of land and labour, lowering regulations and taxes are the most direct and effective means of making their territory attractive to MNCs.

The reality of multinational firms' behaviour is not so simple, however. They seek lower regulations only when, according to Spar and Yoffie (2000: 1), four conditions obtain: 'the products or key inputs for the firms are homogeneous, cross-border differentials are significant, and both sunk and transaction costs are minimal'. But all these conditions are rarely met in reality. Products and key inputs are frequently too different to be comparable in ways that reveal clear-cut choice. And even when meaningful comparison is possible, sunk and transaction costs may be too high to be worth the cost of relocation. As a result, firms rarely have the inclination or capacity to shift or even credibly threaten to shift to other sites and instead learn to cope with existing regulations and, if possible, seek a more conducive regulatory environment in their home country through reform (Vogel and Kagan 2002: 5).

In any case, the cost of regulations is not always as burdensome as portrayed and may provide little incentive to relocate. Wheeler (2000: 3) points out that the cost of complying with environmental regulations is modest especially when compared with the costs and uncertainties of relocating to a new site. There is no certainty that the country to which they relocate would not later increase its standards. Firms may also find it less expensive to standardise their performance to higher standards (Vogel and Kagan 2002: 4). The fact vast majority of international investment and trade occurs among industrialised countries, which tend to have comparable and generally higher standards, also obviates the need for firms to constantly seek lower standards (Anderson and Kagan 2000, cited in Vogel and Kagan 2002: 5). Even in the most globalised financial sectors, firms have not urged adoption of standards prevailing in tax havens. Lack of credibility, stability and security are costly for financial firms, indeed to varying degrees for all firms, and they would rather comply with stringent conditions than operate under uncertainty (Kahler 2004: 22–3).

More significantly, regulations do not necessarily erode national economic competitiveness and, consequently, there may be no pressure on governments to deregulate and, indeed, the opposite may be the case in practice. There is no observed positive relationship between economic openness and deregulation. Indeed Eliste and Fredriksson (1998) found that more open economies have more stringent regulations. Similarly, some of the most competitive economies in the world are also the most highly regulated: for instance, Denmark, Finland, Germany, the Netherlands, Norway, Sweden and Switzerland rank in the top 15 in the competitiveness ranking despite a tough regulatory environment (World Economic Forum 2005). This is not unexpected because firms do not prefer lower regulations per se: what they instead prefer is lower costs, including transaction costs. Regulations may offer lower transaction costs under some circumstances, as when it is a part of a larger institutional setup such as organised capitalism (Gourevitch 2004). Scharpf (1998) is correct in his assertion that:

> governments attempting to improve international competitiveness are by no means limited to reducing production costs through tax cuts, deregulation, or currency devaluation. Comparative advantages can also be achieved through policies stimulating productivity, innovation and specialization. In other words, states are not necessarily compelled to enter a 'race to the bottom' in order to defend market shares at the expense of welfare losses.

Some industries may well require deregulations to be competitive in the global economy but others may require more, depending on the industry and circumstances it faces.

Instead of just not seeking lower regulatory standards, in certain circumstances firms may actually seek higher standards or seek new standards in areas where none exist, that is, engage in a race to the top rather than the bottom (Vogel and Kagan 2002: 10–11). First, in the realm of product standards (in contrast to process standards), firms are under constant pressure to improve quality lest their products lose out to competition and are hence less likely to ask for lowering of standards. Second, if the market size of the country with stricter standards is larger than the standards in the less strict country, then the latter will be pressured to raise its standards. Third, and related to the preceding, standards are likely to go up when a country's major export market has stricter regulations and firms are used to complying with them. Fourth, producers may ask for strengthening rather than weakening of standards if the costs of the change is lower than the benefits of market access expected from the change.

The growing economic and political interdependence that globalisation involves affords expanded opportunities for influencing other governments' policies. Powerful nations are especially able to bilaterally pressure other governments to change their regulatory and other barriers in ways that make it possible for their firms to compete in the host country (Vogel and Kagan 2002: 13). The pressure is not always for weakening of regulations but may be for strengthening as well if it is in their interest, as in the case of protection of intellectual property rights.

However, bilateral arrangements are not as common as multilateral arrangements on regulatory changes because of the higher level of confidence they offer. International agreements providing for regulations exist in areas as diverse as banking, information privacy, biological diversity, civil aviation and disposal of hazardous waste (for a sample, see Electronic Information System for International Law, www.eisil.org/ and the Multilaterals Project, fletcher.tufts.edu/multilaterals.html). The nature and scope of the regulatory obligations imposed by such agreements vary considerably. Some of the arrangements require relaxing of regulatory standards while others require their raise.

Trade is of course the area in which there exist the most elaborate international regulations. Here too both deregulation and reregulation trends are evident. Some trade agreements are explicitly designed to weaken or eliminate national regulations that impede trade: for instance, General Agreement on Services on Banking, Telecommunications, etc. and Trade Related Investment Measures (TRIM). There are, however, other agreements that increase the scope or stringency of regulations: Trade in Intellectual Property rights (TRIPS) and Basel Capital Accord, for example.

Environment is a particularly apt example of globalisation's conflicting effects on national regulations. On the one hand, we have the GATT decision in the tuna-dolphin case where the international organisation hindered establishment of higher standards while the Montreal Protocol on CFC and Basel accord on hazardous waste trade embodied international efforts to raise standards (Vogel and Kagan 2002: 22–3). Labour standards are another such example. On the one hand, countries with regulation-induced higher wage costs are pressured to reduce the burden on their firms. On the other hand, the more powerful states with stronger labour regulations protect their interests by pressuring other governments to raise their standards. It is unsurprising that in many industrialised countries regulations regarding hiring and firing have been eased at the same time as those related to discrimination and workplace safety have been increased (Gitterman 2002).

Many international agreements affecting national regulations have emerged under the aegis of, or sponsored by, international governmental organisations (IGOs) dealing with an issue on a continuing basis. Expanded economic and political exchange that globalisation involves creates expanded opportunities for cross-national interaction among policy practitioners and commentators. There exist countless international governmental organisations which bring people with common policy interests together at formal and informal meetings (for a partial list of major IGOs, see www.lib.msu.edu/publ_ser/docs/igos/igoswww.htm). They provide a forum for learning from each other's experiences as well as a vehicle for socialisation which promotes common understanding of policy problems and solutions to them (see Bernstein and Cashore 2000: 73; Keck and Sikkink 1998).

Opportunities for policy learning at the international level can be about deregulation or reregulation. The IGOs are also a main vehicle for popularising policy ideas that form a basis for emulation elsewhere. Simmons and Elkins (2003) emphasise emulation in their explanation of similar financial liberalisation patterns across countries. The deregulation of air transportation and telecommunications in the UK and the US in the 1980s, and the decline in prices that followed, was widely emulated around the world in the following decades. But there were also experiences that led to stricter regulatory standards, in the electricity sector for example.

International non-governmental organisations (INGOs) have proliferated even more rapidly than IGOs in recent decades. These new entrants to international politics are shaping regulations by monitoring common policy problems, proposing solutions, and collaborating with their counterparts in other countries to secure regulatory changes. According to Kahler and Lake (2004), 'As economic integration expands, new groups are mobilized into politics because of transnational spillovers, including environmentalists, consumers, and other activists who are increasingly concerned with not only where but also how goods are produced.' While there may be business-related NGOs seeking reduction in regulations, a large number of NGOs concentrate on the rights of labour, women, and consumers involving collective actions to make regulations more stringent. Gelb (2002) for instance highlights the role of NGOs in promoting international norms to advance women's causes through legislative and regulatory changes in the areas of maternity leave, child-care, equal pay, non-discrimination and sexual harassment.

Domestic Factors

While recent commentators rightly highlight global factors' impact on national regulations, they unnecessarily and unjustifiably ignore the importance of domestic forces in shaping regulations. The importance of domestic factors in shaping globalisation and its effects on national polity is, fortunately, gradually beginning to be acknowledged (Weiss 2002). But domestic political actors, institutions and traditions do more than just intermediate global factors' effects: they are often the primary determinant with global forces playing only a supplementary role. It is not surprising that the underlying causes of the shift towards deregulation and reregulation are often domestic rather than global.

Different sectors in a market economy are related to each other in complex and subtle ways and action in one area often necessitates a corresponding action in another. Deregulation of telecommunication prices in many countries, for example, had to be followed by deregulation of market entry by new firms. Sometimes deregulation requires further reregulation rather than deregulation: deregulation of utilities pricing, for instance, requires imposition of new regulations on the existing dominant player lest it muzzles competition from new entrants.

Domestic groups' political pursuit of self-interest is also behind contradictory regulatory trends. Export-interests and those businesses trying to get into industries from which they are shut out by regulations favour removal of the restrictions. Domestic firms that expect to better compete at home and abroad if subjected to fewer restrictions pressure their governments to lower regulations. The same is true for domestic firms who expect to enter new product lines or industries from which they are shut out by regulations. They are especially likely to ask for laxity in process standards – environmental and labour standards, for instance – which involve significant production costs but about which consumers don't much care.

Many deregulation measures are intended to iron out anomalies and obsolescence rather than a response to any particular economic or political pressure (Wilson 2003). The campaign for removal or at least weakening of regulations is often led by small businesses, which find the cost of complying particularly onerous. Their demand cannot be ignored because of the considerable political clout they wield at the local level due to their large numbers and central position in the community. The campaign finds ready support among voters who may have their own reason for disaffection with what they see as bureaucratic red tape. The regulators' frustration with implementing further reinforces the calls for streamlining regulations.

However, there are businesses that gain from enhanced regulations and use political opportunities available to them to raise standards. Examples include firms seeking protection from competition and industries in which certainty and stability is important, such as financial products. Another situation promoting increased regulations is newly privatised sectors in which governments seek to promote competition through greater regulations. Bad experiences with deregulation elsewhere also promotes reregulation (see Trebing and Miller 2004) – for example, deregulation of electricity production in California or of bus services in Sri Lanka.

The vicissitude of changes in regulations has also been shaped by the rough and tumble of national politics with governments and opposition seeking to differentiate themselves from each other by adopting opposite positions on regulatory issues. In the 1980s, many governments were elected on the plank to reduce 'red tape' and generally roll back the state while their opponents emphasised the virtues of state protection. Beginning in the 1990s, many political parties – for example, Labour in Australia and the UK, Clinton Democrats in the US, Social Democrats in Germany – adopted a 'third way' platform promising a non-doctrinaire approach to public policy which promoted economic efficiency while protecting citizens from its undesirable consequences.

The changes in regulatory conditions involving both deregulation and reregulation is also a by-product of the New Public Management movement which seeks to introduce public sector practices to government while recognising the government's unique functions (see Borins 2001; Christensen and Laegreid 2001; Gruening 2001; Hood 1995; Shields and Evans 1998). While critics often find it convenient to describe proponents of NPM as doctrinaire free marketeers, the reality is more complex, as they seek marketisation (and its corollary deregulation) of some aspects and increased control over others. NPM is no doubt about winding back the direct role of the state in the economy ('steering rather than rowing'), devolution of responsibility, partnership with the private sector, but it is also about greater accountability, performance evaluation and competition in both private and public sectors.

It is also arguable that increased regulations are intended to compensate for, or offset, various changes that have occurred in recent years. Governments increase regulations to compensate for loss of control resulting from privatisation and public management reforms granting expanded autonomy to public managers (Levi-Faur and Gillard 2005). The need for maintaining quality in recently deregulated sectors is yet another reason for enhanced deregulation because it is feared that producers will reduce costs by compromising the quality and safety of the product. Similarly, it is arguable that new regulations at times compensate for the destruction of 'club government' based on trust and informal norms (Moran 2004). What used to be done informally through peer review or norm-conforming behaviours must now be done formally under government requirement. Many of the reforms are intended to promote goals – accountability, transparency, plurality of representation – that are an integral part of governance in a liberal democracy.

CONCLUSIONS

The chapter surveyed contemporary trends in regulations with the purpose of assessing globalisation's role in shaping them. While much of the literature speaks of the homogenising effects of globalisation which is leading governments to engage in a regulatory race in which they must either lower or raise standards, there is no evidence demonstrating unilinear shift in either direction. What we find instead is conflicting patterns with greater regulatory laxity and stringency occurring at the same time.

The observation of inconsistent regulatory patterns is not as contradictory as may superficially appear. The heightened international competition that globalisation involves no doubt exerts pressures on governments to allow freer reign to market forces, but market forces require expanded government involvement in order to operate smoothly. The situation is further complicated by imperatives of domestic politics which lead governments to respond to their citizens' need for greater security, safety, equity and accountability. The net result of these imperatives is that contemporary governments are required to engage in deregulation and reregulation at the same time. This is hardly surprising given that governments unavoidably pursue competing objectives.

The simultaneous pursuit of deregulation and reregulation is entirely consistent with the imperatives of globalisation. What globalisation requires of national governments is establishment of conditions that promote competitiveness of their firms, not deregulation per se. In fact deregulation designed to promote competition may require tougher regulations to force firms to compete and not use their market position to stifle competition.

NOTES

1. In contrast, 'product-related' regulations are not subject to downward pressures due to global competition ('race to the bottom'). The 'California effect', named after the diffusion of stricter Californian car gas emission standards to other jurisdictions, is perhaps the norm for product standards. Consumers prefer higher quality products and it is in producers' interest to meet the demand, regardless of the regulations in place. When a local or international producer raises its product standards, its competitors immediately come under pressure to at least match if not do better. Certainly no industry player wishes to be associated with lower standards, other things being equal. If the product competiton is global, then we would expect global increase rather than decrease in standards.

REFERENCES

Armstrong, David (1998) 'Globalization and the Social State', *Review of International Studies*, **24**, 461–78.

Bennett, Colin J. and Michael Howlett (1992) 'The Lessons of Learning: Reconciling Theories of Policy Learning and Policy Change', *Policy Sciences*, **25**(3), 275–94.

Bernhagen, Patrick (2003) 'Is Globalization What States Make of It? Micro-Foundations of the State-Market Condominium in the Global Political Economy', *Contemporary Politics*, **9**(3), 257–76.

Bernstein, Steven, and Benjamin Cashore (2000) 'Globalization, Four Paths of Internationalization, and Domestic Policy Change: The Case of Ecoforestry in British Columbia, Canada', *Canadian Journal of Political Science*, **33**, 67–99.

Borins, Sandford (2001) 'Public Management Innovation in Economically Advanced and Developing Countries', *International Review of Administrative Sciences*, **67**, 715–31.

Busch, Andreas (2002) *Divergence or Convergence? State Regulation of the Banking System in Western Europe and the United States*, Contribution to the Workshop on Theories of Regulation, Nuffield College, Oxford, 25–26 May.

Cerny, Philip G. (1990) *The Changing Architecture of Politics*, Thousand Oaks, CA: Sage.

Cerny, P. G. (1996) 'International Finance and the Erosion of State Policy Capacity', in P. Gummett (ed.), *Globalization and Public Policy*, Cheltenham: Edward Elgar, pp. 83–104.

Christensen, Tom and Per Laegreid (eds) (2001) *New Public Management: The Transformation of Ideas and Practice*, Aldershot: Ashgate.

Clark, Ian (1998) 'Beyond the Great Divide: Globalization and the Theory of International Relations', *Review of International Studies*, **24**, 479–98.

Cox, Robert W. (1996) *Approaches to World Order*, Cambridge: Cambridge University Press, pp. 296–313.

Dowd, Kevin (1999) 'Too Big to Fail?: Long-Term Capital Management and the Federal Reserve', Cato Institute Briefing Papers #52, http://www.cato.org/pubs/briefs/bp52.pdf.

Drezner, D. W. (2001) 'Globalization and Policy Convergence', *The International Studies Review*, **3**(1), 53–78.

Eliste, P. and Fredriksson, P. G. (1998) *Does Open Trade Result in a Race to the Bottom? Cross Country Evidence*, unpublished manuscript, World Bank.

Evans, Peter (1997) 'The Eclipse of the State? Reflections on Stateness in an Era of Globalization', *World Politics*, **50**(1), 62–87.

Falk, Richard A. (1997) 'State of Siege: Will Globalization Win Out?', *International Affairs*, **73**(1), 123–36.

Friedman, Thomas L. (1999) *The Lexus and the Olive Tree*, London: HarperCollins.

Friedman, Thomas L. (2005) *The World Is Flat: A Brief History of the Twenty-first Century*, New York: Farrar, Straus and Giroux.

Gelb, Joyce (2002) 'Feminism, NGOs, and the Impact of the New Transnationalisms', in David Vogel and Robert Kagan (eds) *Dynamics of Regulatory Change: How Globalization Affects National Regulatory Policies*, Berkeley, CA: University of California Press, http://repositories.cdlib.org/uciaspubs/editedvolumes/1/9.

Gitterman, Daniel P. (2002) 'A Race to the Bottom, a Race to the Top or the March to a Minimum Floor? Economic Integration and Labor Standards in Comparative Perspective', in David Vogel and Robert Kagan (eds) *Dynamics of Regulatory*

Change: How Globalization Affects National Regulatory Policies, Berkeley, CA: University of California Press, http://repositories.cdlib.org/uciaspubs/editedvolumes/1/10.

Gourevitch, Peter (2004) 'Corporate Governance: Global Markets, National Politics', in M. Kahler and D. Lake (eds) *Governance in a Global Economy*, Princeton: Princeton University Press, Chapter 12.

Gruening, Gernod (2001) 'Origin and Theoretical Basis of New Public Management', *International Public Management Journal*, **4**, 1–25.

Hayek, Friedrich A. Von (1944) *The Road to Serfdom*, Chicago: University of Chicago Press.

Helleiner, Eric (1995) *States and the Reemergence of Global Finance*, Ithaca, NY: Cornell University Press.

Hobson, John and M. Ramesh (2002) 'Globalisation Makes of States What States Make of It: Between Agency and Structure in the State/Globalisation Debate', *New Political Economy*, **7**(1), 5–22.

Hood, Christopher (1995) 'Contemporary Public Management: A New Global Paradigm?', *Public Policy and Administration*, **10**(2), 104–17.

Hoogvelt, Ankie (1997) *Globalisation and the Postcolonial World*, Basingstoke: Macmillan.

Jayasuriya, Kanishka (2001) 'Globalization and the Changing Architecture of the State: The Politics of the Regulatory State and the Politics of Negative Co-ordination', *Journal of European Public Policy*, **8**(1), 101–23.

Kahler, Miles (2004) *Modeling Races to the Bottom*, unpublished paper http://irpshome.ucsd.edu/faculty/mkahler/RaceBott.pdf.

Kahler, M. and D. Lake (eds) (2004) *Governance in a Global Economy*, Princeton: Princeton University Press.

Kapstein, Ethan B. (1994) *Governing the Global Economy*, Cambridge, MA: Harvard University Press.

Keck, Margaret E. and Kathryn Sikkink (1998) *Activists Beyond Borders: Advocacy Networks in International Politics*, Ithaca, NY: Cornell University Press.

Kiesling, Lynne (2001) 'Flimsy excuse for more regulation', *Houston Chronicle*, 2 December.

Levi-Faur, David (2005) 'The Global Diffusion of Regulatory Capitalism', *The Annals of the American Academy of Political and Social Science*, **598**, 12–32.

Levi-Faur, D. and S. Gillard (2005) 'The Rise of the British Regulatory State – Transcending the Privatization Debate', *Comparative Politics*, **37**(1), 105.

Majone, Giandomenico (1997) 'From the Positive to the Regulatory State. Causes and Consequences of Changes in the Mode of Governance', *Journal of Public Policy*, **17**(2), 139–67.

McCourt, Willy and Martin Minogue (eds) (2001) *The Internationalization of Public Management: Reinventing the Third World State*, Cheltenham: Edward Elgar.

Moran, Michael (2004) *The British Regulatory State: High Modernism and Hyper-Innovation*, Oxford: Oxford University Press.

OECD (1995) *Governance in Transition: Public Management Reforms in OECD Countries*, Paris: Organization for Economic Co-operation and Development.

Ohmae, Kenichi (1990) *The Borderless World*, London: HarperCollins.

Palan, Ronen and Jason Abbott (1996) *State Strategies in the Global Political Economy*, London: Pinter.

Peters, B. Guy (2000) 'Public-Service Reform: Comparative Perspectives', in E. Lindquist (eds), *Government Restructuring and Career Public Services*, Toronto:

Institute of Public Administration of Canada, 27–40.

Porter, Gareth (1999) 'Trade Competition and Pollution Standards: "Race to the Bottom" or "Stuck at the Bottom"?', *Journal of Environment and Development*, **8**(2), 133–51.

Reich, Robert B. (1991) *The Work of Nations*, New York: A. Knopf.

Rodrik, Dani (1997) *Has Globalization Gone Too Far?*, Washington, DC: Institute for International Economics.

Rodrik, Dani (1998) 'Why Do Open Economies Have Bigger Governments?', *Journal of Political Economy*, **106**(5), 997–1032.

Scharpf, Fritz W. (1998) 'Globalization: The Limitations on State Capacity', *Swiss Political Science Review*, **4**(1), 2–8.

Scholte, Jan Aart (1997) 'Global Capitalism and the State', *International Affairs*, **73**, 440–51.

Shields, John and B. Mitchell Evans (1998) *Shrinking the State: Globalization and Public Administration 'Reform'*, Halifax: Fernwood.

Simmons, Beth and Zachary Elkins (2003) 'Globalization and Policy Diffusion: Explaining Three Decades of Liberalization', in Miles Kahler and David Lake (eds), *Governance in a Global Economy: Political Authority in Transition*, Princeton: Princeton University Press, chapter 11.

Spar, Debora, and David B. Yoffie (2000) 'A Race to the Bottom or Governance from the Top?', in A. Prakash and J. A. Hart (eds) *Coping with Globalization*, London: Routledge.

Strange, Susan (1996) *The Retreat of the State*, Cambridge: Cambridge University Press.

Trebing, H. M. and E. S. Miller (2004) 'The Limitations of Deregulation Revisited', *Utilities Policy*, **12**(3), 105–8.

Vogel, David (1995) *Trading Up: Consumer and Environmental Regulation in a Global Economy*, Cambridge, MA: Harvard University Press.

Vogel, David and Robert A. Kagan (2002) 'National Regulations in a Global Economy', in David Vogel and Robert Kagan (eds) *Dynamics of Regulatory Change: How Globalization Affects National Regulatory Policies*, Berkeley, CA: University of California Press, http://repositories.cdlib.org/uciaspubs/editedvolumes/1/Introduction.

Vogel, Stephen (1996) *Freer Markets, More Rules: Regulatory Reform in Advanced Industrial Countries*, Studies in Political Economy. Ithaca, NY and London: Cornell University Press

Weiss, Linda (1998) *The Myth of the Powerless State: Governing the Economy in a Global Era*, Oxford: Polity Press.

Weiss, Linda (1999) 'Globalization and National Governance: Antinomy or Interdependence?', *Review of International Studies*, **25**(5), 1–30.

Weiss, Linda (eds) (2002) *States in the Global Economy: Bringing Domestic Institutions Back In*, New York and Cambridge: Cambridge University Press.

Wheeler, D. (2000) Racing to the Bottom? Foreign Investment and Air Pollution in Developing Countries, *Journal of Environment & Development*, **10**(3), 225–45.

Wilson, Graham K. (2003) 'Changing Regulatory Systems', A Paper for the Annual Convention of the American Political Science Association, Philadelphia, August, http://www.lafollette.wisc.edu/facultystaff/wilson/ChangingRegulatorySystems.pdf.

World Economic Forum (2005) *Global Competitiveness Report 2004-2005*, Geneva: author. http://www.weforum.org/site/homepublic.nsf/Content/Global+Competitiveness+Programme%5CGlobal+Competitiveness+Report.

PART II

Deregulation and its discontents: cases in
East Asian regulatory reform

4. Power's promise: electricity reforms in Eastern Europe and Central Asia

J. A. Lampietti, S. G. Banerjee, J. Ebinger, M. Shkaratan, G. Sargsyan, I. Klytchnikova and K. Van den Berg

Energy sector reforms remain among the most controversial development issues in transition economies, as these countries continue to tread the path toward sustainable growth. The legacy of central planning left the electricity sector highly centralized, vertically integrated, and often inefficient and deeply in debt. Falling service quality, continuing lack of investment, and persistent sector deficits made the reforms urgent in the Eastern Europe and Central Asia (ECA) region. International financial institutions have spent millions of dollars on power sector reforms in these economies, but a number of such operations are now in difficulty with controversies, delays, and opposition surrounding them. This immediately begs the question: What are the outcomes, particularly the social and environmental effects or the 'cost' of reform?

Using data compiled from a number of sources including local consultant reports, reviews of project documents, Household Budget Surveys (HBS), and Living Standards Measurement Study (LSMS) surveys, this chapter takes a closer look at the unintended consequences of reform. The transition economies in this study – Armenia, Azerbaijan, Georgia, Hungary, Kazakhstan, Moldova, and Poland – started reforming their electricity sectors in the 1990s. Caution is required in drawing conclusions because reforms are a dynamic process and the countries examined are at different points in the reform process. Of course, it has to be kept in mind that most of the CIS economies became countries only at the beginning of the decade and tasks of nation-building took precedence. It may thus be too early to draw conclusions about outcomes where the process is not complete. In addition, the time elapsed does not imply anything about the quality or pace of reforms.

Studying reform outcomes is complicated because it requires a counterfactual – what would have happened without reforms? Creating this counterfactual to evaluate the performance of the entire electricity sector is difficult because it requires many assumptions – not only about a particular company,[1] but about the entire domestic political and economic situation (for example, alternative scenarios of economic growth, private investment and political stability). The alternative of trying to compare outcomes before and after reform ignoring the counterfactual is also difficult because of the debate over the appropriate baseline (pre-transition or transition), the fact that reforms are dynamic, and the scarcity of pre-reform data. Given the nature of the data before the transition, it is difficult if not impossible to simulate what would have happened in the absence of reforms.

BACKGROUND

ECA is Different

The starting point for energy reforms in ECA is different from the other regions, further complicating program design and implementation. Incomes, measured by GDP per capita, are higher than in other parts of the world except Latin America. Similarly, other development indicators – such as infant mortality rate, illiteracy rate, and access to basic infrastructure such as water – suggest that the situation in ECA is better. GDP per unit of energy use is substantially lower – due in part to the cold winters, the legacy of central planning, and substantial declines in household incomes following transition. The Soviet legacy resulted in a highly centralized power infrastructure designed to provide reliable electricity to all households at little or no cost. Studies indicate that access to electricity is substantially higher than in other regions with similar incomes (Komives *et al.* 2001; Wallsten and Clarke 2002). Electricity consumption levels are also thought to be higher than in other parts of the world, suggesting substantial potential efficiency gains (Cornille and Frankhauser 2002).

Need for Reform

Providing large numbers of consumers with reliable electricity at little or no cost requires substantial power infrastructure. When this infrastructure was built, energy prices in the Soviet Union were well below international prices. With the onset of transition and the end of central transfers, the sector's large investment needs were neglected because revenues were low, if positive at all. Low tariffs, high consumption levels, and low collections characterized the sector. The net result was a power sector supported through fiscal and quasi-fiscal budget operations and asset depreciation, especially in countries of the former Soviet Union. In Armenia, Georgia and Moldova the power sector deficit was among the largest items in the budget deficit. The energy (electricity and gas) sector's quasi-fiscal deficit has been estimated at 5 percent of GDP in Moldova in 1999, 3.5 percent in Armenia in 2001, and 2 percent in Georgia in 2000 (International Monetary Fund 2001a, 2001b, 2001c).

Thus, the opportunity cost of subsidizing the energy sector is large. As countries struggle to balance their budgets and reduce quasi-fiscal operations, transfers of this magnitude take limited funds away from other sectors. Public spending on health and education has fallen dramatically since the beginning of the transition. In Azerbaijan, Georgia and Moldova spending on health is less than a quarter of what it was in the early 1990s – and in Kazakhstan, about half. Spending on education is a mere sixth of the level in the early 1990s in Armenia, and a third in Azerbaijan. As shares of GDP, total public expenditures on education, health, and social assistance and welfare remained stable or fell (Public Expenditure database 2002).

Timeline of Reforms

A comprehensive review of the reform experience in ECA reveals that no universal recipe for reforms can fit the specific conditions of each country (Krishnaswamy and Stuggins 2003). Hungary and Poland engaged in reform the earliest, followed by Kazakhstan, Moldova and Georgia (Table 4.1). Though Armenia entered late, significant progress was made in restructuring the sector. It made a number of abortive attempts to sell the loss-making distribution network to foreign strategic investors before the sale finally went through. In 2002, a controlling stake in its power distribution network was sold to an offshore company – Midland Resources Holding. It happened after substantial attempts by the government to reorganize the sector, improve service, and align prices. Kazakhstan privatized 80–90 percent of its generating capacity using asset sales and concessions in 1996, and it completed privatization of the rest of generation assets between 1999 and 2002 except for a hydro plant.

SOCIAL IMPACT

The electricity sector reforms have confronted households with a tradeoff between prices and service quality, and the perception of high political costs has had an adverse impact on the reform progress. Azerbaijan and Georgia experienced the highest tariff increases during this period. Therefore, unless accompanied by improvement in service quality, welfare loss would be substantial. Tariff increases and disconnections are very unpopular, and the public often views the sale of state assets to the private sector with skepticism.

Table 4.1 *Timeline of reforms in the electricity sector in ECA*

	Date of passage of Energy Law and creation of an independent regulator	Corporatization and unbundling	Privatization of distribution	Privatization of generation	Market liberalization
Armenia	1997	1997	2002	None	None
Azerbaijan	1998	1996	2001–2003[c]	None	None
Georgia	1997	1999–2000	1998	2000	1999–2000
Hungary	1993–94	1993–94	1995	1996–97	2001
Kazakhstan	1998–99	1996	1996, 1999	1996, 1999–2002[b]	
Moldova	1998	1997	1999	None	None
Poland	1997	1993	Ongoing	None[a]	Ongoing

Notes:

[a] Except for new entry of private strategic investors.
[b] Large customers and generators are allowed to enter in bilateral contracts. In 2001 the government set up KOREM (Kazakh market operator for electric energy and capacity) to organize the spot and 'day ahead' markets.
[c] Concession contracts.

Source: Adapted from Krishnaswamy and Stuggins, 2003.

This is especially true when the public expects that the privatization of a public monopoly would result in a higher price without any improvement in the quality of service. If there is an improvement in service quality, it takes place a few years after privatization, while the price rises early on in the process. This mismatch between the timing of the gains and costs of reform and the uncertainty about the gains causes consumers to be skeptical.

Even though the official statistics and household surveys suggest that access to service is nearly universal, supply is often rationed. The low investment in electricity generation and distribution infrastructure in the last decade resulted in severe deteriorations in service quality. Some countries experience frequent interruptions in electricity supply. Others experience voltage fluctuations that destroy household appliances (Markandya *et al.* 2001). Unless investments are made in rehabilitation and maintenance of the infrastructure, households may experience widespread supply shortages in the future.

Household Energy Use Patterns Differ

There are systematic differences in energy use in urban areas in the ECA region. Separating network and non-network energy use provides insight into energy use patterns (Table 4.2). Almost all households use electricity, with small differences between the poor and the non-poor. But poor people use much less central heat and gas.

If poor people are not using network energy, what are they using? Primarily dirty non-network energy (Table 4.3). Wood and coal use are consistently higher among the poor – except in Tajikistan, where coal is heavily subsidized for everyone. Except in Latvia, the non-poor are more likely to use liquefied petroleum gas (LPG), the cleanest non-network energy. The poor may favor dirty non-network energy because it is less expensive or because they do not have the resources to spend on network appliances. But as noted, burning dirty fuels has social costs – mainly air pollution and deforestation – that require careful, country-specific analysis of the economic implications of raising the price of clean energy (Lampietti and Meyer 2002).

Tariffs Rose

In an effort to reach cost-recovery levels, the residential electricity tariffs were increased in all countries.[2] In nominal dollar terms they nearly doubled in Azerbaijan, Georgia and Hungary between the mid-1990s and 2002; Poland and Hungary currently have the highest tariffs. In Kazakhstan, Azerbaijan and Moldova the tariffs first increased or remained stable and then fell in the late 1990s due to the depreciation of local currency and the 1999 devaluation triggered by the financial crisis in Russia. In real terms the tariff increase

Table 4.2 Urban network energy use in ECA (percentage of households)

Country	Central heat		Central gas		Electricity	
	Poor	Non-poor	Poor	Non-poor	Poor	Non-poor
Armenia (1999)	11	14	4	16	97	99
Croatia (1997)	15	39	19	30	99	100
Kyrgyz Rep. (1999)	17	55	13	33	100	99
Latvia (1997)	70	83	57	68	99	100
Lithuania (1998)	31	46	47	56	85	94
Moldova (1999)	17	57	37	70	65	89
Tajikistan (1999)	1	1	3	6	100	100

Source: Lampietti and Meyer (2002).

Table 4.3 Urban non-network energy use in ECA (percentage of households)

Country	LPG		Kerosene		Coal		Wood	
	Poor	Non-poor	Poor	Non-poor	Poor	Non-poor	Poor	Non-poor
Armenia (1999)	17	27	14	11	n/a	n/a	47	50
Croatia (1997)	44	45	3	7	1	1	51	26
Kyrgyz Rep. (1999)	24	39	31	17	60	31	46	22
Latvia (1997)	37	28	n/a	n/a	<1	<1	1	2
Lithuania (1998)	n/a	n/a	n/a	n/a	<1	<1	1	2
Moldova (1999)	6	7	n/a	n/a	9	5	12	9
Tajikistan (1999)	n/a	n/a	<1	1	11	18	47	32

Note: n/a - not available from household survey.

Source: Lampietti and Meyer (2002).

during this period was the highest in Azerbaijan and Georgia, where the tariffs quadrupled and tripled, respectively. By 2002 the tariffs doubled in Armenia and Moldova, increased by about 160 percent in Hungary, remained unchanged in Poland and fell in Kazakhstan (Figure 4.1). Such substantial tariff increases are unlikely to be welfare neutral unless accompanied by improvements in service quality or cushioned by income transfers.

A complete analysis of the tradeoffs between tariffs and service quality requires comparing the welfare losses from price increases with the gains from improved service quality (which may take place with a lag). Aggregate service quality is thought to have improved since the early 1990s, the crisis period in Armenia, Azerbaijan and Georgia, implying welfare gains for consumers.[3] In Kazakhstan service quality remained unchanged. But it is not clear what the situation would have been in the absence of privatization of generation facilities, which were in dire need of investments. It is also not clear how much of the improvement, where it did take place, can be attributed to the general political and economic changes, and how much to power sector reforms. So instead of evaluating the welfare gains from service quality improvements, the welfare impact of reforms is first assessed by examining changes in the share of electricity expenditures in income (using total expenditure as a proxy),

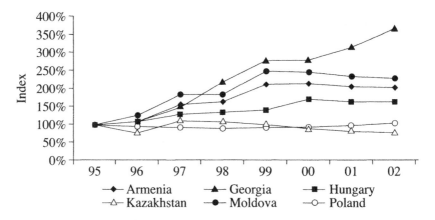

Note: Nominal tariffs in local currency were adjusted by the CPI. Base year is 1995 (1996 for Georgia). The first year for which data for all countries are available is 1995. In Poland and Hungary most of the tariff increase occurred before that. Azerbaijan is not included in the graph. Though its nominal tariffs, when calculated in US cents/kWh, is among the lowest in the regions, the CPI adjusted real tariff is the highest.

Source: Authors' calculations based on data provided by local consultants and Counterpart International (for Moldova).

Figure 4.1   Residential electricity tariff – index of CPI adjusted real tariffs

particularly for the poor and non-poor and then by assessing the loss in consumer surplus.

The Burden Increased

Mean expenditures on electricity range from 2 to 10 percent of income on average, with a high of 14 percent for the bottom quintile in Armenia in 2001 and a low of less than 1 percent for the bottom quintile in Kazakhstan in 2001 (Table 4.4). The share increased slightly in all countries and for all welfare quintiles.[4] Bottom quintile annual change in electricity share varied between −1.9 percentage points (Poland 2000) to 4 percentage points (Moldova 2002). Moldova emerges as the one especially hard-hit from reforms: of the four highest increases in electricity shares for the bottom quintile, three occurred in Moldova (2000 – 2.9 percentage points, 2001 – 2.5 and 2002 – 4). The fourth highest yearly increase of 2.7 percentage points took place in Georgia in 2002. The results are conditional on the households reporting positive expenditures on electricity.[5]

The increasing share of expenditures on electricity can be explained by rising tariffs, falling income, reduced rationing (as service quality improved), or inelastic demand. That the share falls monotonically across the welfare distribution is consistent with findings that the poor devote a higher share of total expenditures to energy (Lampietti and Meyer 2002) and that electricity is a necessary good. It also implies a greater proportionate welfare loss for the poor and a more active search for substitutes when electricity tariffs increase.

The overall welfare impact of the reforms can be measured by the change in consumer surplus. Consumers gain from an improvement in service quality and the removal of rationing, but lose from an increase in price. Since we cannot measure the gains from the service quality improvement from the existing data, we focus on the consumer surplus change of a price increase. The magnitude of the welfare effect of a price increase depends on the household's dependence on the energy source, measured by its budget share, the price change, and the household's access to substitute energy sources and other goods and services. The third is measured by the elasticity of demand. For electricity the elasticity of demand is typically low: it has been estimated between −0.08 and −0.32 for a range of countries (Hope and Singh 1995).[6] The budget share of electricity in household income varies depending on income and the geographic location of a household. Typically network energy budget shares are inversely related to income, with the poor urban households spending a highest share of their total income compared to all other groups of households (Hope and Singh 1995). This is also the case in these countries in ECA.

We present the consumer surplus calculation[7] in a range of demand

Table 4.4 Shares of spending on electricity went up, 1993–2002 (mean of household electricity shares)

	1993	1994	1995	1996	1997	1998	1999	2000	2001	2002
Armenia[a]										
Bottom quintile	na	na	na	18.2	na	na	10.2	na	13.9	na
Top quintile	na	na	na	3.6	na	na	5.3	na	6.5	na
All quintiles	na	na	na	9.0	na	na	7.2	na	8.8	na
Georgia										
Bottom quintile	na	na	na	3.1	3.8	5.7	4.4	3.7	3.6	6.3
Top quintile	na	na	na	1.5	1.5	1.6	1.5	1.5	2.3	2.0
All quintiles	na	na	na	2.0	2.3	2.9	2.5	2.4	2.7	3.4
Hungary										
Bottom quintile	4.3	na	na	na	na	5.6	6.3	6.5	na	na
Top quintile	2.2	na	na	na	na	3.6	3.7	3.7	na	na
All quintiles	3.4	na	na	na	na	4.9	5.4	5.4	na	na
Kazakhstan										
Bottom quintile	na	na	na	0.16	na	na	na	na	0.92	na
Top quintile	na	na	na	0.11	na	na	na	na	0.56	na
All quintiles	na	na	na	0.14	na	na	na	na	0.69	na
Moldova										
Bottom quintile	na	na	na	na	6.5	7.6	10.8	8.4	7.7	6.3
Top quintile	na	na	na	na	2.7	3.2	4.2	4.1	3.7	5.1
All quintiles	na	na	na	na	4.1	4.6	6.1	5.5	5.2	4.3
Poland										
Bottom quintile	4.5	4.6	4.6	4.5	4.5	6.6	7.2	5.3	5.8	na

| Top quintile | 2.4 | 2.3 | 2.4 | 2.3 | 2.1 | 3.5 | 3.7 | 2.6 | 2.9 | na |
| All quintiles | 3.4 | 3.4 | 3.4 | 3.3 | 3.3 | 3.8 | 4.1 | 4.1 | 4.3 | na |

Notes: [a] For 1999 the results reported are based on 1999 Household Budget Survey. The results for the 1999 Energy Survey for Armenia are similar: the average expenditure share is 6.2 percent, that of the bottom quintile 8.8 percent, and that of the top quintile 5.0 percent.

Source: Authors' calculations from household survey data.

elasticity scenarios. Zero elasticity means that the household is unable to adjust, so this provides an upper bound of the welfare loss. At a price elasticity of -1, the household is able to reduce electricity consumption in response to the price increase, so reducing the magnitude of the welfare loss. Households in Armenia and Georgia experienced the largest welfare loss, expressed as a percentage of total household budget, because of the high magnitude of the price increase and the high shares of electricity expenditures in the total budget (Table 4.5). In real terms the electricity price fell slightly in Kazakhstan, so households did not experience a welfare loss.

Consumption is Low

Studying consumption using household survey data is confounded by the presence of arrears (nonpayments), which make it impossible to determine whether reported electricity expenditures represent current or historical consumption. But it is possible to examine a sample of household electricity consumption records from distribution companies in Armenia and Georgia.[8] These data do not take into account households not included in the utility's database and thus might be an underestimate of household consumption. In Armenia, where service quality has been consistently high since 1996 (provided 24 hours a day, seven days a week), mean household consumption fell steadily from an average of 160 kilowatt-hours (kWh) a month in 1998 to 117 kWh a month in 2001.[9] In Tbilisi, where service quality has been improving since 2000, consumption remained constant at about 150 kWh a month (Figure 4.2). Greater seasonal fluctuations in electricity consumption in Armenia than Georgia suggest greater access to inexpensive substitutes for heating in Georgia.

Household electricity consumption is close to basic minimum needs, sufficient only for lighting and refrigeration.[10] The median consumption was as low as 84–100 kWh a month during 2002 in Armenia and Georgia. The assumption is that an electricity demand function is kinked, as is characteristic of necessary goods, sloping steeply around the minimum required for basic needs and then rapidly leveling off as the quantity of electricity consumed moves from necessity to luxury.

This leads to two conclusions. First, the welfare losses from a price increase are high for households with very low electricity consumption. Second, there may now be little scope for efficiency gains from the household sector in Armenia, Georgia and Moldova. There was such scope at the beginning of the transition because the former CIS countries have traditionally been energy intensive, but the move toward cost-recovery tariffs and regulatory improvements had little scope for further reductions in consumption. The decline in household incomes associated with transition also added to the

Table 4.5 Consumer surplus fell

Country	Real price increase		Starting point budget share	Lost (gained) Consumer surplus (percent of total household budget)		
	Period	%	Change %	η=20.1	η=20.5	η=20.9
Armenia	1996–2002	98%	9.0	−8.38	−8.39	−8.40
Georgia	1996–2002	267%	2.0	−5.33	−5.33	−5.33
Hungary	1993–2002	57%	3.4	−2.36	−2.36	−2.36
Kazakhstan	1996–2002	2%	0.2	0.00	0.00	0.00
Moldova	1997–2002	43%	4.1	−0.95	−0.95	−0.95
Poland	1994–2002	9%	3.4	−0.14	−0.14	−0.14

Source: Budget shares calculated from household survey data.

61

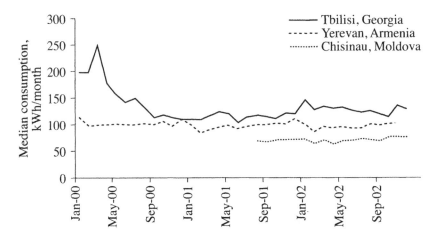

Note: Calculations include only households with positive electricity consumption.

Source: Authors' calculations using AES Telasi data (reported in Lampietti *et al*. 2003) and electric utility records for 1197 households in Yerevan and 2092 households in Chisinau.

Figure 4.2   Enough for three light bulbs and a refrigerator

decline in electricity use. If the price of electricity increases further, there will only be a small reduction in household energy consumption.

Gas May be Filling the Gap

Electricity is the single largest item in the household energy budget in Armenia, Georgia, Moldova, and Poland, and the share is largest for the bottom quintile (Table 4.6). Assuming that it consumes less than the top quintile, this implies that electricity is used for the most basic needs for which other fuels are poor substitutes, so demand by the poor is inelastic.

Given the large price increases and the inelastic demand, it is surprising that expenditures went up by only 1.5 percentage points on average. The impact may have been mitigated by improvements in service quality or substitutions of other energy sources. While there are no perfect substitutes for electric lighting, refrigeration, and television, given a choice of substitutes for electricity in heating and cooking, households are likely to choose natural gas because it is clean, convenient, and low priced. Other alternatives – such as kerosene, coal and wood – are less convenient.

Relative fuel prices and fuel availability influence household energy consumption choices. Even at full import prices gas is substantially less expensive than electricity (Figure 4.3). While there may be additional costs

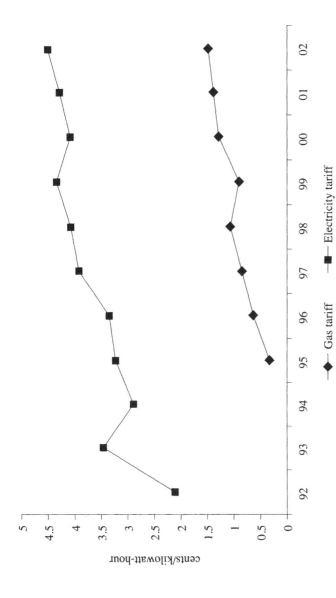

Note: The applied conversion factor was 277.8 kWh per Giga-Joule (GJ) of natural gas (International Energy Agency). Average tariffs were calculated for Armenia, Azerbaijan, Georgia, Hungary, Kazakhstan, Moldova, and Poland. Note that this is a simple average. The number of observations varies by year depending on data availability.

Source: Authors' calculations based on data from local consultants, Counterpart International (for Moldova), and ERRANET database

Figure 4.3 Electricity tariffs are higher than those for gas, 1992–2002

Table 4.6 Electricity expenditure as a share of total energy expenditure, 1993–2002 (mean of household electricity shares)

	1993	1994	1995	1996	1997	1998	1999	2000	2001	2002
Armenia[a]										
Bottom quintile	na	na	na	na	na	na	73	na	96	na
Top quintile	na	na	na	na	na	na	57	na	88	na
All quintales	na	na	na	na	na	na	62	na	90	na
Georgia										
Bottom quintile	na	na	na	83	65	68	68	68	67	na
Top quintile	na	na	na	54	38	41	40	40	45	na
All quintales	na	na	na	65	48	51	53	53	53	na
Hungary										
Bottom quintile	32	na	na	na	na	37	38	39	na	na
Top quintile	33	na	na	na	na	37	38	39	na	na
All quintales	31	na	na	na	na	36	37	38	na	na
Kazakhstan										
Bottom quintile	na	na	na	41	na	na	na	na	47	na
Top quintile	na	na	na	30	na	na	na	na	65	na
All quintales	na	na	na	34	na	na	na	na	56	na
Moldova[b]										
Bottom quintile	na	na	na	na	86	87	92	89	87	86
Top quintile	na	na	na	na	80	74	77	81	79	76
All quintales	na	na	na	na	83	80	84	86	84	81
Poland										
Bottom quintile	62	61	61	60	60	68	68	67	69	na

| Top quintile | 35 | 33 | 33 | 32 | 32 | 39 | 41 | 43 | 44 | na |
| All quintiles | 47 | 45 | 45 | 43 | 44 | 39 | 40 | 43 | 41 | na |

Notes:

[a] The 2001 survey, unlike the 1999 survey, does not capture well energy sources other than electricity.

[b] The share is high in Moldova because none of the surveys captures a larger portion of other energy sources.

Source: Authors' calculations from household survey data.

65

associated with the technology required to use gas (metering and gas-fired appliances), the convenience and savings suggest that, given access, it is the household fuel of choice.

Back-of-the-envelope calculations confirm the rising use of natural gas. In Armenia residential consumption of natural gas more than tripled from 1996 to 2001 (from 29 000 tons of oil equivalent to 90 000), while monthly electricity consumption dropped from 187 000 tons of oil equivalent to 106 000.[11] For Georgia the number of gas connections in the capital quadrupled from 2000 to 2003.[12]

Enforcement is Necessary

Nonpayments, or arrears, are one of the most vexing problems. A key reform objective has been to resolve it, and collection rates indeed appear to rise after privatization.[13] Understanding who accumulates arrears has important implications for the welfare effect of reforms. If it is mainly the poor, affordability may be a problem and special care must be taken by the state to provide adequate assistance to the poor. If it is all households, free-riding may be the problem and stricter enforcement will not disproportionately hurt the poor.

Evidence on the absolute amount of cumulative arrears (in kilowatt-hours) in Georgia suggests that the problem may be free-riding. In some periods cumulative arrears[14] of the bottom quintile exceed those of the top quintile,[15] but in others there is no statistical difference between the two groups (Figure 4.4). However, the cumulative arrears of the bottom quintile are higher than those of the top when arrears are measured relative to electricity consumption. The top quintile consumes more than the bottom quintile in 6 of 12 quarters (all quarters of 2002), and this difference is statistically significant.[16]

Searching for Better Transfers

In addition to improving service quality, the government can mitigate the welfare effects of price increases by providing assistance to vulnerable households and by stimulating income growth. There is much debate about the validity of each assistance measure. Lovei *et al.* (2000) found that instruments that perform well on some criteria tend to perform poorly on others. So no single instrument has been identified that would outperform all others.

One of the most contentious debates is between lifeline tariffs, which subsidize an initial block of electricity for all users, and direct income transfers. Proponents of direct transfers argue that lifelines are not targeted and thus encourage inefficient energy use. Opponents claim that transfers through

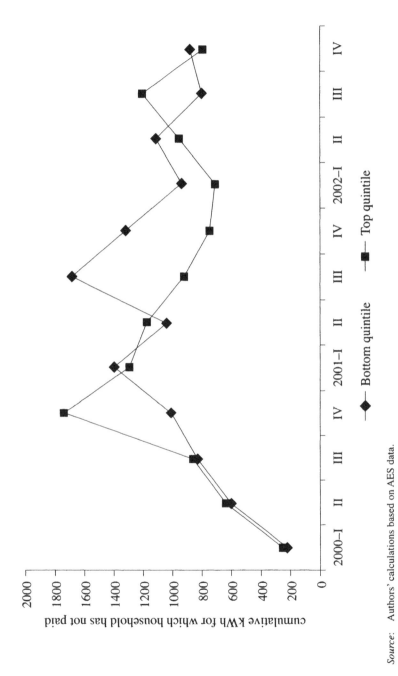

Source: Authors' calculations based on AES data.

Figure 4.4 Burden of arrears is the same for the poor and non-poor, 2000–2002

the general social assistance system, while theoretically attractive, fail to reach a large share of the poor because of inadequate targeting.

Income transfers tend to be well targeted in countries with less than 10 percent of the population below the poverty line, with enough funds to finance the administration of social assistance, and with a small informal sector so that means testing is easy. Examples include Hungary and Poland.[17] The transfers are less well targeted in countries such as Armenia and Georgia, where nearly half the population is poor, budget resources are insufficient, and means testing is very difficult. The case for lifeline tariffs is stronger in countries with high poverty rates and poor targeting – so long as there is sufficient political will to keep the size of the blocks small (say below 50 or 100 kWh) and to reimburse the utility for its costs – than in the countries with low poverty rates and well targeted social assistance.

Where tariff-based subsidies are in use, it may be possible to reorient their design to maximize consumer welfare gains and minimize the cost to the government budget. An electricity demand function is kinked, sloping steeply around the minimum required for basic needs and then rapidly leveling off as the quantity consumed moves from necessity to luxury. Ideally a subsidy would provide just enough compensation to ensure that each household consuming in the steeply sloping (inelastic) portion of the demand curve (where welfare losses are large) consumes in the flat (elastic) portion where welfare losses are small. Since the exact location of the kink[18] cannot be identified, an upper and lower bound approach can be used. The lower bound eliminates incentives for gaming the system (such as installing multiple meters) and excludes residences with very low electricity usage, such as houses that are not primary residences. The utility would implement the program, using their billing database, and the government would be responsible for transferring the necessary resources to them.

ENVIRONMENTAL IMPACT

Reforms and Environmental Benefits

Power sector reforms are expected to produce environmental benefits. Increased production efficiency, new investment, and environmentally friendly technology all contribute to lower fossil fuel consumption and lower emissions. With falling demand (the result of higher prices) this would lead to better ambient air quality and presumably to better health outcomes for the local population. There may well be unanticipated environmental costs as well. The cold climate, rising price of electricity, and collapse of clean, safe heating alternatives (such as district heating) may push households, especially the poor, to substitute less expensive dirty energy (such as wood, coal or kerosene) for electricity in heating. Burning dirty fuels lowers indoor and outdoor air quality, leading to worse health outcomes. Burning wood can also contribute to deforestation and the loss of valuable forest functions.

World Bank projects in power sector reform are expected to result in specific environmental benefits. These include a variety of emissions reductions and, in some cases, improvements in ambient air quality, especially around generation plants. Unfortunately, claims about improvements in ambient air quality are difficult to verify for most pollutants. Indicators for pollutants and monitoring programs were never established – or if they were, collection collapsed with the breakup of the Soviet Union. During the transition the collection of accurate air quality data decreased substantially in the countries of the Caucasus and Central Asia.

The environmental performance of the electricity sector, measured by fuel efficiency of electricity production, has improved slightly over the last decade, leading to reductions in carbon dioxide emissions. However, these benefits are global rather than local. Increasing energy efficiency in electricity production does not automatically improve environmental health. Health improvements resulting from increased efficiency can be insignificant when compared with emissions of sulfur dioxide, nitrogen oxides, and fine particulates (PM_{10}), the pollutants that cause the most health damage.[19] The health effects of particulate matter may be very low even if energy intensity is high if abatement equipment is used. If power plant stacks are high[20] or located in sparsely populated areas, as in many of the countries in Eastern Europe, Caucasus and Central Asia, they may not have much influence on ambient air quality, so increasing efficiency may not translate into local health benefits.

The raw data suggest that urban air pollution decreased slightly in the major cities during the reforms, yet it continues to be a major health hazard. Ambient standards for PM_{10} continue to be surpassed regularly in Yerevan, Tbilisi and Katowice. The key question is how much the power sector reforms contributed to this change. A crude dispersion model was used to estimate the magnitude of the impact of the sector on air quality and health in selected cities. If the sector does not play an important role in determining local air quality, the reforms will produce small health benefits even if emission reductions are large. Conversely, if the sector plays an important role, the health benefits may be large.

Within the countries under study the power sector contributed less than 1 percent of health damage from all emissions. The share is small because the power stations account for a small amount of total ambient air quality. Between 1990 and 2000 the share of the electricity sector in the disability adjusted life years (DALYs) originating from low air quality ranged from 0.1 to 2.0 percent. The highest shares attributed to the sector are in Almaty and Warsaw. In the other cities the contribution is less than 0.5 percent.[21]

The analysis reveals five reasons for the low contribution of the electricity sector to health damages. First, the amount of electricity produced dropped substantially in Armenia, Georgia and Kazakhstan. Second, the fuel mix used for thermal power plants shifted more toward natural gas in Armenia and Azerbaijan. Third, high-capacity power plants are often located far from populated cities. Fourth, improvements in fuel quality[22] and abatement technologies for particulate matter were already in place before the reforms started in Hungary, Kazakhstan and Poland, with average removal efficiencies of 97–99.9 percent. Fifth, power station stacks were built high to reduce deterioration of ambient air quality and were regulated by Soviet norms and regulations.

Private transport is now a major source of urban air pollution in the large cities of Eastern Europe, the Caucasus,[23] and Central Asia. These emissions are increasing due to the aging vehicle fleet, the low quality and high sulfur content of the fuel, and the decline in the provision of public transport. In contrast, the share of emissions from power stations and other stationary sources is falling. In sum, sector reforms are most closely associated with a reduction in carbon dioxide emissions, which produces global, not local, benefits. At the same time, sector reforms are unlikely to have any significant impact on ambient air quality related to sulphur dioxide, nitrous oxides, and fine particulate matter, the pollutants that cause the most local health damage.

There were Unintended Environmental Costs

There may also be unintended environmental costs associated with the reforms – particularly from household fuel-switching. As residential tariffs are brought to cost-recovery levels, households may switch to less expensive but dirtier energy (such as wood, coal or kerosene) contributing to indoor and outdoor air pollution. Health damage may be substantial, especially in densely populated urban areas where household chimneys are low and there is little opportunity for the pollution to disperse. Cumulative damage from household emissions may well exceed the benefits from reduced power plant emissions.

While there are no comprehensive data on household emissions, there is some evidence that some households, especially the poor, are more likely to use dirty fuels for heating. In Armenia 80 percent of households and 95 percent of poor households reported using additional alternative fuel sources to reduce reliance on electricity and district heating, primarily wood (60 percent) and/or gas (24 percent) (Lampietti *et al.* 2001).

Burning dirty fuels can cause indoor air pollution. Worldwide, inhalation of smoke from combustion of solid fuels causes about 36 percent of lower respiratory infections, 22 percent of chronic obstructive pulmonary disease, and 1 percent of trachea, bronchus and lung cancer (WHO 2002). It is also associated with tuberculosis, cataracts and asthma, but the evidence here is weaker. Nearly 3 percent of disability adjusted life years worldwide are attributed to indoor smoke, 2.5 percent for males and 2.8 percent for females (WHO 2002). The health threat depends on the local technology and ventilation. Unfortunately, little information is available on household technology, ventilation, or indoor air pollution levels.

Damage from Dirty Fuel Use may be Large

Burning dirty fuels for heating is likely to be a significant source of urban/ambient air pollution. A recent note by UNEP (2002) indicated rising air pollution due to increased low temperature emissions, a large share of which is attributable to household heating. The dispersion model developed earlier, with assumptions about household fuel use, is used to estimate the share of ambient air pollution attributable to household wood and coal use.[24,25] The total share of DALYs attributable to households using 'dirty' fuels ranges between 6 percent and 39 percent over the past decade (Figure 4.5), considerably higher than the contribution of the electricity sector to the DALYS originating from ambient air pollution (0.5 to 2.4 percent)[26].

Back-of-the-envelope estimates of the possible maximum extent of health damage from indoor air pollution in three cities in the Caucasus puts the number of premature deaths at the same order of magnitude as that from outdoor air pollution (Table 4.7).

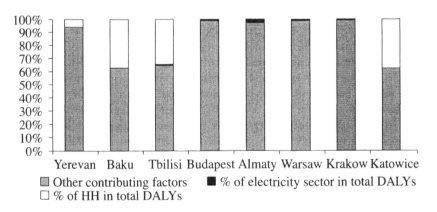

Source: Authors' calculations.

Figure 4.5   Electricity contributes in small measure to health damages (average DALYs for 1990–2000)

Table 4.7   Potential loss of life and life years due to indoor air pollution

	Armenia (Yerevan)	Georgia (Tbilisi)	Azerbaijan (Baku)
Number of premature deaths			
Children under five	52 (19)	62 (20)	36 (17)
Women	164 (60)	147 (47)	114 (54)
Total	216 (79)	210 (66)	150 (71)
DALYs			
Children under five	1820 (664)	2186 (690)	1260 (597)
Women	3287 (1,199)	2928 (931)	2275 (1,078)
Total	5107 (1,863)	5134 (1,621)	3535 (1,675)

Source: Authors' calculations based on WHO statistics, mortality database, and household surveys.

The number of premature deaths is higher among women than children, counterintuitive given the evidence in other continents. But in ECA the number of women compared with the number of children is very different from that in other continents: in Azerbaijan the ratio of women to children is 6, in Georgia 10, and in Armenia 8.5. The total estimated potential loss of life due to indoor air pollution amounts to 7 percent of all deaths related to respiratory diseases and 1 percent of the total deaths in Armenia, 10 percent of all deaths related to respiratory diseases and 1 percent of the total deaths in Georgia, and 2 percent of all deaths related to respiratory diseases and 0.3 percent of total deaths in Azerbaijan. However, these estimates are based on the assumption that there is a lack of ventilation at the location of dirty fuel burning. More research is needed to identify the precise availability and usage of fuel burning technologies and chimneys in households to establish the precise relation between dirty fuel use, indoor air pollution and health outcomes.

Fuel wood use may also contribute to deforestation and the loss of important forest resources. However the magnitude of the problem is unclear, because data on deforestation, particularly deforestation attributable to fuel wood collection are notoriously difficult to obtain. Several studies (such as UNEP 2002) and observations of forestry specialists visiting the Caucasus show a significant decrease of local forest cover and deterioration in forest quality. But these trends are often not reflected in national or international statistics. The United Nations Economic Commission for Europe and Food and Agriculture Organization report (2000) on forest resources of Europe[27] does not indicate a decline in forest resources.[28] Indeed, the forested area appears to be increasing from 0.2 percent a year in Poland to 2.2 percent a year in Kazakhstan in the last 10–15 years.[29] But these data are unlikely to be reliable. Few ministries have the resources to monitor forest cover consistently and rigorously.

Changes in forest canopy cover, which can be monitored using conventional remote sensing approaches, often do not reflect changes in forest health, yield, species mix, or density, which can be captured only by more rigorous ground based inventories and assessments. The low-intensity harvesting of fuel wood from trees growing in agricultural land, around houses, and along roads is seldom shown to have a significant impact on overall forest canopy cover – and is difficult to measure with remote sensing. Particularly when trees are coppiced or pollarded to provide these supplies, the overall impact of rural firewood harvesting can be negligible.

The situation is much different in meeting urban demands for firewood. Heavy urban household use of fuel wood creates market conditions that favor the clearance of sometimes large forested areas. When urban household energy use is constrained as a result of utility reform, the negative environmental impact on forested areas can be significant because of a shift from electricity to firewood. It may also happen that there is no visible change in total forest cover, even though the quality and density is decreasing (UNEP 2002).

From the household surveys it is clear that the majority of rural households and a substantial number of urban households used wood for their energy needs. With average expected consumption of 5–10 cubic meters of fuelwood per year, this can lead to substantial (local) deforestation. More research is necessary on the amounts of fuelwood that households burn, the sustainability of this practice, and the incremental use of fuelwood due to electricity reforms.

CONCLUSIONS AND EMERGING LESSONS

1. Increasing access and extending networks has been one of the most significant benefits of private participation in the power sector (Foster *et al*. 2004). But ECA is different from other regions because the socialist legacy provided almost all households with access to electricity. Thus private operators in the region are not faced with the challenge of increasing access, but rather with the challenge of figuring out which parts of the network to disconnect because they are not economically viable. Ultimately this leads to large welfare losses. The traditional model of private participation may not be appropriate in these economies and it may be time to identify and create public-private partnerships to ease the transition.

2. Greater emphasis must be placed on explicitly linking and timing tariff increases with improved service quality in order to minimize negative

welfare effects. This is also likely to generate more political will to support the reform. But this may not always be possible. Where it is not, improving access to and efficiency in the use of clean alternatives can mitigate the adverse impact of tariff increases, especially on low-income consumers. In some locations, especially urban areas where households heat with electricity, natural gas may be a viable substitute.

3. Where the data are available, household electricity consumption is surprisingly close to basic minimum needs. Thus the large efficiency gains from tariff reform may not materialize, as households are unable to further reduce consumption. This signals the importance of carefully aligning the timing of mitigating measures to coincide with the timing of tariff reform in order to minimize welfare losses.

4. Compared to the non-poor, poor households mostly use non-network fuels. A rise in prices of clean fuels can exacerbate this trend. Given the potential welfare losses of using dirty fuels, poor households should be encouraged to use clean and inexpensive substitutes, such as natural gas. An example would be bidding out competitive subsidies to encourage the extension of natural gas networks to poor neighborhoods.

NOTES

1. A methodology for this type of analysis is detailed in Galal *et al.* (1994).
2. In Kazakhstan tariffs also increased in nominal terms after 1993, but the increase was negligible, unlike the other countries in this study.
3. In Georgia supply improved in Tbilisi after privatization of the distribution company. The company was not always able to provide 24-hour supply for reasons beyond its control, such as interconnectedness of the power grid with the rest of the country. Power supply in other areas where distribution is still publicly owned, is worse (Project Appraisal Document for an Electricity Market Support Project in Georgia, World Bank, April, 2001, p. 5).
4. Average yearly change in electricity shares was positive for bottom, top, and all quintiles for Georgia (1997–2002), Moldova (1999–2002), and Poland (1994–2001). There was a similar positive change in electricity shares for all quintiles in Armenia (between 1999 and 2001), Hungary (between 1993 and 1998, 1998 and 1999), and Kazakhstan (between 1996 and 2001).
5. The share of households with zero expenditures varies across surveys due to different survey design. Surveys in which respondents are asked about the previous month's expenditures frequently have over half the respondents reporting zero expenditures, a result more likely due to the nature of the question than to the fact that none of them pay for electricity. If the whole sample is included, it is not clear whether the calculated shares of electricity expenditures in income vary due to different survey structures or because the share actually changed. So only the subsample with households with positive expenditures is included. A series of tests reveals that these households are systematically different from the other households in the sample. Household size and total expenditure levels are similar for both groups, while the share of urban households is substantially higher in the group with non-positive expenditures (excluded from the calculations). The sample thus underrepresents urban households.
6. Electricity price increase of the late 1980s for Zimbabwe, Colombia and Turkey.
7. In most cases, the welfare loss or gain calculation includes information on access. For the

ECA region, access to electricity is close to 100 percent. The welfare loss calculation should also include information on disconnection as a result of price rise, but we could not get accurate data.

8. In Armenia, the sample consists of (usable) monthly records for 1197 households for the period from March 1998 to September 2002, and in Georgia for 288–408 households, depending on the month, for the period from January 2000 to September 2002. Data were provided by electricity utilities.

9. The median consumption for the same period fell from an average of 143 kWh a month to 95 kWh a month.

10. A refrigerator (manual defrost, 5–15 years old) consumes about 95 kWh a month and three incandescent light bulbs another 30 kWh a month.

11. Total residential consumption from the energy balance data in Armenia (Ministry of Energy). Converted to kilowatt-hours using the conversion factor of 1000 kWk = 0.086 tons oil equivalent, this is equivalent to an increase in natural gas consumption from 337 million kWh in 1996 to 1046 million in 2001, and a reduction in electricity consumption from 2174 million kWh in 1996 to 1232 million in 2001 (conversion factor is from the World Energy Council).

12. Tbilgazi's customer base increased from 39 000 households in June 2000 to 164 000 households in January of 2003 (Lampietti *et al.* 2003).

13. Lampietti *et al.* (2003) reach a similar finding, using collection rates (Figures 13, p. 30).

14. Cumulative arrears take into account that some households may carry arrears for many months before being disconnected.

15. According to *t*-test results, this difference is significant in the fourth quarter of 2000 and in the third and fourth quarters of 2001. In the fourth quarter of 2000 arrears of the top quintile exceed those of the bottom, and in 2001 the reverse is true.

16. According to *t*-test results, this difference is significant in the fourth quarter of 2000, the fourth quarter of 2001, and in all quarters of 2002.

17. With a poverty line of $2.15 a day, the poverty headcount index is 44 percent in Armenia, 24 percent in Azerbaijan, 19 percent in Georgia, 6 percent in Kazakhstan, and less than 2 percent in Hungary and Poland. With a poverty line of $4.30 a day, these numbers change to more than 50 percent in Armenia, Azerbaijan and Georgia; 30 percent in Kazakhstan – and less than 20 percent in Poland and Hungary (results of household surveys, reported in World Bank (2000c).

18. A kink in the demand curve is a specific instance of non-linearity.

19. Different pollutants are associated with different health risks, commonly measured in terms of the disability adjusted life years (DALY), a measure used internationally to compare health effects of different causes. One DALY is equal to the loss of one healthy life year.

20. In the former Soviet Union a number of state norms and rules regulated the height and design of the chimneys of power plants. These rules and norms were in general close to western norms. The Ekibastuz Power Plant in Kazakhstan, which uses coal as fuel, has two stacks of 330 meters each. Other known stacks in Russia and Ukraine range from 250 meters to 1370 meters.

21. Total DALYs from ambient air pollution range from around 4000 on average in Krakow to around 50 000 on averge in Katowice.

22. Sulfur and ash content of the coal; sulfur content of liquid fuel.

23. In Tbilisi, for instance, transport accounts for 80 percent of total air pollutants.

24. The following assumptions are made: (1) share of population using wood is as reported earlier, (2) the urban exposed population of Baku is estimated at 50 percent, (3) the average quantity of wood per household is 8 m³ per household per year, (4) the density factor of wood 0.5 ton/m³, and (5) average household size is taken from UN World Prospects Population Database.

25. In the recently released results of the 2002 census of Georgia, the actual population appears to be smaller than originally listed in international databases of UN and World Bank. The contribution of the household sector to atmospheric air pollution comes down from 34 percent to 29 percent on average for the last ten years. The relative contribution of the electricity sector to health effects will accordingly be lower, since it also depends on the

number of people affected.
26. These are total and not incremental figures.
27. Forest resources of Europe, CIS, North America, Australia, Japan and New Zealand: contribution to the global Forest Resources Assessment 2000. Geneva Timber and Forest Study Papers 17, New York and Geneva, United Nations.
28. A forest is defined as a forest when composed primarily of indigenous (native) tree species. Natural forests include closed forests and open forests (where at least 10 percent tree cover). Total forests consist of all forest area (plantations and natural forests) for temperate developed countries.
29. Reference periods for the different countries are Armenia 1983–1996, Azerbaijan 1983–1988, Kazakhstan 1988–1993, Poland 1987–1991 and 1992–1996, and Moldova 1990–1995. There is no information available for Georgia.

REFERENCES

Bourdaire, J. M. (1999) 'Empowering the End-User: Market Reform Lessons from IEA Countries', in *Energy After the Financial Crises. Energy Development Report 1999*, Washington, DC: The World Bank.

Bucknall, J. and G. Hughes (2000) 'Poland – Complying with EU environmental legislation', World Bank Technical Paper No. 454, Washington, DC: The World Bank.

Bucknall, J. (1999) 'Poland – Program for air protection in Silesia project', Project Information Document, Washington, DC: The World Bank.

Cornille, J., and S. Frankhauser (2002) 'The energy intensity of transition countries' Working Paper 72, European Bank for Reconstruction and Development.

Estache, A., V. Foster and Q. Wodon (2001) *Accounting for Poverty in Infrastructure Reform*, World Bank Institute, Washington, DC: The World Bank.

European Environmental Agency (2003) Europe's Environment, the Third Assessment, Air Quality in Europe', Environmental Assessment Report No. 10.

Foster, V., E. R. Tiongson and C. R. Laderchi (2004) 'Poverty and social impact analysis: Key issues in utility reforms', Mimeo, Washington, DC: The World Bank.

Freinkman, L., G. Gyulumyan and A. Kyurumyan (2003) 'Quasi-Fiscal Activities, Hidden Government Subsidies, and Fiscal Adjustment in Armenia', Mimeo, Washington, DC: The World Bank.

Freund, C. L. and C. I. Wallich (1995) 'Raising Household Energy Prices in Poland: Who Gains? Who Loses', Policy Research Working Paper 1495, Washington, DC: The World Bank.

Galal, A., L. Jones, P. Tandan and I. Vogelsang (1994) *Welfare Consequences of Selling Public Enterprises: An Empirical Analysis*, New York: Oxford University Press.

Hope, E. and B. Singh (1995) Energy Price Increases in Developing Countries, Policy Research Paper 1442, Washington, DC: The World Bank.

International Monetary Fund (2001a) 'Republic of Armenia: Recent Economic Developments and Selected Issues', IMF Country Report 01/78.

International Monetary Fund (2001b) 'Republic of Moldova: Recent Economic Developments and Selected Issues', IMF Country Report No. 01/22.

International Monetary Fund (2001c) 'Republic of Georgia: Recent Economic Developments and Selected Issues', IMF Country Report 01/211.

International Energy Agency (Various years) 'Energy Balances of OECD- and non-OECD countries'.

Katyshev, S. and G. Mandrovskaya (2003) 'Social and Environmental Impact of Electricity Reform in Kazakhstan', Mimeo, ECSSD, Washington, DC: The World Bank.
Kennedy, D. (1996) 'Competition in the Power Sector of Transition Economies', Working Paper 41, European Bank of Reconstruction and Development.
Kennedy, D. (2003) 'Power Sector Regulatory Reform in Transition Economies: Progress and Lessons Learned', Working Paper 78, European Bank of Reconstruction and Development.
Klytchnikova, I. (2003) 'Deforestation, Poverty and Household use of Fuel Wood in the Caucasus Region. A Household Level Analysis of Azerbaijan', Mimeo, University of Maryland, College Park.
Komives, K. D. Whittington and X. Wu (2001) 'Infrastructure Coverage and the Poor: A Global Perspective', Policy Research Working Paper 2551, Washington, DC: The World Bank.
Krishnaswamy, V. and G. Stuggins (2003) 'Private Participation in the Power Sector in Europe and Central Asia, Lessons from the Last Decade', World Bank Working Paper No. 8, Washington, DC: The World Bank.
Lampietti, J. A. (2004) 'Power's Promise: Electricity Reforms in Eastern Europe and Central Asia', Working Paper 40, Washington, DC: The World Bank.
Lampietti, J. A. and B. Kropp (2002) 'Climbing Down the Energy Ladder? Household Energy Trends in Eastern Europe and Central Asia', Mimeo, ECSSD, Washington, DC: The World Bank.
Lampietti, J. A., S. G. Banerjee, and A. Branczik (forthcoming), 'Power and People: Electricity Sector Reforms and the Poor in Eastern Europe and Central Asia', Washington, DC: The World Bank.
Lampietti, J. A., A. A. Kolb, S. Gulyani and V. Avenesyan (2001) 'Utility Pricing and the Poor: Lessons from Armenia', World Bank Technical Paper No. 497. Washington, DC.
Lampietti, J. A., H. Gonzalez, E. Hamilton, and M. Wilson (2003) 'Revisiting reform: Lessons from Georgia', Mimeo, ECSSD, Washington, DC: The World Bank.
Lengyel, L. (2003) 'Status of Power Sector in Hungary', Eurocorp Commerz Ltd., Mimeo, ECSSD, Washington, DC: The World Bank.
Lieberman, I., M. Gobbo, A. Sukiasyan, S. L. Travers and J. R. D. Welch (2003) 'Privatization Practice Note: Europe and Central Asia Region', Mimeo, Washington, DC: The World Bank.
Lovei, L., E. Gurenko, M. Haney, P. O'Keefe and M. Shkaratan (2000) 'Maintaining utility services for the poor: policies and practices in Central and Eastern Europe and former Soviet Union', Washington, DC: The World Bank.
Lvovsky, K. (2000) 'Environmental Costs of Fossil Fuels', World Bank Environment Department Papers No 78, Pollution Management Series.
Markandya, A., M. Jayawardena and R. Sharma (2001) 'The Impact of Infrastructure Investments on Measured Poverty', A Viewpoint Note, unpublished manuscript, Washington, DC: The World Bank.
Nadiradze, N.(2003) 'Study of Social and Environmental Impacts of Electricity Reform in Georgia', Mimeo, ECSSD, Washington, DC: The World Bank.
Nersisyan, E. and A. Marjanyan (2003) 'Armenia Consultants Report on Power Sector and the Environment', Mimeo, ECSSD, Washington, DC: The World Bank.
Petri, M., G. Taube and A. Tsyvinski (2002) 'Energy Sector Quasi-Fiscal Activities in the Countries of the Former Soviet Union', IMF Working Paper WP/02/60, Washington, DC.

Public Expenditure Database (2002) *Eastern Europe and Central Asia Region*, Washington, DC: The World Bank.

Rodrik, D. (1994) 'The Rush to Free Trade in the Developing World: Why So Late? Why Now? Will It Last?', in S. Haggard and S. Webb (eds), *Voting for Reform: Democracy, Political Liberalization, and Economic Adjustment*, New York, Oxford University Press.

Ryszard G. (2003) 'Status of Power Sector in Poland', Agency for Energy Market, mimeo, ECSSD, Washington, DC: The World Bank.

Saavalainen, T. O. and J. ten Berge (2003) 'Energy Conditionality in Poor CIS Countries', Mimeo, Washington, DC: International Monetary Fund.

Smith, K. (2000) 'National Burden of Disease in India from Indoor Air Pollution', School of Public Health, University of California, Berkeley, Contribution to special series of Inaugural Articles by members of National Academy of Sciences, 2000.

European Bank for Reconstruction and Development (2001) 'Transition Report 2001: Energy in Transition'.

United Nations Environment Program (2002) 'Caucasus Environment Outlook'.

United Nations Secretariat (2002) 'World Population Prospects: The 2002 Revision Population Division of the Department of Economic and Social Affairs of the United Nations Secretariat'.

United Nations Secretariat (2003) 'World Urbanization Prospects: The 2001 Revision.'

UNECE/FAO (2000) 'Forest Resources of Europe, CIS, North America, Australia, Japan and New Zealand: Contribution to the Global Forest Resources Assessment 2000', Geneva Timber and Forest Study Papers 17, New York and Geneva: United Nations.

Valiyev, V. (2003) 'State of Azerbaijan Republic Electric Power Industry (1990–2002)', Shems Energy Ltd.

Wallsten, Scott, J. and George R. G. Clarke (2002) 'Universal(ly bad) service – providing infrastructure services to poor urban consumers', Policy Research Working Paper Series 2868, Washington, DC: The World Bank.

Wodon, Q, M. I. Ajwad, J. Baker, R. Jayasuriya, C. Siaens and J.P. Tre (2003) 'Poverty and Public Spending in Latin America', Mimeo, Washington, DC: The World Bank.

World Bank (1993a) 'Energy Efficiency and Conservation in the Developing World: The World Bank's Role', A World Bank Policy Paper, Washington DC.

World Bank (1993b) 'Poland – Energy Sector Restructuring Program, volume 1: Main Report', Washington, DC.

World Bank (1993c) 'Armenia: Energy Sector Review', Washington, DC.

World Bank (1996) 'Republic of Moldova: Energy Project', Staff Appraisal Report, Washington, DC.

World Bank (1997) 'Georgia: Power rehabilitation project', Staff Appraisal Report, Washington, DC.

World Bank (1999) 'Privatization of Power and Natural Gas Industries in Hungary and Kazakhstan', World Bank Technical Paper No. 451, Washington, DC.

World Bank (2000b) 'Making Transition Work for Everyone: Poverty and Inequality in Europe and Central Asia', Washington, DC.

World Bank (2000c) 'Kazakhstan Public Expenditure Review – I, II, and III', Report No. 20489-KZ, Poverty Reduction and Economic Management Unit, Europe and Central Asia.

World Bank (2002a) 'Description of the Existing Power Networks in Armenia – Bank Mission aide memoires', Unprocessed, ECSIE, Washington, DC.

World Bank (2002a) 'Georgia Public Expenditure Review', Report No. 22913-GE, Poverty Reduction and Economic Management Unit, Europe and Central Asia.

World Bank (2002b) 'Private Sector Development in the Electric Power Sector: A Joint OED/OEG/OEU Review of the World Bank's assistance in the 1990s', Mimeo, Washington, DC.

World Bank (2003a) World Development Indicators, CD-ROM.

World Bank (2003b) 'Armenia Public Expenditure Review', Report No. 24434-AM, Poverty Reduction and Economic Management Unit, Europe and Central Asia.

World Bank (2003c) 'Azerbaijan Public Expenditure Review', Report No. 25233-AZ, Poverty Reduction and Economic Management Unit, Europe and Central Asia.

World Bank (2003d) 'Moldova Public Economic Management Review', Report No. 25423-MD, Poverty Reduction and Economic Management Unit, Europe and Central Asia.

World Bank (2003e) 'Poland – Toward a Fiscal Framework for Growth – a Public Expenditure and Institutional Review', Report No. 25033-POL, Poverty Reduction and Economic Management Unit, Europe and Central Asia.

World Bank (2003f) 'ECSPF Private Sector Strategy Paper', Mimeo, Washington, DC: The World Bank.

World Bank (2004) 'World Development Report – Making Services Work for Poor People', Washington, DC.

World Health Organization (1989) 'Management and Control of the Environment'.

World Health Organization (2002) 'Reducing Risk, Promoting Healthy Life', World Health Report.

5. Privatization and regulation of competition in the electricity sector

Lucas A. Skoufa

The privatisation and reform of electricity supply industries in many countries around the world has seen a transformation in the thinking of senior management of organisations had to become more commercially focused. For these privatised firms the old paradigm of meeting government obligations is no longer an objective, in a commercial world maximising shareholder wealth is now important. For almost a century beforehand electricity sectors in most countries around the world were 'natural monopoly' industries where government or private suppliers were subjected to regulation based on prices entry, investment, service quality, and other aspects of a firm's behaviour (Joskow 1998).

Privatisation and reform has meant that ownership of generation firms has either moved to the private sector or been retained by governments; government owned electricity is now expected to run like a business. Whatever the style of ownership of electricity firms the spectre of regulation has been such that it is a major consideration in a firm's strategic choices and behaviours. There is a lack of strategic planning literature of firms in regulated environments which has been acknowledged by Mahon and Murray (1981); Smith and Grimm (1987); Reger *et al.* (1992); Russo (1992); Parker (2002) and Bonardi (2004). It is the intention of this chapter to address some of the issues involved with this.

The general issues involved with regulation are presented first in this chapter and then regulation with regards to electricity generation firms is discussed. Thereafter a 'Governance-Strategic Choice (GSC) Framework', which is meant to assist electricity generation firms understand its choice of strategy and also assist in predicting the likely strategic behaviours of rivals, is presented. The framework is a process or sequence of events model, and it attempts to match strategic decisions to exchange conditions. It is hoped that this framework will demonstrate to policy-makers that strategic behaviours of electricity generating firms is not just the providence of the principles of neo-classical economics which is the ideological basis of privatisation and reform for such industries in the UK and Australia. The results of four studies as analysed by the framework are then highlighted with specific reference being on the effects of the regulatory environment on generation firms in the United Kingdom (UK) and Australia. It is noted here that the UK electricity supply industry (ESI) is fully privatised, as is the Victorian ESI in Australia, the Queensland and New South Wales ESIs have been reformed and are referred to as being 'corporatised' meaning that they are to 'run like a business' but are still government owned. Finally, some implications for electricity supply industries in Asia are discussed with specific reference to the industries in India and China.

MANAGEMENT OF PRIVATISED FIRMS

From a managerial point of view the privatisation (and reform) of an industry presents two main challenges for incumbent firms (Emmons 2000). First, the challenge of transforming the formerly government-owned enterprises into profitable enterprises; this brings both problems and opportunities for these firms. At a broad level the strategic issues that are important for these 'new' firms include determining the level of governance and leadership required and also the new corporate direction of the firm. Second, firms face the challenge of competing in a post-reform industry, which is totally different from the previously closed markets in which they operated under a set of physical and intangible assets that would likely be inappropriate in a competitive environment. Senior managers of privatised/reformed firms would have incentives to plan and develop strategies based on the analysis of industry and market conditions (Zahra *et al.* 2000) because of the need to compete subject to market forces.

Privatisation of an industry instigates a market disruption and allows new entrants to shape competitive terms through their strategies (Doh 2000). The privatisation process encourages firms to utilise strategies that shape and exploit market imperfections, earn monopoly rents, collaborate with other firms, and finally exploit relationships with government officials (Doh 2000) of which some managers were not previously exposed to. Managers of privatised firms have the incentive to take advantage of opportunities and corporate-level strategies, for example mergers, to expand their scope of activities (Cuervo and Villalonga 2000). At the business-level a firm's strategy is expected to change upon privatisation and it can be predicted that new entrants will bring about an increased range of product offerings, former state-owned enterprises may have previously used a cost-leader strategy and may have to compete with new entrants offering more variety but at slightly increased prices.

The Need for Regulation

There is a boundary between the state and the market and the transfer of
ownership by privatisation does not imply that state controls are removed
(Newbery 2001). Indeed privatising utility industries does not really change
the amount of regulation faced by utilities; this can be achieved by introducing
competition in utilities through the process of liberalisation (Newbery 2001).
Liberalisation is where state-owned utilities are deregulated and broken-up
into several companies, the service provided by the utilities is open to private
intervention and ownership can be transferred from state to private ownership
through privatisation (Vickers and Yarrow 1989; Peacock 1992). However, the
liberalisation of state-owned utilities may not actually see highly competitive
markets emerge which need little regulation since these industries are capital
intensive; entry is difficult and merger/acquisition activity is likely amongst
the incumbents (Newbery 2001). In Australia the Australian Competition and
Consumer Commission (ACCC) recognises the need for regulation which
replicates the outcomes of highly competitive markets whilst also being
guided by principles of economic efficiency (Utility Regulators Forum
2004).

There is a need for a regulatory regime of some sort with regards to the
management of utility services such as electricity generation (Ernst 1994).
Without such a regime the overall operation of utilities would most likely be
characterised by 'disparateness, conflicting objectives, and insular behaviour
premised on short-term planning horizons' (Ernst 1994: 55). Reforming an
industry such as electricity supply may result in replacement of regulation by
market forces, but regulators will remain important because some long-run
decisions will require public intervention because they involve important
externalities or public goods (Chao and Huntington 1998). Regulation
involves government action by itself or through agencies to control price, sale
and production decisions of firms in an avowed effort to prevent private
decision-making that would not take into account the 'public interest'
(Amendola and Bruno 1998). The 'public interest' is open to interpretation and
will not be elaborated on here; however, the public interest has its place in the
ideas of Australia's National Competition Policy in that this policy seeks to
facilitate competition whilst making sure there is no conflict with social
objectives (Hilmer *et al.* 1993).

The case or need for regulation is supported when the positive theory of
regulation is considered (Newbery 2001). This theory observes that both
customers and utilities demand regulation. Consumers want protection from
the undesirable consequences of potential market power and utilities want to
protect their investments and also ensure there is some certainty in the future.
In contrast a normative theory of regulation (Vietor 1994; Newbery 2001) is

based on theoretical approaches to optimal taxation which is open to criticisms such as (a) it is static and (b) social welfare is meaningless in operational terms since choices about policy will likely conflict between different groups. For example, in the UK the Monopolies and Mergers Commission which governs the relations between electricity generators and the regulator has the power to advise the British government on whether a generator has acted against the public interest and what should be done to remedy this (Newbery 2001).

It is suggested the competing 'interests' of electricity generation firms and customers might be conflicting which causes distortions and thus returns are reallocated in socially undesirable ways. In this case the regulator will be an arbitrator between the interest groups and attempt to accommodate the utility maximising preferences of each group which also is influenced by how much bargaining power each group possesses (Newbery 2001). Groups that will be more favoured are those with which the benefits of regulatory outcomes will be greater than the organisational costs of their operations (managers, workers, trade associations) and also large consumers (who may form lobby groups) who compete globally, whilst some political entrepreneurs will lobby on behalf of some consumer/voter groups (Newbery 2001).

One goal of regulation is to ensure that economically efficient prices are charged (Newbery 2001) by firms. However, regulators will have problems assessing if this is the case since they are not privy to the decisions made by the firms, thus an information asymmetry exists. However, regulators rely on getting firms' detailed cost and demand data and their deliberate administrative procedures may represent a very invasive form of government regulation which is just short of government ownership (Foer and Moss 2003).

The notion of 'market failure' provides a justification for regulation since electricity markets, if allowed to their own devices, would be incapable of providing efficient and equitable electricity supply, may encourage the emergence of monopoly power, and not provide protection from environmental externalities (Ernst 1994; Chao and Huntington 1998; Parker 1999). However, these possible outcomes/effects of regulation are contradicted by two views (Carlton and Perloff 2000); one holds that governments should regulate to correct market inefficiencies. Second, another view suggests that governments do not possess the necessary information for optimal regulation, otherwise special-interest groups would pressure governments/regulators so much so that regulations would create market inefficiencies. In the context of electricity generation the fact that electricity is a non-storable commodity with little demand elasticity that requires real-time supply/demand balancing (Borenstein and Bushnell 2000) suggests regulation is necessary to avoid security of supply and opportunistic pricing behaviour.

Regulatory Issues with Privatised/reformed Electricity Generation Industries

Electricity supply is a network utility and assets used to generate, transmit and distribute electricity are capital intensive, durable, long-lived and immovable (Newbery 2001). Public utilities such as electricity generation acquire financing which will be, provided that regulation is credible enough to satisfy the demands of consumers, firms and investors (Newbery 2001). For firms an uncertain future regulatory setting may suspend or cancel investment in plant, which ultimately can lead to supply shortages. Also, firms are expected from a regulatory perspective to offer efficient and competitively low prices but not so low as to discourage investment (Newbery 2001; Shepherd 1997; Joskow 1998).

With regards to electricity generation there are four regulatory instruments that can be used by regulatory agencies (Newbery 2001; Yajima 1997; Parker 2002). First is rate of return regulation, a popular approach around the world and used in the USA whereby a satisfactory profit or rate of return is established for a firm's asset base after allowing for efficient capital and operating costs. An issue with this type of regulation would be that generation firms could create allocative distortions in that they built units that employ excessive capital.

Second is price cap regulation, because it links revenues to costs rate of return regulation does not provide incentive for firms to lower costs and thus economists have argued for other forms of regulation such as price which was adopted by the UK for regulating privatised utilities such as electricity supply and has been implemented in other countries around the world, for example Australia. If it is properly applied price regulation has the advantage of providing firms with the incentive to become more efficient because firms can increase their price-cost margin from increased efficiency. However, some critics of price cap regulation have stated that whilst electricity firms have become more efficient and lowered costs they have also accrued large profits. Furthermore, for regulators to set a price cap they have to have access to financial and economic data of the firms involved and also be able to forecast a multitude of figures such as potential growth in demand for electricity, future input price changes, and appropriate cost of capital to name a few. In the UK the price cap is such that a generation firm's prices cannot rise for a specified period (five years) at a rate faster than the rate of $RPI - X$ (Beesley and Littlechild 1989). RPI is the Retail Price Index (that is, rate of inflation); X is an efficiency improvement term (MacKerron and Boira-Segarra 1996: 101) that is set by the government/regulator. In the UK $RPI - X$ formula is one of many constraining conditions contained in a regulated company's licence conditions. The initial value of X is set upon the privatisation of an industry and it is adjusted every few years depending on government choices. *X* should motivate generation firms to reduce costs and also make sound investment decisions (MacKerron and Boira-Segarra 1996).

Third is known as sliding scale regulation. This form of regulation is a mixture of rate of return and price cap regulation. This is a hybrid of rate of return and price cap regulation whereby once an agreed rate of return is achieved for a firm then it is subjected to price cap regulation and prices would most likely be adjusted downwards. However, this form of regulation has not been implemented in the UK or Australia.

Fourth includes the use of licences; in the UK and Australia generation firms are required to obtain licences before they can supply electricity into their respective systems. Unless a generator has failed to meet licence obligations it will not be revoked, in the UK a license continues until the Secretary of State has given any electricity generator 25 years' notice and then they may not do so for at least 10 years, so effectively a generator has at least a 35-year licence. Licences can also been modified and in the UK the licences of three incumbents were modified in 1992 such that the Director General of Electricity Supply was able to receive information and monitor generators' behaviour to see whether they were restricting, distorting, or preventing competition. The UK has adopted this system whereby the details of regulation are largely contained in the licences because primary legislation can be changed quickly especially with changes of government; licences are legally enforceable contracts which are contestable in court by independent judiciaries and cannot be readily changed without the consent of the licence holder (generation firm).

Table 5.1 highlights and represents the scope of UK utility economic and social regulations, with respect to the domains and instruments used, and the sources of power used by regulators. For a privatised utility such as an electricity generation firm compliance to these has been restrictive, especially the price cap mechanism.

The preceding discussion in this section has been mainly on the issue of economic regulation. However, the issue of environmental regulations on electricity generating firms is also important. Three important air pollution issues that can affect generation firms are (a) carbon dioxide emissions, (b) control of sulphur and nitrogen emissions from large combustion plants, and (c) requirements for an integrated pollution control framework for discharges from individual power stations (MacKerron and Boira-Segarra 1996). Furthermore, there is a very important issue of control philosophies between national and international requirements. That is, the requirements of the Kyoto Protocol for tighter emission standards have not been ratified by the Australian government and such a decision means that generation firms in Australia may not be duly concerned with environmental constraints in their daily operation

Table 5.1   The regulatory setting for the UK ESI

Regulatory domains	Regulatory instruments	Source of powers
Economic regulation		
1. Competition	Policing, promoting restructuring and market entry, 'Yardstick competition'	Legislation and licence
2. Financial viability of companies	Price controls/tariff review	Licence
3. Efficiency	Price controls/tariff review	Licence
4. Capital investment	Monitoring regulatory accounts	Licence
5. Price protection (monopoly sectors)	Price controls/tariff review	Licence
6. Diversification – protection of core business	Monitoring regulatory accounts	Licence and legislation
Social regulation		
1. Obligation to supply	Determinations	Legislation
2. Service quality	Performance standards/ complaint handling/ tariff reviews	Legislation and licence
3. Protection of 'vulnerable consumers' e.g., elderly, disabled	Codes of practice	Legislation and licence
4. Tariff protection for rural consumers	Price controls	Legislation and licence
5. Debt and disconnection	Codes of practice	Legislation and licence
6. Consumer representation	Consumer committees	Legislation
7. Occupational health and safety		Legislation
8. Quasi-environmental protection, e.g., energy efficiency	Codes of practice/performance standards	Legislation

Source: Ernst (1994), p. 57; Table 9: The regulatory setting for the UK ESI.

and investment decisions. However, in the future, global environmental summits or conferences will most likely mean tighter environmental laws will be introduced in Australia which will undoubtedly change the operating and investment outlook of generation firms.

In the UK ESI environmental regulation was not an influential factor in the decision-making process of generation firms adopting cleaner gas-fired power stations (MacKerron and Boira-Segarra 1996). It was more to do with investment decisions being made to use cheaper, and fortuitously cleaner, gas-fired systems rather than retrofitting older, polluting coal-fired systems (MacKerron and Boira-Segarra 1996; Newbery 2001).

Ownership in Electricity Supply Industries (ESIs)

Figure 5.1 below depicts the central actors (stakeholders) in the electricity

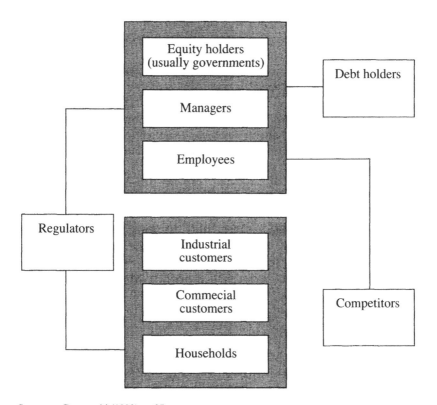

Source: Czamanski (1999), p. 27.

Figure 5.1   The central actors in the electricity sector

sector. The actors depicted all have diverse interests and this can lead to conflicts between goals and the agency problem might be prevalent. The agency problem was found in the UK ESI study; the industry's management having to deal with conflicting goals between the government's community obligations and commercial requirements to be profitable.

The changes that have occurred in electricity supply industries around the world relate to changes in ownership and management. The three most common forms of ownership/management are now detailed (Hunt and Shuttleworth 1996). First, there is direct government ownership where the government owns and manages the industry. This was the case for the UK and Australia until the 1990s and investment was carried out under government appropriations. The industry was viewed as national infrastructure and the focus was on central planning usually in conjunction with other industries. Second, the government-owned corporation is where the government owns a corporation, which manages the industry so that government is one step removed from day-to-day control. A board of directors is appointed which sets the goals and appoints management to achieve those goals. The corporation is under some obligation to make a profit but may also be required to carry out other government policies such as supporting supplying industries such as coal (UK); there may be an independent regulating authority, which is the case for ESIs in New South Wales and Queensland (Australia). Third, the privately owned corporation is where the UK and Victorian ESIs are now placed, the corporation may be listed and is obviously expected to make profits for the shareholders and independent regulators usually regulate them.

A GOVERNANCE – STRATEGIC CHOICE FRAMEWORK

Regulated firms take into account their business environment, which comprises of two contexts (Vietor 1994: 315–16). These are (a) the regulation-defined marketplace and (b) the political arenas of vested interests of the relationships amongst market place participants. The broad conceptual relation of a firm's strategy to these two contexts shows that a regulated firm that desires to be effective needs strategies that enable it to compete in an actual regulated market and amongst the political arena of vested interests (Vietor 1994) as shown in Figure 5.2.

The Governance–Strategic Choice (GSC) framework presented in this chapter (see Figure 5.3) has been developed with strategic choice (Child 1997) and strategic process research in mind. Strategic process involves organisational power holders, senior management, deciding upon an organisation's strategic action based on the environment it is operating in (for example, highly competitive or not) and also the standards of performance

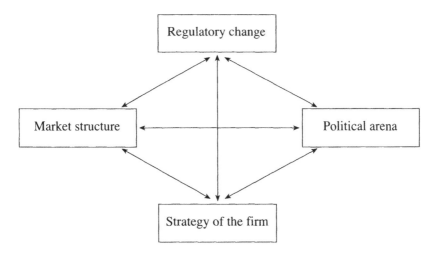

Source: Vietor (1994), p. 316.

Figure 5.2   Regulatory reform and strategic adjustment

required (for example, maximising profits or shareholder wealth). The effectiveness of strategic actions is evaluated in a feedback system and further changes can be made if required. It is not the intention of this chapter to explain the framework in detail but to point out that the regulatory environment and government intervention has the potential to affect the strategies and investment decisions of electricity generation firms.

In some industries managers may share a common set of 'strategic recipes', which are assumptions as to what strategies would be appropriate to perform well in an industry (Child 1997). For electricity generation, producing power that meets frequency and reliability standards would be one such possible strategic recipe followed in the industry. Furthermore firms share strategic recipes they may also be able to facilitate the interpretation of the environment (Child 1997). Hatten and Schendel (1975-75: 195) stated that, 'in formulating strategy, management must cope with uncertainty and must rely on the accuracy of its perceptions'. The thoughts of Murray (1978 as cited in Fredrickson, 1983: 568) are also relevant here; he suggested that firms in regulated environments, of which an electricity supply industry is typical, must 'negotiate' their actions (strategic choices) with outside constituents.

The GSC Framework is now presented on the page thereafter. The major components of the framework in this chapter include:

1.   the mode of entry for firms, that is either as privatised incumbents or new

entrants;
2. strategic events that may influence the chosen strategies;
3. the possible strategic deceits that firms may use and which may also influence the chosen strategies;
4. the actual strategies chosen; and
5. the remediableness of the governance regime used in conjunction with the chosen strategies employed.

Firms may also choose to exit the industry if the conditions are not appropriate to their strategic needs. The feedback loop is utilised in this model as verification that the chosen strategy is remediable under the criteria set in Williamson (1999a).

Implications of GSC Framework for Government Policy

Two main areas of policy affect electricity supply industries of which the generation sector is one of three components. First of all competition policy seeks to promote competition in an industry for the benefit of consumers (President's Council of Economic Advisers 2002). The fundamental challenge with development of such policy is to ensure government measures do not actually restrict or handicap the ability of firms to lower costs or improve products, which in turn does not benefit consumers and society at large (President's Council of Economic Advisers 2002). In Australia the 1993 National Competition Policy document and the Council of Australian Government have helped to shape policy for the electricity supply industry in that country.

Second, specific government policies with regards to electricity supply industries come under the umbrella of broad national energy policies. For the case of the UK and Australia two distinct statements are now shown. The UK government's objectives for its energy policy are (DTI 2003):

1. to put ourselves on a path to cut the UK's carbon dioxide emissions – the main contributor to global warming – by some 60 per cent by about 2050, as recommended by the RCEP, with real progress by 2020;
2. to maintain the reliability of energy supplies;
3. to promote competitive markets in the UK and beyond, helping to raise the rate of sustainable economic growth and to improve our productivity; and
4. to ensure that every home is adequately and affordably heated.

In a similar fashion the Australian government's energy policy (COAG, 2001) is about:

The GSC Framework

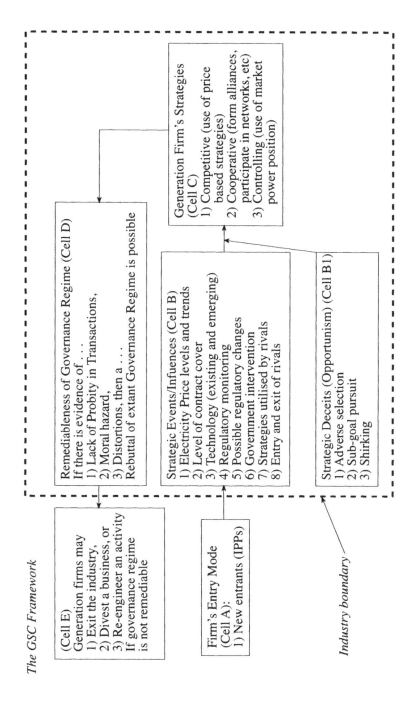

Figure 5.3   The GSC framework

1. encouraging efficient provision of reliable, competitively-priced energy
    services to Australians, underpinning wealth and job creation and
    improved quality of life, taking into account the needs of regional, rural
    and remote areas;
2. encouraging responsible development of Australia's energy resources,
    technology and expertise, their efficient use by industries and households
    and their exploitation in export markets; and
3. mitigating local and global environmental impacts, notably greenhouse
    impacts, of energy production, transformation, supply and use.

The GSC Framework has been developed to highlight that several events or
influences will have an impact on the strategies adopted by electricity
generation firms and that some of these include regulatory influences. There
seems to be little coverage in literature of the strategic behaviour of firms;
according to Vietor (1991: 20) 'neither economic or policy explanations take
into account the strategic conduct of the firm or its surprising effects'. In
contrast to the economists' approach researchers in the area of strategic
management have begun to examine the effects of regulation using the
individual firm as the unit of analysis (Ramaswamy *et al.* 1994). Another view
suggests that very little is known about how regulation and deregulation
affects the strategic choices made by firms in utility industries (Parker 2002).

Within the framework presented in Figure 5.3 the strategic events of (a)
regulatory monitoring, (b) possible regulatory changes and (c) government
intervention are important factors. The practical effects of these factors are
discussed more in the next section of this chapter but it is pertinent to state the
likely corollaries/implications that these factors would have for government
policy. First the level or amount of regulatory monitoring is important since
firms in regulated industries such as electricity generation have to manage not
only their business context but also their relationships with external entities
(Mahon and Murray Jr. 1981); such as government departments and regulatory
agencies. Parker (2002) stated that regulation involves the development of
trust between the regulator, the regulated, and the public. In electricity
generation the regulator's actions will influence the distribution of efficiency
gains between profits for generators and lower prices/improved services for
consumers (Parker 2002).

Second, the amount/level of regulatory changes has potential to affect
competitive responses (Mahon and Murray Jr. 1981) due to legislative
requirements for approvals of firms' potential strategies and the fact that the
rules of the game might change frequently, thus firms may face a great deal of
uncertainty. Privatised firms will face normal commercial risks associated
with investing; producing and competing but also may face regulatory risks
from the nature of the regulatory rules and practices (Parker 2003). Third, the

occurrence of government intervention is interesting in that it can conflict with regulated firms' assessment/outlook of certainty about the future (Mahon and Murray Jr. 1981).

Energy policy issues have been relevant of late with the California power problems well covered in the media and also the failure to liberalise European energy markets (Helm 2002). The energy market, which includes electricity, is a crucial part of a nation's economy and society so governments remain an important player and have influence on prices, output and capital structures (Helm 2002). This is an important factor at the level of the individual firms and as is shown in the GSC Framework regulatory changes/monitoring and government interventions are influences, which help shape strategy for electricity generation firms.

Firms may act opportunistically by withholding or distorting information (Parker 2003) on prices or output levels and this is accounted for by the strategic deceits cell in the framework as an influence that can affect the strategies of rivals and also the regulatory framework. That is, the information withheld may distort the efficiency of the regulatory system which in turn affects the over efficient market based outcome of the industry.

THE OUTCOMES OF PRIVATISATION?

Four industries have been studied which include the United Kingdom (UK), and the three Australian states jurisdictions of Victoria, Queensland and New South Wales Electricity Generation sectors. For the UK the period 1990 to 2001 has been covered since it is during this time that a pool market trading system was implemented and then replaced ten years later. A major reason for this included that the pool system had not been able to prevent abuse of market power by the initial incumbent and later entrant generation firms. For the Australian jurisdictions the period covered is 1992 to 2003. This is the time in which Australia moved from having separate state based jurisdictions to a national market that now stretches from South Australia to Queensland through interconnections. Only the state of Victoria has fully privatised its electricity supply industry, Queensland and New South Wales have 'corporatised' their respective industries. This means that the incumbent generation firms remain government owned but are required to compete in a fully commercial environment.

The first study on the UK ESI provided a plethora of information from a wide variety of sources; these sources have a time span of over ten years (from 1988–2001). In all, several books and journals from differing authors, including those who had been involved from the regulatory role, both UK and European based have been sourced for information. In addition, the Internet site for the regulatory body in the UK, Office of Electricity Regulation, and the sites for the major generation companies have been utilised. The sources of data for the second, third, and fourth studies comprise of books, journal articles, Internet sites (Federal Government Departments and Agencies such as the ACCC and the NCC) and newspaper articles on the reform process from 1991 until 2003, and interviews.

The persons interviewed for the Australian studies were senior management, and if possible Chief Executive Officers or Managing Directors. This is because these people are the most connected with the longer term strategic directions of the firms and also have contact with regulatory bodies, government ministers, and major customers. One weakness of utilising CEO/MD/Senior Management personnel is that they may not fully reveal their strategic direction/s and also talk favourably about their own organisation but not favourably about other organisations, which could include the regulatory bodies, for example, who might be seen to be operating against their company's strategic direction.

United Kingdom ESI (UK ESI)

In 1996 it was stated that with respect to regulation (Robinson 1996) two government failures had made the UK electricity regulator's job unnecessarily difficult: these were:

1. the failure to isolate naturally monopolistic activities (for example, transmission) and regulate those only; and
2. the failure to establish conditions in which potentially competitive sectors of electricity would actually be competitive (for example, generation).

Other overall with respect to the regulation of the privatised UK ESI reveal that the unregulated market power of the non-nuclear generation duopoly (National Power (NP) and PowerGen (PG)) in the period 1990–1994 did not attract sufficient entry due to their large combined market share and manipulation of Pool prices (Armstrong *et al.* 1994).

The generators NP and PG arguably cannot be criticised for retaining their market power because they played the game according to the rules set down by the government at the time of privatisation (Robinson 1996).

The role of government had been reduced, but not entirely eliminated and regulation was far more transparent than under the old government controlled regulation, which was perceived as 'secretive' (Robinson 1996).

Insufficient competition in generation had led to the introduction of some price controls by the electricity regulator; it was envisaged in 1990 that this regulation would not be necessary (Armstrong *et al.* 1994).

The lessons from the UK privatisation suggested that there should be effective mechanisms for smaller consumers to influence the market and have some power base (Murray 1998). What this mechanism might be had not been detailed at the time; however domestic consumers now have the choice of electricity supplier, be it a retail or generation company. They are no longer held captive because of what area they live in.

Because of the British government's 'botched' privatisation of the UK ESI and subsequent 'limp-wristed' regulation, a process of natural selection would take place and that the UK ESI would eventually consist of two or three vertically integrated generation/distribution companies (Pitcher 1995). Further, a British Labour government would not have to re-nationalise the UK ESI, as the companies would be able to do it themselves (Pitcher 1995). This has actually not occurred as yet in 2004.

Major consumer groups have been concerned about the prices charged in the first few years after privatisation. For example, the Major Users Group of electricity that represents companies such as British Steel and ICI demanded an investigation into an apparent 'price fixing' conspiracy in the Pool system in 1994 (Boscheck 1994). The electricity regulator at the time decided not to refer NP and PG to the Monopoly and Mergers Commission (MMC) on the condition that they would use 'all reasonable endeavours' to dispose of plant within two years of 1994 and to reduce their respective market shares (Boscheck 1994).

Conflict between the privatised generators' corporate strategy and the UK regulatory setting occurred in 1995. Regulatory provisions meant that takeovers of the Regional Electricity Companies (RECs) by UK generators were forbidden until April 1995. Soon after this date expired, July 1995, PG announced a formal bid for Midlands REC and NP responded with its own formal bid for Southern REC (Green and Newbery 1998). The proposed bids were referred to the UK Monopoly and Merger Commission (MMC), which found that the bids could be expected to act against the public interest but recommended they be allowed to proceed (Green and Newbery 1998).

If these mergers by NP and PG were allowed to proceed then it would be against the principles of public interest (*Economist* 1996). The public interest was stated as electricity being available at the lowest pricing that is compatible with an adequate, reliable supply (*Economist* 1996) and thus to permit a vertical merger between a generator and distributor would contradict the original ideas of privatisation. The MMC however, supported the mergers because it would: 'help British electricity firms compete abroad' (*Economist* 1996: 14). Finally in 1996 the UK Government's Secretary of State for Trade and Industry rejected both bids and most commentators noted that this rejection of the MMC's recommendation left the UK ESI unsure of the government's intentions for its desired evolution and its policy more generally on competition (Green and Newbery 1998).

The constant threat of regulation has been a good and powerful tool in gaining compliance by participants (Helm and Jenkinson 1998). The voluntary undertakings by NP and PG in 1994 to divest 6000 MW of plant and adhere to a pool price cap for 1994–1996 is an illustration of such compliance (Helm and Jenkinson 1998). The level that is set, the structure, and the duration of price caps gives regulators considerable scope to influence the development of competition (Helm and Jenkinson 1998). The institutional environment may not have been as well defined as the participants would have liked and the major participants in generation sector used this to their advantage and, consequently, regulation was heavier than expected.

The regulated companies in the United Kingdom, which includes those in electricity supply, telecommunications and gas supply, have complained about the costs of satisfying regulators' requests for data (Parker 1999). For example, a senior manager of PG commented about regulation that 'From a regulated firm's perspective, [the] uncertainty is significant. We have to commit resources to trying to guess what is around the next corner' (Reidy 1995: 124). Even though companies have complained about regulation they have been criticised about increases in management pay and bonuses for the privatised firms (Parker 1999). This has been in contrast to more modest pay increases for ordinary employees and at a time of large reductions (around 50 per cent of employees) in work forces (Parker 1999).

However, consumers have not been disadvantaged. For domestic consumers prices dropped approximately 26 per cent in real terms for the 1990s period (Parker 2003) and for industrial and commercial consumers the price drops in the 1990s were between 25 per cent and 34 per cent respectively (Parker 2003). Other studies found that consumer prices did fall but also argued that these drops in prices could have been larger (Newbery 2001; de Olivera and Tolmasquim 2004). Newbery (2001) indicated that costs (fuel and staff) had fallen dramatically for generation firms since privatisation, and this coupled with efficiency gains in the other sectors of the electricity supply industry was not passed on to consumers until 1995. That is, part of the fall in fuel costs was passed on to the companies in the form of increased profits and to investors in the form of increased share prices (Newbery 2001; de Olivera and Tolmasquim 2004). Although it is difficult to measure, the service quality of electricity supply in the UK has improved since privatisation (Parker 1999 and 2003).

In the mid-late 1990s the electricity regulatory office, OFFER, was given virtually no power to make regulatory rules and when it did make imaginative use of its limited powers to modify licences, electricity firms complained vigorously that the actions were illegitimate and that they amounted to legal challenges (Loughlin and Scott 1997). In 1998 the regulator had proposed that the pool system in the UK had allowed the two big generators (NP and PG), and even smaller generators, to bid up the pool prices on many occasions since privatisation in 1990 (Energy Economist 1998). A new system of bilateral trading arrangements between generation firms and customers was suggested and thus the pool system could be abolished (Energy Economist 1998). The pool trading system that was established upon privatisation on 31 March 1990 was abolished in April 2001 and replaced by the new trading arrangements.

Australia's National Electricity Market (NEM)

Various regulatory agencies are 'involved' with Australia's National Electricity Market (NEM). These are the National Electricity Market Management Company (NEMMCO), the National Electricity Code Administrator (NECA), the Australian Competition and Consumer Commission (ACCC), and each state based jurisdiction has its own state-level regulator, for example in Victoria it is the Victorian Office of the Regulator-General. Senior management of all of the major generators in the states of Victoria, Queensland and New South Wales were asked to be interviewed on their views of the industry reforms and whilst not all agreed to be interviewed the responses of those interviewed (fictitious company names are used) in regards to the following question are now detailed. The question asked was 'Have the regulatory bodies become more rigorous in their enforcement of legislation/regulations? How do they enforce these?'

VicPower stated that there was a credible threat from regulators, 'if you misbehave, we'll drop in'. The volume of new or modified regulations was said to be high with about five papers per week sent out to the company; these papers are anywhere from 5 to 200 pages in length and come from a variety of regulators (five to six major bodies are involved). The company does not have the time to look through all these changes thoroughly. A major problem for the company's management was that regulators change the 'rules of the game' very rapidly. Therefore, VicPower could not really plan ahead as much as it would like to, especially when negotiating contracts with customers for long-term supply.

Aussie Power stated some contrast to the view above; regulatory bodies had not been that rigorous in their application of legislation/regulations. It was mentioned that it was almost a relationship now with the regulatory bodies; there is much more discussion now and the generators get representation on some committees.

Country Power mentioned that it is essential that every participant have a close association with the regulatory bodies and that compliance with Codes is necessary. Comments were made that the level of government intervention was too high. Further investment is possible if the financial returns are attractive but the risks are that government intervention could affect these returns.

Q Power stated that the regulatory bodies had become more rigorous and that companies were exposed to more of them. It was perceived that the ACCC and NECA were the regulators that mattered the most. NECA, the industry regulator, was perceived as being good. The ACCC was regarded as being a 'little too consumer-focused' and consequently did not give much concern to the firms.

Northern Electric was concerned that no one was driving the industry forward ('there is no driver in the bus') and that market rules were changing too quickly for the participants to absorb them. Regulation has become more rigorous over time and compliance was very important. This company affirmed that regulation could provide certainty on the 'rules of the game'. The company suggested that a 'Utilities Commission' should be established to incorporate all regulators; federal and state-based, and to leave the market operator as a separate entity.

Banana Power stated that regulation could be 'out of control' in Australia, and there are too many bodies involved at both federal and state level. For example, it was stated that the ACCC was not really an energy industry regulator because it is a body that represents consumer interests. Only one overall regulatory body should be present; amongst other things it would make sure that investment for new power stations is not curtailed.

Harbour Power stated that there are in all 16 regulators involved in the NEM. This creates a lot of 'choke' and in the eyes of Harbour Power regulation is too great.

Power NSW stated that regulation had been more watchful and that the ACCC and NECA were too involved with the practice of rebidding by generators.

In summary the interviews presented some conflicting views on the effects of regulation on the individual firms. Taken collectively the views do indicate that regulatory changes and monitoring have impacted upon the way firms do business and on the level of investment for new power stations. Also, some interviewees did indicate that the number of regulatory bodies involved with the industry is high and implied one wide-ranging body would be best for the industry. At the time of writing this chapter the establishment of two new regulatory bodies had been approved by the Australian Parliament. The two new bodies will be the Australian Energy Regulator (AER) and the Australian Energy Market Commission (AEMC). The AER will be responsible for the National Electricity Code and economic regulation of the electricity transmission system. The AEMC will be responsible for rule-making (through the electricity code) and electricity market development. The ACCC will retain responsibility for competition regulation and industry access.

In Australia an unincorporated association called the National Generators' Forum (NGF) is made up of all the major generation firms in the Australian NEM; the CEOs of each member generator convene to lobby regulators on market governance issues. One CEO stated that 'NGF membership plays a key role in influencing the market rules direction for generators'. There are good working relations between the NGF and the main regulators involved with the NEM. Each generator provides funds toward the NGF and because it is an unincorporated association it does lack authority to challenge regulators, for example, to challenge the ACCC in the Competition Tribunal.

Table 5.2 shows a tabulated summary of the regulatory outcomes and price levels/trends for the four industries studied with reference to the framework presented in this chapter.

CONCLUSIONS

The strategies used by generators in all four ESIs have been in part determined by (a) the amount of monitoring by regulatory bodies, (b) the amount of regulatory changes (especially for the Australian generators) and (c) the level of government intervention. These factors have provided generators the opportunity for gaming strategies if they so desired but also restricted their long-term objectives for investment and negotiating long-term supply contracts with customers. Government intervention in Australia has encouraged gas-fired plants over coal-fired plants but in the UK this intervention has protected coal-fired and nuclear plants and also barred entry of gas-fired plant in 1998. It is very apparent that government intervention and regulatory bodies have a major say in an industry that was originally set up under the ideals of competitive markets.

A dominant and emerging theme in the evidence and data from the four industries was that regulation seemed to be much more heavy-handed than was originally expected and this has impacted on the strategic direction and operations of generators in all four studies. The Australian studies interview data revealed that all generators were concerned with the regulatory setting in the NEM and with the mix of several federal and state-level regulators. These issues make it very hard for generators to adjust to proposed changes and also impedes their ability to negotiate long-term contracts since such rapid changes bring more uncertainty into transactions. A recommendation here is that regulatory monitoring/changes have an effect on the strategies used by generators, whether this is a positive or negative effect on a generator's competitive advantage seems to be situational and needs further investigation as to whether associations such as the Australian NGF play a role in improving generators' competitive advantages.

Table 5.2 Summary of regulatory outcomes for UK and Australian electricity generation sectors

GSC framework elements	Characteristics and measurement unit	Outcome for each industry				Overall outcome
		UK ESI	Victoria (Australia)	Queensland (Australia)	New South Wales (Australia)	
Strategic events and influences	Electricity prices/trends (up/down)	Volatility in pool prices; basic average prices were static over ten years, major and minor players manipulated pool system to gain market power	Volatility in pool prices and downward trend of prices from 1997 to 2000	Higher prices were evident in QESI than other NEM states in the period 1997–2000	Average prices have been lower than other NEM states	A major influence with respect to levels of investment, and competitiveness outcomes
	Regulatory monitoring (how much?)	After two years it became evident the regulation had to be more heavy-handed than originally perceived, monitoring has remained this way since	Perception there is too much monitoring and too many bodies involved. However relations between regulators and gencos should be amicable	Lack of leadership in the industry; regulation is more important now, the rules of the game seem to change too quickly and the ACCC is too consumer-focused	Too many regulators, which choke company operations. Regulators are more watchful	There is too much regulation and there are too many regulators involved in these ESIs of which no one has a lead role

Regulatory changes (how often?)	Regulatory changes were made to combat the market power of the major players, a new system of trading electricity started in 2001	Changes are too many too quickly; insufficient time to digest the changes	Changes are too quick but regulations could provide some certainty to potential investors	Changes are too quick and there is not enough time to digest the implications of the changes	The 'rules of the game' change quickly and in some cases these are ignored by firms due to time and costs involved
Government intervention (how often?)	UK government intervened on occasions to (a) block mergers and (b) support the domestic coal industry	Government intervention used on occasions when supply is threatened. Government established a commission to oversee industry and was trying to facilitate new investment in 2002/3	Queensland government introduced a Cleaner Fuel Strategy in May 2000, may force gencos to use more expensive but cleaner burning fuels. As an owner of generators the government encourages public/private partnerships for new investments	Support for full privatisation is not present but there has been privatisation of the wholesale electricity trading functions because of a history of losses	In all cases the government has intervened, periodic crisis intervention has been more apparent in the privatised UK and Victorian ESIs.

Implications for Electricity Supply Industries in Asia

The industries, regulatory instruments and settings covered in this chapter have been applied and are 'located' in western Anglo-Saxon countries. Even though regulatory reform has been progressing in Southeast and East Asia one comment was that it would 'be interesting to see if Asian countries can evolve comparably efficient and credible regulation if they choose to privatize their networks' (Newbery 2001: 396). Such a comment has to be considered with the relevant institutions that are in place in Asian countries. Of the various definitions of institutions, North (1991: 97) is comprehensive in that institutions are 'the humanly devised constraints that structure political, economic, and social interactions. They consist of both informal constraints (sanctions, taboos, customs, traditions, and codes of conduct), and formal rules (constitutions, laws, property rights)'. Given that some Asian countries have historical links with the United Kingdom and Europe (for example, Singapore) an 'Anglo' style regulatory philosophy and system might be suitable. However this has to be tempered with the relevant level of government involvement in society, the social systems in place and the ultimate market philosophy that exists in Asian countries.

In the Asian region the demand for electricity (exceeding 10 per cent per annum) seems to be growing faster than GNP in many countries (Gabriele 2004). The consequent financing needs for such growth in electricity demand requires funds from both domestic and international sources (Gabriele 2004). A comparison between the electricity sectors in India and China is provided by Gabriele (2004) and policy implications are offered here. Both countries have populations over 1 billion and are still rapidly industrialising their economies, per capita consumption of electricity in India is amongst the lowest in the world.

India's federal structure has created some problems since the various states are at different stages of implementing electricity sector reform. The Indian government has actively facilitated foreign direct investment (FDI) but annual flows of FDI into India have been about 5 per cent of that for China. The political structure in India between the central government and the states has resulted in an unpredictable investment climate which is reflected in the above-mentioned FDI flows. India should examine the operation and experiences of Australia's National Electricity Market since both countries are federations, albeit with very different populations, cultures and stages of economic development. Possibly the establishment of an Indian electricity market along the lines of Australia's market may not only foster competition between the various Indian states but also provide a nation-wide industry which will attract FDI.

As mentioned above China, has attracted large inflows of FDI which has allowed for construction of new power plants. However, these projects have not been without their problems such as long approval delays or outright cancellation. Some of the provinces have been experimenting with more market based systems as used in the UK and Australia, for example, merit-order dispatch of individual generating units. The reality is that even though ownership may be undergoing change in China it would be very difficult to foresee total privatisation of China's electricity industry. The state can use the electricity industry as a policy tool to, for instance, control inflation or promote rural electrification. It will take time for competitive market based systems to be fully implemented in China, 5 to 10 years, so foreign firms will need to take stock of the regulatory requirements and utilize joint ventures with a local partner. Whether or not China can utilise the experiences of the reform of the UK and Australian electricity industries is hard to judge due to the vast differences in national systems.

Whatever systems of regulation are chosen in Asian countries can only benefit from the experiences of privatisation and deregulation not only in the UK and Australia but also the United States and developing countries.

Recommendations

From a government policy and regulatory perspective this chapter has briefly highlighted that regulatory monitoring and changes have impacted on the ability of generators to not only compete within their market but also make reasonable returns on their investment. Neo-classical economic principles may well guide policymaking but the actual behaviours of firms, be it to compete, co-operate or control, must be considered in further policymaking. The corporate strategy used by generators seemed to be that controlling (market power) strategies are preferred first, then co-operative (bilateral) strategies, then competitive (price based) last in the pursuit of reasonable profits and maximising shareholder wealth. Also, regulators need to note that firms in an industrial network are in effect citizens of a small self-governing community and as such have the capacity to act for the common good of the industry participants.

From a practitioner perspective, the expected contribution is that practitioners/senior management should appreciate that strategic management is a complex and pluralistic area in which shareholder wealth maximisation is just one consideration. Other considerations are that regulators and overseers impact upon strategies in sometimes-significant ways. In addition it was apparent that collective and cooperative behaviours yield better financial outcomes for generators, as was the situation for all the ESIs with respect to the use of long-term relationship focused hedged supply contracts. The GSC Framework hopefully provides senior management with a model to assist in their short-, medium- and long-term strategic plans and highlights that generators should be wary of the strategic deceits highlighted in the model.

One possible alternate regulatory system is that of industry self-regulation (King and Lenox 2000). In such a system generation firms could join together to regulate their collective action to avoid a common threat or provide a common good by introducing appropriate codes of conduct. Since many economists have argued that without explicit penalties and sanctions self-regulation will fail (King and Lenox 2000) it not might be appropriate for such issues as prices charged or profits accrued by generation firms since the threat of opportunistic behaviour would most likely be high. Self-regulation might be more appropriate for issues such as (a) obligation to supply, (b) quality/security of supply and for the more proactive industries, (c) the protection of vulnerable consumers with regards to prices.

One thing is for sure, privatisation and deregulation in the UK and Australia has been successful only to a point; it can be argued that prices may have fallen but larger consumers got much lower prices than domestic consumers did.

REFERENCES

Amendola, V. and S. Bruno (1998) 'Regulation and Deregulation', in R. Arena and C. Longhi (eds), *Markets and Organization*, Berlin: Springer.

Ansoff, H. I. (1988) *The New Corporate Strategy*, New York: John Wiley & Sons.

Arena, R. and C. Longhi (eds) (1998) *Introduction to 'Markets and Organization'*, Berlin: Springer-Verlag.

Arend, R. J. (2003) 'Revisiting the Logical and Research Considerations of Competitive Advantage', *Strategic Management Journal*, **24**, 279–84.

Armstrong, M., S. Cowan and J. Vickers (1994) *Regulatory Reform: Economic Analysis and British Experience*, Cambridge, MA: The MIT Press.

Barney, J. B. and W. Hesterly (1999) 'Organizational Economics: Understanding the Relationship between Organizations and Economic Analysis', in S. R. Clegg and C. Hardy (eds), *Studying Organization: Theory and Method*, London: Sage Publications.

Beesley, M. E. and S. C. Littlechild (1989) 'The Regulation of Privatized Monopolies in the United Kingdom', *The RAND Journal of Economics*, **20**(3), 454–72.

Bonardi, J. P. (2004) 'Global and Political Strategies in Deregulated Industries: The Asymmetric Behaviors of Former Monopolies', *Strategic Management Journal*, **25**, 101–20.

Borenstein, S. and J. Bushnell (2000) 'Electricity Restructuring: Deregulation or Reregulation?', *Regulation*, **23**(2), 46–52.

Boscheck, R. (1994) 'Deregulating European Electricity Supply: Issues and Implications', *Long Range Planning*, **27**(5), 111–23.

Bowman, E. H. and C. E. Helfat (2001) 'Does Corporate Strategy Matter?', *Strategic Management Journal*, **22**, 1–23.

Carlton, D. W. and J. M. Perloff (2000) *Modern Industrial Organization*, Reading, MA: Addison-Wesley.

Chao, H. P. and H. G. Huntington (1998) 'Introduction: Economic and Technological Principles in Designing Power Markets' in H. P. Chao and H. G. Huntington (eds), *Designing Competitive Electricity Markets*, Boston, MA: Kluwer Academic Publishers.

Chakravarthy, B. S. and Y. Doz (1992) 'Strategy Process Research: Focusing on Corporate Self-Renewal', *Strategic Management Journal*, **13**, 5–14.

Child, J. (1997) 'Strategic Choice in the Analysis of Action, Structure, Organizations and Environment: Retrospect and Prospect', *Organization Studies*, **18**(1), 43–76.

Combs, J. G. and D. J. Ketchen (1999) 'Explaining Interfirm Cooperation and Performance: Toward a Reconciliation of Predictions from the Resource-based View and Organizational Economics', *Strategic Management Journal*, **20**, 867–88.

Council of Australian Governments (COAG) (2001) 'Commonwealth/State Agreement on Energy Policy – Extract from Council of Australian Governments' Communiqué 8 June 2001', accessed via http://www.industry.gov.au.

Cuervo, A. and B. Villalonga (2000) 'Explaining the Variance in the Performance Effects of Privatization', *Academy of Management Review*, **25**(3), 581–90.

Czamanski, D. (1999) *Privatization and Restructuring of Electricity Provision*, Westport, CT: Praeger Publishers.

de Olivera, R. G. and M. T. Tolmasquim (2004) 'Regulatory Performance Analysis Case Study: Britain's Electricity Industry', *Energy Policy*, **32**, 1261–76.

De Wit, B. and R. Meyer, R. (1998) *Strategy: Process, Content, Context – An International Perspective*, 2nd Edition, London: International Thomson Business Press.

Department of Trade and Industry (DTI) UK (2003) *Energy White Paper: Our Energy Future – Creating a Low Carbon Economy*, Norwich: The Stationery Office.

Doh, J. P. (2000) 'Entrepreneurial Privatisation Strategies: Order of Entry and Local Partner Collaboration as Sources of Competitive Advantage', *Academy of Management Review*, **25**(3), 551–71.

Dyer, J. H. and H. Singh (1998) 'The Relational View: Cooperative Strategy and Sources of Interorganizational Competitive Advantage', *Academy of Management Review*, **23**(4),660–79.

Emmons, W. (2000) *The Evolving Bargain: Strategic Implications of Deregulation and Privatization*, Boston, MA: Harvard Business School Press.

Energy Economist (1998) *Uncertain Times*, 201, July, 1.

Ernst, J. (1994) *Whose utility? The Social Impact of Public Utility Privatization and Regulation in Britain*, Buckingham: Open University Press.

Foer, A. A. and D. L. Moss (2003) 'Electricity in Transition: Implications for Regulation and Antitrust', *Energy Law Journal*, **24**(1), 89–105.

Fredrickson, J. W. (1983) 'Strategic Process Research: Questions and Recommendations', *Academy of Management Review*, **8**(4), 565–75.

Gabriele, A. (2004) 'Policy Alternatives in Reforming Energy Utilities in Developing Countries', *Energy Policy*, **32**, 1319–37.

Ghobadian, A. and H. Viney (2002) 'Strategic Reorientation in Former Public Utilities: the Example of UK Electricity', *Management Decision*, **40**(7/8), 634–46.

Ghosh, M. and G. John (1999), 'Governance Value Analysis and Marketing Strategy', *Journal of Marketing*, **63**, 131–45.

Ginsberg, A. (1988) 'Measuring and Modelling Changes in Strategy: Theoretical Foundations and Empirical Directions', *Strategic Management Journal*, **9**, 559–75.

Green, R. and D. M. Newbery (1998) 'The Electricity Industry in England and Wales', in D. Helm and T. Jenkinson (eds), *Competition in Regulated Industries*, Oxford:

Oxford University Press.

Gulati, R.; N. Nohria and A. Zaheer (2000) *'Strategic Networks'*, *Strategic Management Journal*, **21**, 203–15.

Hatten, K. J. and D. E. Schendel (1974–75) 'Strategy's Role in Policy Research', *Journal of Economics and Business*, **28**, 195–202.

Helm, D. (2002) 'Energy Policy: Security of Supply, Sustainability, and Competition', *Energy Policy*, **30**, 173–84.

Helm, D. and T. Jenkinson (1998) 'Introducing Competition into Regulated Industries', in D. Helm and T. Jenkinson (eds), *Competition in Regulated Industries*, Oxford: Oxford University Press.

Hilmer, F. G., M. R. Rayner and G. Q. Taperell (Independent Committee of Inquiry) (1993) *National Competition Policy*, Canberra: Australian Government Publishing Service.

Hite, J. M. and W. S. Hesterly (2001) 'The Evolution of Firm Networks: From Emergence to Early Growth of the Firm', *Strategic Management Journal*, **22**, 275–86.

Hunt, S. and G. Shuttleworth (1996) *Competition and Choice in Electricity*, Chichester: John Wiley & Sons.

Joskow, P.L. (1998) 'Electricity Sectors in Transition', *The Energy Journal*, **19**(2), 25–52.

King, A .A. and M. J. Lenox (2000), 'Industry Self-Regulation without Sanctions: The Chemical Industry's Care Program', *Academy of Management Journal*, **43**(4), 698–716.

Loughlin, M. and C. Scott (1997) 'The Regulatory State', in P. Dunleavy, A. Gamble, I. Holliday and G. Peele, *Developments in British Politics: 5*, Houndsmill: MacMillan Press Ltd.

MacKerron, G. and I. Boira-Segarra (1996) 'Regulation', in J. Surrey (ed.), *The British Electricity Experiment – Privatization: the Record, the Issues, the Lessons*, London: Earthscan.

Madhavan, R., B. R. Koka and J. E. Prescott (1998) 'Networks in Transition: How Industry Events (Re)shape Interfirm Relationships', *Strategic Management Journal*, **19**, 439–59.

Madhok, A. (2002) 'Reassessing the Fundamentals and Beyond: Ronald Coase, the Transaction Cost and Resource-Based Theories of the Firm and the Institutional Structure of Production', *Strategic Management Journal*, **23**, 535–50.

Mahon, J. F. and E. A. Murray Jr (1981) 'Strategic Planning for Regulated Companies', *Strategic Management Journal*, **2**, 251–62.

Mohr, L. B. (1982) *Explaining Organizational Behaviour*, San Francisco: Jossey-Bass Publishers.

Murray, B. (1998) *Electricity Markets: Investment, Performance and Analysis*, Chichester: John Wiley & Sons.

Murray, E. A. (1978) 'Strategic choice as a negotiated outcome', *Management Science*, **24**, 960–72.

Newbery, D. M. (1998) *Freer electricity markets in the UK: a progress report*, Energy Policy, 26(10), 743–49.

Newbery, D. M. (2001) *Privatization, Restructuring, and Regulation of Network Utilities*, Cambridge, MA: The MIT Press.

Nickerson, J. A. (1997) 'Toward an Economizing Theory of Strategy', Olin working paper, 97–107.

Nickerson, J.A.; B. H. Hamilton and T. Wada (2001) 'Market Position, Resource

Profile, and Governance: Linking Porter and Williamson in the Context of International Courier and Small Package Services in Japan', *Strategic Management Journal*, **22**, 251–73.

North, D. (1991) 'Institutions', *Journal of Economic Perspectives*, **5**(Winter), 97–112.

Oster, S. M. (1999) *Modern Competitive Analysis*, 3rd Edition, New York: Oxford University Press.

Parker, D. (1999) 'Regulation of privatised public utilities in the UK: performance and governance', *International Journal of Public Sector Management*, **12**(3), 213–35.

Parker, D. (2002) 'Economic Regulation: a Review of the Issues', *Annals of Public and Cooperative Economics*, **73**(4), 493–519.

Parker, D. (2003) 'Performance, Risk and Strategy in Privatised, Regulated Industries', *The International Journal of Public Sector Management*, **16**(1), 75–100.

Peacock, A. (1992) *Public Choice in Historical Perspective*, Cambridge: Cambridge University Press.

Pitcher, G. (1995) 'Breaking the Charmed Circle', *Marketing Week*, **18**(20), 25.

Porter, M. E. (1980) *Competitive Strategy: Techniques for Analyzing Industries and Competitors*, New York: The Free Press.

Porter, M. E. (1985) *Competitive Advantage: Creating and Sustaining Superior Performance*, New York: The Free Press.

Powell, T. C. (2001) 'Competitive Advantage: Logical and Philosophical Considerations', *Strategic Management Journal*, **22**, 875–88.

Powell, W.W. and L. Smith-Doerr (1994) 'Networks and Economic Life', in N. J. Smelser and R. Swedberg (eds), *The Handbook of Economic Sociology*, Princeton, NJ: University Press.

President's Council of Economic Advisers (2002) 'Economic Organization and Competition Policy', *Yale Journal on Regulation*, **19**(2), 541–97.

Ramaswamy, K., A. S. Thomas and R. J. Litschert (1994) 'Organizational Performance in a Regulated Environment: The Role of Strategic Orientation', *Strategic Management Journal*, **15**, 63–74.

Reger, R. K.; I. M. Duhaime and J. L. Stimpert (1992) 'Deregulation, Strategic Choice, Risk and Financial Performance', *Strategic Management Journal*, **13**(3), 189–204.

Reidy, M. (1995), 'Privatisation, regulation and the electricity market', in D. Helm (ed.) *British Utility Regulation: Principles, Experience, and Reform*, Oxford: Oxera Press.

Robinson, C. (1996) 'Profit, Discovery and the Role of Entry: The Case of Electricity', in *Regulating Utilities: A Time For Change?*, London: The Institute of Economic Affairs.

Rowlinson, M. (1997) *Organisations and Institutions: Perspectives in Economics and Sociology*, London: Macmillan Press Limited.

Russo, M. V. (1992) 'Power Plays: Regulation, Diversification, and Backward Integration in the Electric Utility Industry', *Strategic Management Journal*, **13**(1), 13–27.

Self, P. (2000) *Rolling Back the Market: Economic Dogma and Political Choice*, London: Macmillan Press Limited.

Shepherd, W. G. (1997) *The Economics of Industrial Organization – Analysis, Markets, Policies*, 4th Edition, Upper Saddle River, NJ: Prentice-Hall International.

Smith, K. G. and C. M. Grimm (1987) 'Environmental Variation, Strategic Change and Firm Performance: a Study of Railroad Deregulation', *Strategic Management Journal*, **8**(4), 363–76.

Spanos, Y. E. and S. Lioukas, S. (2001) 'An Examination into the Causal Logic of Rent

Generation: Contrasting Porter's Competitive Strategy Framework and the Resource-Based Perspective', *Strategic Management Journal*, **22**, 907–34.

The Economist (1996) 'Britain's Electricity Shocker', **339**(7961), 13 April, 14.

Utility Regulators Forum (2004) 'Is the building block model based on static, perfectly competitive market paradigm?', *Network*, **16**, Published by the Australian Competition and Consumer Commission, Melbourne, 1–3.

Utility Regulators Forum (2004) 'National Energy Market Reforms', *Network*, **17**, published by the Australian Competition and Consumer Commission, Melbourne, 8.

Van de Ven, A. H. (1992) 'Suggestions for Studying Strategy Process: A Research Note', *Strategic Management Journal*, **13**, 169–88.

Vickers, J. and G. Yarrow (1989) *Privatization: An Economic Analysis*, Cambridge, MA: MIT Press.

Vietor, R. H. K. (1991) 'The Hubris of Regulated Competition: Airlines, 1925–1988', in J. High (ed.), *Regulation: Economic Theory and History*, Ann Arbor, MI: University of Michigan Press.

Vietor, R. H. K. (1994) *Contrived Competition: Regulation and Deregulation in America*, Cambridge, MA: Harvard University Press.

Wheare, H. and A. Adcock (2001) 'Asia Overview: Competition Law – The Asian Perspective', *International Financial Law Review*, April, 33–44.

Williamson, O. E. (1981) 'The Economics of Organization: The Transaction Cost Approach', *American Journal of Sociology*, **87**(3), 548–77.

Williamson, O. E. (1985) *The Economic Institutions of Capitalism*, New York: Free Press.

Williamson, O. E. (1991) 'Strategizing, Economizing, and Economic Organization', in *Strategic Management Journal*, **12**, 75–94.

Williamson, O. E. (1996) *The Mechanisms of Governance*, New York: Oxford University Press.

Williamson, O. E. (1999a) 'Public and Private Bureaucracies: A Transaction Cost Economics Perspective', *The Journal of Law, Economics, & Organization*, **15**(1), 306–42.

Williamson, O. E. (1999b) 'Strategy Research: Governance and Competence Perspectives', *Strategic Management Journal*, **20**, 1087–108.

Yajima, M. (1997) *Deregulatory Reforms of the Electricity Supply Industry*, Westport, CO: Quorum Books.

Zahra, S. A., R. D. Ireland, I. Gutierrez and M. A. Hitt (2000), 'Privatization and Entrepreneurial Transformation: Emerging Issues and a Future Research Agenda', *Academy of Management Review*, **25**(3), 509–24.

6. Independent power producers in Indonesia and the Philippines

Xun Wu and Priyambudi Sulistiyanto

After decades of state monopoly on electricity production, in the early 1990s private sector participation in electricity generation through Independent Power Producer (IPP) was perceived as an inevitable policy option to deal with severe power shortages in several Southeast Asian countries (Haggard and Noble 2001; Dubash 2002). This initiative was encouraged and facilitated by development agencies that considered it an important step toward deregulation and privatization of the power sector. It was argued that IPP would not only relieve governments from the financial burden of capacity expansion in the power sector, but also lead to more competition, higher efficiency, and ultimately, lower electricity rate for consumers.

Calls for the participation of private investors in electricity generation were met with great enthusiasm in Southeast Asia. Private investors, especially the utility companies from the US and Europe, acted quickly to take advantage of this opportunity, pouring billions of dollars into electricity generation for Southeast Asian countries. By 1997, when the region was hit by the Asian financial crisis, 27 IPP contracts in Indonesia had been signed between *Perusahaan Umum Listrik Negara* (PLN), the state-owned electricity company, and private investors. In the Philippines, agreements for 37 IPPs, accounting for 40 percent of the generation capacity of the country, had been reached. Other Southeast Asian countries such as Malaysia and Thailand also experienced similar growth in IPP during the period.

However, the boom collapsed abruptly during the Asian financial crisis. Suddenly, the state-owned electricity companies in these countries found themselves in deep financial trouble in honoring the IPP contracts, mostly with the take-or-pay clause under which they have to pay for electricity no longer in need due to the economic downturn. To make things worse, the payment for many of these IPPs was denominated in the US dollar while revenues for the electricity companies were in local currencies, resulting in sky-rocketing financial debts for the electricity companies because of the depreciation of local currencies. For example, the exchange rate for rupiah went down from 2450 to 10000 for a dollar, and the electricity rate would have had to increase by 70 percent to just stay at its pre-crisis level. Electricity companies saw no way out but to pass on the cost increases to consumers, but the rate hikes couldn't have come at a worse time. The rate hikes prompted dramatic public reactions and stirred political turmoil in these countries.

The increased media attention brought about by the public outcry to the rate hikes led to the uncovering of some dark sides of IPP. Corruption and other irregularities were found to be widespread in the IPP contracting process. For example, a recent review of the IPP contracts in the Philippines showed that half of them were subject to irregularities in either financial or management aspects or both (*Philippine Center for Investigative Journalism* 2002). In Indonesia, most of the 27 IPPs have local partners who are either relatives or close friends of the former president Suharto (Henisz and Zelner 2001). Under enormous pressure from both the public and the electricity companies, the governments in Indonesia and the Philippines chose to renegotiate the terms in the power purchase agreements (PPAs) for IPPs, but reneging on these contractual arrangements severely undermined governments' efforts in restoring the confidence of foreign investors. In less than a decade, the initial enthusiasm about IPP has descended into skepticism, distress, and agony.

While the IPP debacle in Southeast Asia has received a lot of attention both in the academic literature and the media, several critical aspects in the initiation and implementation of IPP have not been addressed fully. In particular, few have attempted to analyze the timing and sequence of introducing private power in these countries. This chapter aims at filling the gap. First of all, our analysis challenges a conventional wisdom that introducing private power was an inevitable choice in Southeast Asia given the power shortages in the early 1990s. We argue that, while private power can potentially improve the welfare of the public in the long run, proper regulatory framework is imperative to prevent opportunistic behaviors that could erode the chances of success. Second, we test the notion that the IPP debacle in Southeast Asia was largely due to the unpredictable circumstances brought about by the Asian financial crisis. While the Asian financial crisis was indeed the catalyst for the collapse of the IPPs, the roots of the vulnerability of IPPs were planted deeply in the weaknesses in governance of these countries. Third, while much of the attention has been focused on some short-run impacts of IPPs, such as excess capacity and rate hikes, the nature and magnitude of the long-term impacts have been largely neglected. These long-term effects might be irreversible because of path dependence and lock-in, and the stigma that emerged from the IPP debacle may have negative impacts far beyond the power sector.

The experience in developing countries in the last two decades suggests that the timing and sequence are critical to the success of deregulation and privatization (Roland 1994; Brown 2002; Fink *et al*. 2002). In the context of the privatization in transition economies, Roland (1994) argues that privatization without first establishing effective institutional infrastructures may spoil the emerging private financial sector and prevent a gradual hardening of budget constraints. Brown (2002) attributes the success in infrastructure privatization in Argentina, Chile, New Zealand and Spain to the fact that all these governments had decided and articulated, either before or concurrently with privatization, the policy objectives, market structures, and regulatory systems. Fink *et al.* (2002) test the hypothesis regarding sequence of privatization and the introduction of competition in telecommunication reforms in developing countries, and they find that delays in the introduction of competition may adversely affect performance even after competition is eventually introduced.

While much of the literature focuses on the optimal sequence of reform measures from a normative perspective, this chapter provides a political economy explanation of why governments are tempted to get the wrong sequence of reform measures in the context of the IPP debacle in Indonesia and the Philippines. The study is organized as follows. In the next section, we describe the power shortages in Indonesia and the Philippines and various potential policy options (or different sequences of policy measures) to deal with the problem. In the third section, we focus on the political economy of IPPs in explaining the prominence and fast penetration of the IPP in Indonesia and the Philippines. The fourth section analyzes the impacts of the Asian financial crisis on the IPPs and some unintended consequences of the IPP debacle beyond the power sector, and the fifth section discusses the impacts of the IPP debacle on power sector restructuring. We conclude in the last section with some observations on both the importance and political economy considerations of the timing and sequence of reform policies in developing countries.

POWER CRISIS AND POLICY OPTIONS

Indonesia's economic growth in the early 1990s was quite impressive. Its average real GDP grew at about 7.6 percent per year from 1990 to 1995. The Philippine economy also grew at 2.3 percent per year after nearly a decade of recession. Fast economic growth contributed to the increase in electricity demand by increasing the total amount of economic activities and by shifting towards more electricity-intensive industries (Henisz and Zelner, 2001)

The fast growing demand for electricity put tremendous pressure on an electricity supply industry already in stress. Demand for electricity in Indonesia grew at about 11.8 percent per annum for over a decade prior to 1994/95, and according to PLN's forecast, the electricity demand could increase at 16.7 percent to 17.8 percent annually up to year 2005 (IEA 1997). A power crisis was looming as PLN's total installed capacity fell short of meeting the total demand (*Far East Economic Review* 1990). In comparison, the situation in the Philippines was even worse. Brownouts often ranged from four to ten hours in the country, and in 1992, the excess demand amounted to 48 percent of total system capacity (*Far East Economic Review* 1993). Power shortage decreased industry output, reduced worker productivity, and undermined the governments' efforts to attract foreign direct investment.

Aside from the fast growing demand for electricity, the power shortage in Indonesia and the Philippines in the early 1990s stemmed from several fundamental structural issues in the power sector. First of all, the electricity had been provided by the state-owned electricity companies that were poorly run. Porter and McKinlay (1999) found that many of the outages were not from inadequate capacity, but from breakdowns and poor maintenance, and there were no incentives for improving efficiency in management or maintenance. The system losses were 13.4 percent for PLN and 14 percent for National Power Corporation in the Philippines (NAPOCOR), considerably higher than other electricity companies in the region. Malhotra (1997) commented that, while the installed capacity expanded sharply, the overall technical, institutional, and financial performance of these state-owned utilities had actually deteriorated.

Second, electricity rates had been kept at low level in these countries, particularly in Indonesia, where electricity was subsidized heavily by the government and electricity rates could barely cover the marginal production costs. In the Philippines, where the electricity rates were much higher than in Indonesia, the rates were still set at below the long-run marginal production costs. The low electricity rate dampened the incentives for reducing electricity consumption, and created a bias toward electricity-intensive industries. In addition, there was no mechanism by which to link the rates to increases in inflation, fuel costs, exchange-rate movements or other components of cost structure for supplying electricity, making it impossible for price adjustment according to the imbalance between supply and demand.

Third, the responsibility of providing electricity at reasonable prices was transferred from the governments to the state-owned electricity companies, but adequate resources were not given to these companies to fulfill their mandates. Governments were increasingly reluctant to use public sector funding or borrowing to finance capacity expansion, leaving limited options for the state-owned electricity companies to meet their obligations. In addition, the fact that the electricity price was set at below the long-run marginal costs created perverse incentives for the state-owned electricity companies to finance capacity expansion.

While the looming power crisis and state-owned electricity companies' inability to adequately finance the capacity expansion certainly made a compelling case for the private sector participation in electricity generation, other policy alternatives as well as the timing and sequence of private sector participation should be examined. For example, raising electricity rates to the long-run marginal cost level (including the marginal cost of production and cost of expansion) may not only dampen the demand for electricity but also provide both the means and the incentives for the state-owned electricity to finance the expansion on their own. The removal of electricity price subsidies may increase interests in more efficient and careful use of electricity (Friedman *et al.* 1993).

Other non-pricing demand-side-management (DSM) strategies can also be quite effective in reducing electricity demand. Such strategies might include the use of energy saving and efficient electric appliances, energy conservation awareness campaigns, and load management techniques. For example, a DSM program introduced by the Electricity Generating Authority of Thailand (EGAT) since 1993 reduced peak demand by 182 MW in 1998, and the average cost of savings from the DSM measures was US$ 0.018 per kWh, well below EGAT's long-term cost of US$ 0.043 per kWh to provide a new electricity supply.

Furthermore, even if the participation of private investors is both necessary and appropriate, the importance of the timing and sequence in which private investment is introduced should not be underestimated. Izaguirre (1998) points out that introducing private participation in generation without first – or at least simultaneously – undertaking deeper sectoral reforms is potentially problematic because it would reduce pressures to implement cost-covering retail tariffs. Newbery (2000) argues that the separation of the transmission from generation should precede the private participation in the generation because ownership stakes in generation is likely to favor its own generation over that of other owners. In addition, it is essential to establish a credible and effective regulatory regime to protect investors from the opportunistic behavior of governments (Cook 1999; Commander and Killick 2000).

The wrong sequence in introducing private power may also constrain choices over the forms and nature of private participation. For example, postponing tariff adjustments and delaying separation of transmission from generation reduce the creditworthiness of power purchasers, leading to demands from the private investors for long-term PPAs with a take-or-pay clause and (or) government guarantee (Izaguirre 1998). If the IPPs have confidence in the regulatory framework, they will not feel the need to sign long-term contracts; however, without such a framework, the long-term PPAs become the only viable solution to bring private investment into electricity generation (Newbery 2000; Crow 2001).

The rationale for alternative policy options and different sequence, however, was overwhelmed by a set of political economy considerations that are predominant against the backdrop of the political reality in Indonesia and the Philippines in the early 1990s. Improving the financial conditions of the state-owned electricity companies by raising electricity rates would deem to be a politically unpopular move because the electricity has been considered a strategic political resource for politicians in these two countries. Second, introducing competition by restructuring the sector would encounter several difficulties while there aren't apparent winners in the constituencies. The needs for privatizing and breaking-up the vertically-integrated electricity companies would almost certainly encounter fierce resistance from these companies. Third, the restructuring is highly complex, demanding expertise that was not readily available in these countries. Brown (2002) notices that efforts to establish regulatory and market institutions and the availability of the resources to undertake these efforts is rarely commensurate with the enormity of the work to be done. Last, the restructuring would take relatively long period of time to complete, a luxury the decision-makers in these countries felt they wouldn't have given the urgency of a power crisis. From their perspectives, prolonging power shortage could easily turn to a thorny political issues that might be exploited by the opposition.

POLITICAL ECONOMY OF IPPs

An apparent quick solution they found was in IPP. In 1990, the Philippine government passed the Republic Act 6957 which provided the legal framework for private sector participation in infrastructure development. The Electric Power Crisis Act (Republic Act No. 7648) was promulgated to empower the executive branch to fast track the IPP projects in 1991 when the power crisis became full blown (Woodhouse 2005). Indonesia enacted Presidential Degree 37 in 1992 (Keppres 37/1992), which stipulated that private entities could be involved in power generation, transmission and distribution, opening the door to private power. It is no coincidence that the governments in the two countries not only both chose the IPP model to deal with power shortage, but also both decided to do so with negligible restructuring and regulatory reform (Newbery 2000).

The prominence for IPP in both countries can be interpreted as the result of the convergence of interests among private investors, development agencies and politicians. The private investors, especially utilities from the US and Europe, were looking for investment opportunities because of the excess supply in the industrialized world. Malhotra (1997) argues that deregulation in the developed countries forced utilities to look for investment opportunities in developing countries. In the early 1990s, Southeast Asian countries such as

Indonesia and the Philippines presented great prospects for investments because of the strong growth in electricity demand.

Development agencies embraced such a move wholeheartedly as they considered the IPP a part of the overall efforts towards deregulation and privatization of the sector. It was well argued that introducing IPP in the sector would end the monopoly of the state-owned electricity utilities, imposing pressure on them to increase efficiency level. The ideological arguments also got a boost from some early successes of IPP in other developing countries. The World Bank and other development agencies encouraged the development of IPP by conditioning their lending on the private sector participation in the state-controlled sectors and by directly providing technical assistance.

The politicians also found the IPP model appealing because of its seemingly low political risks. Although the state-owned electricity companies would have to give up the monopoly in power generation under this arrangement, they would be better-off than under other alternatives aimed at more fundamental structural changes in the sector, and they felt they still had the upper hand as they would be the single buyers of electricity from IPPs. The injection of capital from the private sector would at least temporarily defer tough decisions such as price increase. In addition, mega-million dollar IPP contracts certainly would project positive images of key decision-makers internationally while assuring voters of their determination and ability to end power shortages.

Along with the looming power crisis, the convergence of interests among private investors, development agencies and politicians created a unique policy window for the fast rise of IPP in Indonesia and the Philippines at the beginning of the 1990s. The power crisis legitimized the fast-tracking of IPP in the policy agenda, while the private sector backed up with financial resources and the development agencies supplied the intellectual capital. Politicians rendered their support to IPP unconditionally as they perceived it as an opportunity to reap sizable political gains at minimal risk.

In retrospect, however, the enthusiasm about IPP was at least partially fueled by misperception and unrealistic expectation. It was assumed that IPPs could relieve the governments of the budgetary burden for financing power projects, but this is a misperception in the context of Indonesia and the Philippines. Under the take-or-pay clause typically found in PPAs, the state-owned electricity companies have to buy a minimum quantity of electricity under specified prices (most denominated in US dollars) even if the electricity is not needed. These PPAs had in effect committed the governments to billions of dollars worth of potential contractual obligations due to exposure to potential risks originating from economic slowdown or currency depreciation or both (as is the case in the Asian financial crisis). In addition, the claim that introducing private power would drive down electricity rates because of increased competition couldn't be further from the truth. The IPPs are protected from any competition by the long-term PPAs, and at the same time they also pose no threat to other generators because they have no spare capacity to increase their market shares. Intentionally or incidentally, however, these potential risks were not communicated effectively to the public as well as the decision-makers, delaying a much needed public discourse on the true costs of private power.

Some peculiarities in the IPP contracting process further eroded the chance of success for IPP, and they reinforce the notion about the importance of an appropriate regulatory framework. First of all, while the competitive bidding could potentially reduce PPA prices by 25 percent (Albony and Bonsba 1998), most of PPAs in Indonesia and the Philippines were concluded by exclusive bilateral negotiations instead of competitive bidding. Second, many IPP deals were initiated from unsolicited bids which might not reflect the needs and preference of the planning agencies for the power sector. The state-owned electricity companies were often forced to respond to these unsolicited bids in a very short period of time. Third, related to the first two peculiarities, the outcome of negotiations of PPAs were often not made available to the public, effectively shielding them from public scrutiny (Cowell 2004).

The reliance on exclusive bilateral negotiation, acceptance of unsolicited bids, and lack of transparency opened the doors for privileged deals and corruptions (Bosshard 2002). In the Philippines, an investigation of 35 IPPs concluded that many were developed through cronyism (Philippine Center for Investigative Journalism 2002). For example, several projects were linked to relatives or close friends of the then President Fidel Ramos. The most illustrative cases of cronyism in IPPs came from Indonesia, where 26 of the total 27 IPPs were concluded without competitive bidding. Not surprisingly, the majority of these IPPs were connected to Suharto's relatives or close associates. The electricity rate concluded in these IPPs ranged from 5.75 to 8 cents per kWh, significantly higher than the long run average costs at the generation plants owned by PLN. Despite their monopoly status, the state-owned electricity companies had little power in negotiation, as bluntly put by Djiteng Marsudi, the former director of PLN, 'the power companies dictated terms to us because they had Indonesia's first family behind them. Resisting them was like suicide.'

The political patronage and cronyism not only explain why the IPPs were overly expensive, but also account for why the expansion was excessive. The development in IPP took on a life of its own as politically connected groups teamed with the private investors to loot the governments through lucrative IPP deals and no one wanted to be left out. The expansion of private power quickly surpassed what was needed to balance supply and demand. In

Indonesia, the PLN was forced to sign contracts with more IPPs with instructions directly from the then President Suharto, despite clearly and repeatedly communi-cating to the government that the electricity from these proposed IPPs would not be needed[1]. In the Philippines, an additional 12 IPPs were signed after warnings from within the government and World Bank that an impending oversupply of electricity could push up prices (Philippine Center for Investigative Journalism 2002).

By 1997, when the region was hit by the Asian financial crisis, 27 IPP contracts in Indonesia had already been signed between the state-owned electricity company PLN and private investors. In the Philippines, the agreements for 37 IPPs, representing 40 percent of the generation capacity of the country, had been reached. It is almost certain that more IPP contracts would have been signed without the Asian financial crisis.

ASIAN FINANCIAL CRISIS, RENEGOTIATION AND SPILLOVER EFFECTS

The IPP frenzy in Indonesia and the Philippines was ground to a halt by the Asian financial crisis in mid-1997. The crisis had several impacts on the IPPs. First of all, the contraction of these economies led to reduced power demand and much of the planned capacity expansion was no longer required in the short-run. Second, under the take-or-pay clause the state-owned electricity companies had to pay for electricity produced by IPPs that was not needed. Third, because the payment for most IPPs was denominated in US dollars, the depreciation of the local currencies during the financial crisis led to a dramatic increase of state-owned electricity companies' financial obligations to IPPs. Over the first six months in 1998, PLN's net loss accumulated to US $1.4 billion.

Contrary to the miscalculation by the politicians that the IPP model carries minimum political risks, the busted IPPs soon turned into political crises in these countries. Unable to meet their financial obligations to the IPPs, the state-owned electricity companies were left with no option but to raise electricity rates at the worst possible time, because the consumers were hit hard on multiple fronts during the financial crisis. PLN raised the electricity tariff by 30 percent in 1998, and power bills in the Philippines doubled to become the second highest in Asia (Cowell 2004). The rate hikes caused dramatic public reactions and stirred social unrest in both countries. By this time, some irregularities in the IPP contracting process were also coming to light, further intensifying the public resentment.

Civil society groups wasted no time calling for the cancellation of the IPP contracts and renegotiation of the terms for the IPPs that were in operation, given the irregularities in the contracting process for many of these IPPs. The Indonesian government responded quickly either to postpone or put on hold many IPPs, and PLN announced its intention to renegotiate all IPP contracts. In February 1998, PLN issued letters to three IPPs, unilaterally setting an exchange rate of 2450 rupiah per dollar for its payment when the rupiah was trading at about 8450. The new government insisted that the project be renegotiated or canceled because of alleged corruption in the contracting process for many of these IPPs. The investors were shocked by the government's decision but were left with no choice but to renegotiate with the government. By March 2003, PLN had reached agreement for 14 IPPs and renegotiated tariffs were mostly in the range of US$ 0.042–0.0493, significantly lower than the US$ 0.0575–0.08 demanded in the original contracts.

The Philippine government's initial response to the crisis was more restrained although the damages of the crisis to NAPOCOR were just as severe as to PLN. By 1999, the losses to NAPOCOR to honor minimum off-take agreements specified in the IPP contacts had grown roughly US $10 million per week. The government went to great lengths trying to honor its contractual agreements to various IPPs, including shutting down the operation of NAPOCOR owned generation facilities that can produce electricity at much lower cost than the IPPs. Under pressure from the public and the Congress, however, the government took a somewhat harder line after 2000, announcing that it would allow IPPs to expand their existing facilities and guarantee their participation in a planned power pool only if they agreed to renegotiate existing PPAs. NAPOCOR tried to reduce the take-or-pay ratio from 70–75 percent of capacity to 55 percent.

Although renegotiation of private funded infrastructure projects are not uncommon in developing countries, such efforts may incur significant costs. In the case of Indonesia and the Philippines, the renegotiation of the IPPs had some unintended consequences that spilled over beyond the power sector. First of all, the renegotiation of IPPs severely undermined the governments' efforts to boost foreign direct investments at the time when such investments were desperately needed. Foreign investors grew increasingly skeptical about these governments' commitment to protect the investors' interests, and it is no coincidence that both Indonesia and the Philippines experienced the slowest recovery from the Asian financial crisis among the Southeast Asian countries. In addition, the overall costs of the financing infrastructure projects became much higher because of investors' concerns over the opportunistic behavior by the government. Both Indonesia and the Philippines have the need for massive capital outlay for infrastructure projects, but investors demand hefty rates of return to compensate for the potential risks of renegotiation as seen in the broken IPP deals. At last, renegotiation has slowed down the development of market for an alterative financing mechanism. The project bond market, for example, had been gaining currency prior to the Asian financial crisis, and many new projects were seeking access to this credit market as a means of achieving financing. However, the renegotiation of IPPs prompted credit risk rating agencies to lower the grades of new issues, effectively turning off the bond market as a means to access US and European investors.

The IPP debacle also had other spillover effects beyond the financial aspects. The irregularities found in the IPP contracting process have fed into the public sentiment against deregulation and privatization in other sectors such as health care and telecommunication. The civil society groups opposed to market-oriented reforms have successfully channeled the public outcry caused by electricity rate hikes to market-oriented reforms in general. For example, they depicted corruption as an unavoidable consequence of privatization. Proponents for market-oriented reforms face bigger hurdles to mobilize support after the IPP debacle.

POWER SECTOR RESTRUCTURING AND IPPs

Although the exact form of power sector restructuring differs from one country to another, it typically involves four components:

1. the breaking-up of the state-owned electricity monopoly into several independent entities such as transmission, generation and distribution;
2. privatization of the state-owned assets;
3. establishment of competitive power markets through market pools or retail competition;
4. creation of an independent regulator (Newbery 2000).

Because of its potential impacts on employment and financial management, the power sector restructuring has often encountered heavy resistance from the state-owned electricity companies, especially the labor unions.

The Asian financial crisis, however, placed the state-owned electricity companies in Indonesia and the Philippines in a weakened position in resisting power sector restructuring. The excess supply induced by the crisis created a more favorable condition for market-oriented reform initiatives because it is more likely to have meaningful competition among the generators when there is excess power. Development agencies have also played a critical role in pushing the reform agenda, and the conditioning of the financial packages on the restructuring of various sectors including the power sector gave a big boost for power sector restructuring. Some development agencies have provided technical assistance through power sector restructuring loans to these countries. The initial progress led to a sense of optimism about the future of power sector reform. According to the Electric Power Industry Act enacted in the Philippines in 2001 and Indonesia's Electricity Law promulgated in 2002, a competitive electricity market would be established by 2004 in the Philippines and 2007 by Indonesia.

However, a close examination of the progress in power sector restructuring in Indonesia and the Philippines up to date indicates that the IPP debacle has created several obstacles to the restructuring. First of all, it is difficult to integrate the IPPs into a competitive market framework. The existing IPPs are incompatible with the establishment of the competitive markets because IPPs don't have the incentive to participate in the markets as they are protected by the PPAs, and this effect is especially pronounced in countries like Indonesia and the Philippines where the IPP plants account for a significant portion of the overall installed capacity. Second, ironically as it may sound, the short-run excess capacity resulting from the IPP contracts actually bought some time for the state-owned electricity companies because the urgency under power shortage are removed. The rate hikes necessary to cover the high costs of IPPs also considerably strengthened the financial position of the state-owned electricity companies and they became increasingly assertive after recovering from the initial shock of the crisis. Third, the privatization of the state-assets becomes more difficult in the aftermath of the IPP debacle because the long-term PPAs with IPPs makes the state-owned electricity companies less attractive for private investors who are contemplating acquiring stakes in these companies. Fourth, the forced renegotiation renewed private investors' concerns over the political risk in investing in the power sector in these countries, and they will seek more assurance from governments and charge a higher premium for capital if they are to return to the power sector in these countries. Last, the failures in IPPs spoil the willingness of the public to make sacrifices to genuine power sector reform (Cowell 2004), and the opponents of power sector reform can exploit the resentment created throughout the IPP debacle to their advantages.

The stagnation of the power sector reform in recent years confirms these points. Eight years after the crisis, not only is there no sign of the wholesale electricity pool as planned, the electricity sector reform in Indonesia was effectively terminated in December 2004, when the constitutional court of the country ruled that the Electricity Law is unconstitutional. The opponents of the reforms have won a crucial battle and the IPP debacle has certainly contributed its fair share to their success. In the Philippines, although a regulatory framework is already in place, the restructuring process has experienced significant delay as the government has encountered immense difficulties in attempting to privatize state-owned assets because of lack of interest from private investors. The IPP debacle significantly diminishes the chances of success in power sector restructuring, and policy options have been severely constrained compared to the situation a decade ago.

CONCLUDING REMARKS

More than a decade after private power was introduced in Indonesia and the Philippines to solve power shortage problems, the governments of these countries find themselves facing the same situation as it was a decade ago. The economies of these countries have performed well in recent years, and demand for electricity has grown steadily. Excess capacity, a short-run consequence from the IPP debacle, will soon be forgotten, and power shortages are once again on the horizon. The IPP has been making a quick return to reclaim their prominence in the power sector, but the governments so far have been unable to take advantage of the favorable opportunity created by the Asian financial crisis to make significant progress towards power sector restructuring. The IPP deals signed in the 1990s created formidable obstacles to establish a competitive market, and private investors became more skeptical about governments' commitment to protect the interests of investors after the forced negotiation of IPP contracts. More importantly, the public support for genuine power sector reform has also eroded as they continue to suffer from ill-planned and corruption-ridden IPP deals.

What was considered as a quick fix to the power shortage problems in the early 1990s has had several unintended consequences. The fact that the decision-makers had chosen to introduce private power without first creating an appropriate regulatory environment has locked the power sector into a path in which contractual power becomes the predominant model for future expansion despite its many shortcomings. The IPP debacle as experienced in the two Southeast Asian countries also has impacts beyond the power sector. It has contributed to the difficulties in attracting foreign investment, confined these countries to a more expansive financing mechanism, and fed into the public sentiment against market-oriented reforms in various sectors. Policy-makers should pay close attention to these unintended consequences when deciding on the right timing and sequence for future reform initiatives.

The IPP debacle also implies that potential economic gains promised by market-oriented reforms such as IPP could quickly become an illusion in an environment where political patronage and corruption are pervasive. Proponents of reform should be mindful about the possibility that their good intentions could be exploited by a coalition between politically connected interests and private capital to legitimize rent-seeking schemes. On the other hand, however, civil society groups should exercise greater care differentiating this possibility from genuine reform efforts that can eventually improve the welfare of the public. The growing power of these groups can be captured and misused by special interest groups to protect their existing gains at the expense of the public interest.

NOTE

1. Interview with a World Bank official in Jakarta, June 2003.

REFERENCES

Albony, Yves and Reda Bonsba (1998) 'The impact of IPPs in developing countries – out of the crisis and into the future', *Public Policy for the Private Sector*, Note No. 162, The World Bank.

Bacon, Robert and John Besant-Jones (2001) 'Global Electric Power Reform: Privatization and Liberalization of the Electric Power Industry in Developing Countries', *Annual Review of Energy and Environment*, **26**, 331–59.

Bosshard, Peter (2002) 'Private Gain – Public Risk? The International Experience with Power Purchase Agreements of Private Power Projects', *International Rivers Network*, 20 November.

Brown, Ashley C. (2002) 'Confusing Means and Ends: Framework Of Restructuring, Not Privatization, Matters Most', *International Journal of Regulation and Governance*, **1** (2), 115–28.

Commander, S. and T. Killick (2000) 'Privatisation in Developing Countries: A Survey of the Issues', in P. Cook and C. Kirkpatrick (eds), *International Library of Comparative Public Policy*, **13** (1), 120–53.

Cook, P. (1999) 'Privatization and Utility Regulation in Developing Countries: the Lessons So Far', *Annals of Public and Cooperative Economics*, **70** (4), 549–87.

Cowell, Ophelia (2004) 'All Hands on Deck: Why Power Sector Reform Is Everybody's Business', Paper presented at the workshop: Electricity Sector Reforms in Asia, Experiences and Strategies, Mumbai, India, 19 January. (www.tni,org, accessed 7 January 2006).

Crow, Robert Thomas (2001) Foreign Direct Investment in New Electricity Generating Capacity In Developing Asia: Stakeholders, Risks, and The Search For A New Paradigm', http://iis-db.stanford.edu/pubs/11908/Crow.pdf (accessed 7 January 2006).

Dubash, Navroz K. (2002) *Power Politics, Equity and Environment in Electricity Reform*, Washington, DC: World Resources Institute.

Far Eastern Economic Review (1990) 'Power Struggle: Indonesia's Electricity Monopoly Is Strained By Demand', 8 November.

Fink, Carsten, Aaditya Mattoo and Randeep Rathindran (2002) 'An Assessment of Telecommunications Reform in Developing Countries', Policy Research Working Paper 2909, Washington, DC: World Bank.

Friedman, Rafael, Steve Meyers, Nina Goldman and Nathan Martin (1993) 'Prospects For The Power Sector In Nine Developing Countries', *Energy Policy*, **21**, 1123–31.

Haggard, Stephan and Gregory W. Noble (2001) 'Power politics, elections and electricity regulation in Taiwan', in Stephan Haggard and Mathew D. McCubbins (eds), *Presidents, Parliaments, and Policy*, Cambridge: Cambridge University Press, pp. 356–90.

Henisz, Witold J. and Bennet A. Zelner (2001) 'The Political Economy of Private Electricity Provision in Southeast Asia', *East Asian Economic Perspectives*, 15 (1), 10–36.

International Energy Agency (IEA) (1997) *Asia Electricity Study*, 165–202.

Izaguirre, Ada Karina (1998) 'Private Participation in the Electricity Sector – Recent Trends', *Viewpoint Note* No. 154, Washington, DC: World Bank.

Izaguirre, Ada Karina (2000) 'Private Participation in Energy', *Viewpoint Note* No. 208, Private Participation In Infrastructure Group, Washington, DC: World Bank.

Malhotra, Anilk (1997) 'Private Participation in Infrastructure: Lessons from Asia's Power Sector', *Finance & Development*, December 1997.

Newbery, David (1995) 'A Template For Power Reform', *Viewpoint Note* No. 54, Washington, DC: World Bank.

Newbery, David (2000) 'Issues and Options For Restructuring Electricity Supply Industries', Cambridge Working Papers in Economics No. 0210.

Philippine Center for Investigative Journalism (2002) 'Trail of Power Leads to Ramos', http://www.pcij.org (accessed 7 January 2006).

Porter, Michael and Calum McKinlay (1999) 'Private Sector Participation and Infrastructure Investment in Asia: The Impact Of The Currency Crisis', consulting report (http://www.tasman.com.au/pdf%20files/CurrencyCrisisand%20Infrastructure_APEC%20Finance.pdf (accessed 7 January 2006).

Roland, Gerard (1994) 'On the Speed and Sequencing of Privatisation and Restructuring', *The Economic Journal*, 104, 1158–68.

Woodhouse, Erik J. (2005) 'The IPP experience in the Philippines', Working Paper no. 37, The Program on Energy and Sustainable Development, Stanford University.

7. Power sector deregulation and the environment: evidence from the Philippines and Thailand

Jessie L. Todoc

Power generation, which accounts for the bulk of the investments in electricity supply that include investments in transmission and distribution networks and customer services, has a number of environmental impacts as shown in Table 7.1. However, emissions from fuel combustion that contribute to local air pollution and global climate change are the most important environmental 'footprint' of the power sector (Dubash 2003).

By one estimate, for example, the electricity sector in East Asia and Pacific account on average for 31 percent of CO_2 emissions and 12 percent of NO_x emissions, which is just a notch below the estimated world average of 32 percent and 13 percent, respectively (Dubash 2003). The choice of fuel and technology is the most fundamental decision affecting power sector emissions (Hagler Bailly 1998).

Similarly, the most important environmental impact of power sector deregulation proceeds directly from the ensuing fuel and technology mix for power generation. 'The market structure put in place by reforms can affect (fuel and) technology choice by changing the relative attractiveness of capital-cost intensive technologies versus those based on high running costs' (Dubash 2002). The resulting fuel and technology mix explains the short-term environmental performance of the power sector after deregulation. Over the long-term, the environmental impacts of deregulation will be determined by, among others, its implications on policies and applications of renewable energy and energy efficiency. 'To mitigate the (global climate change) problem, long-term environmental management within the electricity supply industry involves a continued shift from fossil fuels to fuels causing less environmental damage and risk as well as increased efficiency in production and use of electricity' (Eikeland 1998).

This chapter will address these issues – short-term environmental performance of the power sector after deregulation and its long-term implications on renewable energy and energy efficiency – focusing on the

Table 7.1   The contribution of electricity generation to key environmental problems in Southeast Asia

Key environmental problem	Contribution of electricity generation
Ambient air quality in urban/metropolitan areas	Combustion of fossil fuels is a major source of NO_x, SO_2, and particulate emissions and adds a significant share to air pollution in metropolitan areas
Water pollution	Effluent from coal-fired plants, toxic fluids from geothermal plants, acid drainage from coal mines and ash disposal sites
Solid waste	Coal bottom and fly ashes, gypsum from desulphurization
Acid deposition	SO_2 and NO_x emissions from fossil fuel combustion (most relevant)
Land use and siting	Deforestation from large hydro development, degradation from coal mining
Global climate change	CO_2 emissions from fossil fuel combustion (major contributor), gas leakage during natural gas transport and handling

Source: IEA (1997).

experience of the Philippines and Thailand, which have been at the forefront of electricity deregulation in Asia.[1]

OVERVIEW OF POWER SECTOR DEREGULATION IN ASIA

The traditional structure of the electricity sector comprises four functions: generation, transmission, distribution and supply. Until recently in many countries, these functions had been under vertically integrated state-owned electric utilities because of economies of scale and huge investment requirements, which could be justified only by a natural monopoly, and the view that electricity is a public good and an instrument of social equity. However, changes in economic and political thinking and technological advancements in electric power generation in the 1980s have caused radical changes in the electricity sector functional and ownership structures. The shift in economic and political ideology from policy (dominant role for government) to market (greater role for private enterprises) has been driven by failure of state-owned enterprises (SOEs) in particular and centrally-planned economies in general to deliver expected economic benefits. On the other hand, the development of smaller scale generation and environment-friendly technologies, coupled with increasing supply and popularity of natural gas as a clean fuel, have removed the natural monopoly status of generation. Moreover in Asia, particularly East Asia, the economic miracle in the late 1980s and early 1990s had put additional pressure on energy demand and led government to seek a greater role for the private sector by encouraging private investments to supply energy. All these factors fuelled the spread of independent power producers (IPPs) and opened the generation sector to competition.[2]

Then came the Asian financial and currency crisis in 1997 that exposed some weaknesses of the IPP model and renewed the urgency to introduce more competitive arrangements in the electricity sector (restructuring) and pursue full privatization. The general trend is to completely separate generation from transmission and distribution and introduce competition at the wholesale and retail level, separating the operation of the physical network from the supply of electricity. These structural changes, or restructuring, in the electricity sector are usually accompanied by a change in ownership from government to private, or privatization.[3]

There are four models or stages in the transition from monopoly to competition in the electricity sector (Hunt and Shuttleworth 1996; Tenenbaum *et al.* 1992):

1. *Monopoly – Monopoly at all levels* Generation is not subject to competition and no one has any choice of supplier; a single monopoly company handles generation, transmission and distribution to final consumers, or distribution is separate from generation and transmission.
2. *Purchasing agency – Competition in generation-single buyer* This allows a single buyer, the purchasing agency, to choose from a number of different generators, in some cases including its own, to encourage competition in generation. Independent generators may be created from existing utilities by divestiture, or from new producers who build new plants (independent power producers or IPPs). The purchasing agency retains the monopoly over transmission networks and electricity sale to distribution companies and large industrial and commercial consumers.
3. *Wholesale competition – Competition in generation and choice for distribution companies (discos)* This allows discos to buy directly from an independent producer and deliver over a transmission network. Discos still have a monopoly over final consumers.
4. *Retail competition – Competition in generation and choice for final consumers* This allows customers to choose their supplier. Operation of

the distribution network is separated from retail supply, and the latter is competitive.

Restructuring and privatization need not go together, but there is always a practical logic linking the two decisions (Hunt and Shuttleworth 1996).[4] Restructuring 'is about commercial arrangements for selling energy: separating or "unbundling" integrated industry structures and introducing competition and choice'.[5] Privatization can be defined in broad terms, but strictly speaking is 'a change from government to private ownership, and is the end-point of a continuum of changes in ownership/management'.[6] Privatization is preceded by commercialization and corporatization of the utilities to prepare them towards full privatization.

The main motivation for privatization is to reduce the strain on government budget, including removing losing firms from the budget (Boorsma 1994). Privatization eliminates the need of permanent subsidies to state-owned enterprises. On the other hand, privatization allows government to raise funds in the short term.

> The use of the proceeds from privatization determines to a large extent the impact of privatization on public sector's cash flows. If the revenue from the sales is used to reduce public debt, as has been the case in most countries, we would observe lower interest payments and consequently a stronger cash-flow position of the public sector. The common policy advice has been to use the proceeds for once-and-for-all disbursements, especially if those eliminate future negative cash flows, in lieu of using them for permanent expenditure. The effect of privatization on public sector borrowing requirements should be reflected in lower interest rates, which foster investment, growth, and lower inflation. (Sheshinski and Lopez-Calva 1999)

Most Asian countries have introduced some degree of competition in generation by allowing IPPs to sell to established government utilities, most of which have attained the status of state-owned corporations. Many of these countries are in transition to privatizing their electric utilities and introducing competition in wholesale and retail electricity supply. These include the Philippines and Thailand.[7]

Philippines

The Philippine power sector had a fragmented structure at the time of the reform. Generation and transmission were controlled by the state-owned National Power Corporation (NPC). Distribution and supply to end-users were managed by the Manila Electric Company (Meralco) for the service in Metro Manila and a few neighboring provinces in Luzon, by some 19 private investor-owned distribution utilities in major cities all over the Philippines, and by 116 electric cooperatives in the rest of the country. NPC serves directly few big industrial customers and government offices particularly in Mindanao. Some of the private distribution utilities, including Meralco, and electric cooperatives own small generating facilities, most of them diesel generators particularly in remote islands not connected to the main transmission networks of NPC.

Power sector reform started in 1987 with the promulgation of Executive Order 215, allowing private investors to construct and operate power plants intending to sell their output into the grid and consistent with the development plans of NPC, plants generating electricity for internal use or for sale to NPC, power plants outside the NPC grids desiring to sell directly to end-users, and cogeneration units. The presidential decree was in response to the power shortages in 1986 caused by the mothballing of the politically controversial 625-MW nuclear power plant (which had been scheduled for commissioning in 1985), reduced availability of hydropower plants due to droughts, and the inability of NPC to meet power demand from its aging thermal plants. The high indebtedness of NPC was the other reason for opening up generation to the private sector, partly relieving the pressure on government budget. Although EO 215 ended the monopoly status of NPC in the generation sector, the cancellation of the nuclear power plant created a big gap in the electricity supply-demand balance, precipitating the 8–12 hour power blackouts in 1989–1992. To arrest the power crisis, the government fast-tracked contracts with independent power producers, resulting in the entry of several oil-fired gas turbines that has an installation period of less than one year. A total of 33 IPP projects (excluding private rehabilitation and operation and maintenance projects) with a combined capacity of 5.2 GW were commissioned between 1991 and 1998. In 1999, IPPs accounted for almost 50 percent of total installed generating capacity.

The high indebtedness of NPC, its perceived technical and economic inefficiencies, the high electricity tariffs, and the privatization and restructuring trends elsewhere (notably in Latin America and the UK) continued the pressure in the electricity industry to further institute reforms and in particular privatize NPC. Since 1994 and for more than seven years a law had been pending in the Philippine Congress to privatize NPC and restructure the industry. Finally in June 2001, the Electric Power Industry Reform Act (EPIRA) was approved by the Philippine Congress. The law has set the stage for the break-up and privatization of NPC, establishment of a separate transmission company and its eventual privatization, the divestment of NPC's generation assets, and the creation of a wholesale electricity spot market.

Although EO 215 had allowed the private sector to generate electricity, some of its provisions were called 'lumps in the throat' of prospective developers, particularly of renewable energy projects (Elauria *et al.* 2002). These included the five-year track record of project proponents, 95 percent biomass and 5 percent fossil fuel to start-up hybrid systems, 65 percent thermal efficiency, and availability of spinning reserves at all times. The Philippine Department of Energy, re-established in 1992 as part of the reforms in the energy industry, amended the rules and regulations governing the implementation of EO 215 with respect to renewable energy projects:

- Companies are no longer required to show a five-year track record to receive accreditation for renewable energy generation facilities, provided the technology is commercially available and locally adaptable or the project is for self-generation.
- The thermal efficiency requirement is removed for cogeneration facilities using renewable energy.
- Renewable energy projects are exempted from the 10-year power purchase agreement and are only required to demonstrate potential for foreign exchange savings.

Thailand

Like in the Philippines, generation and transmission are separated from distribution in Thailand's power sector. Unlike the Philippines, however, these functions are controlled by only three entities that are all government-owned. Generation and transmission are the responsibility of the Electricity Generating Authority of Thailand (EGAT), and distribution of the Metropolitan Electricity Authority (MEA) and Provincial Electricity Authority (PEA). MEA distributes electricity in Metropolitan Bangkok and three neighboring provinces, while PEA distributes in the rest of the country.

Power sector reform in Thailand started with the amendment of the EGAT Act[8] in March 1992. EGAT, through this amendment, has been allowed 'to undertake businesses concerning electric energy and other businesses concerning or in continuity with its activities, or to collaborate with other persons for the said activities'. More specifically, EGAT could now (a) establish a limited company or a public limited company for undertaking businesses concerning electric energy and (b) collaborate any activities with other entities, whether internal or external, private or state-owned, including international organizations, or hold shares in any limited or public limited company consistent and in pursuit of EGAT objectives. Then the proposal 'concerning the direction of the future operation of the Electricity Generating Authority of Thailand' was submitted by the National Energy Policy Council (NEPC) and was approved by the Cabinet in September 1992. The proposal, also called the Four-Step Plan, while emphasizing the privatization of EGAT and sale of its generation assets to the private sector, also included privatization proposal for PEA and MEA and allowed private entities (independent power producers or IPPs) to build, own, and operate new power plants.

The IPP guidelines were approved by the Cabinet in May 1994. The guidelines also outlined the terms and conditions for the first IPP solicitation[9] in December 1994. It specified the characteristics of the proposed projects, including type of plant, types of fuel, reference price, and length of the contract with EGAT. It also required prospective IPPs to prepare an environmental impact assessment and secure construction and operation permits and fuel supply contracts. The results of the first solicitation reflected the preference for natural gas over coal. At the closing of bid submission on 30 June 1995, 32 bidders submitted 50 proposals totalling 39 067 MW, more than ten times the original offered capacity. Sixty-two percent (62%), or 24 225 MW of these proposed projects would be fired by natural gas, 35 percent (13 489 MW) would run on coal, and the remaining 1353 MW would use the newly developed orimulsion fuel. Since then, the government has contracted seven IPP projects with a total capacity of close to 6000 MW. Four of these seven IPPs would use natural gas, and two of the remaining three, which originally planned to use coal, has relocated and converted to natural gas, yielding to strong public opposition against their coal power plants.[10] As of 2003, all original four gas-fired power plants had been commissioned.

In April 1997, a new cabinet resolution was issued to boost privatization efforts. First, the new resolution classified the state-owned enterprises (SOEs) due for privatization into two groups, depending on how much of the shareholdings would be kept by the government. EGAT has been placed under the second group, in which the government would keep more than 50 percent of the shareholdings. Second, the resolution also appointed a committee that will oversee the privatization. Lastly, the resolution asked the ministries governing the SOEs to be privatized to prepare action plans on privatization. In this regard, EGAT's plan to create subsidiary companies that will operate its power plants has been confirmed. In addition, the role of private power producers will be promoted through BOO/BOOT schemes.

In 1998, in the aftermath of the financial crisis, the then National Energy Policy Office released a policy statement on privatisation. Subsequently, the Thai government endorsed the Privatization Master Plan. NEPO's Master Plan envisioned that the ESI in Thailand would be gradually opened to wholesale and retail competition in three stages stretching from 1998 through 2003. A reform plan was also developed by a consortium of international consultants for the government in 1999–2000. The blueprint proposed unbundling of the power sector and establishment of a power pool for spot trading. The Energy Act, which focused on the pool model, was approved by the Cabinet in October 2000. 'By spring 2003, however, the Energy Act had not been presented to the Parliament. The Pool Model had been rejected, and the reform blueprints under active consideration did not involve the Pool Model.'[11]

The policy on the restructuring and privatization of the electricity supply industry in Thailand had been ongoing, when serious problems of implementation elsewhere led to power shortages and outages, most notably the California power crisis. Thus, the Thai government has decided to cancel the proposal for a competitive wholesale electricity market or power pool on the pretext that the proposed model was inappropriate for Thailand.

SHORT-TERM ENVIRONMENTAL PERFORMANCE: IMPLICATIONS OF FUEL CHOICE

The state of environmental performance of the Philippines and Thailand during the period of deregulation is assessed using the following indicators:

- CO_2 emissions per kWh from electricity and heat generation; and
- total CO_2 emissions from fossil fuel combustion.

CO_2 Emissions per kWh from Electricity and Heat Generation

During the period of the reform, Thailand had had the higher CO_2 emissions per kWh from electricity and heat generation. In 2001, for example, Thailand emitted 562 gCO_2/kWh compared to the Philippines' 508 gCO_2/kWh. However, the Philippines unit CO_2 emissions in the electricity and heat sector grew by close to 17 percent between 1990 and 2001, while that of Thailand decreased by more than 10 percent (Figure 7.1).

Total CO_2 Emissions from Fossil Fuel Combustion

Similarly, total CO_2 emissions from fossil fuel combustion in Thailand far exceeds that of the Philippines and the gap even grew larger during the period of the reform. However, a closer inspection shows a big drop in the growth of total CO_2 emissions in Thailand, from 14.1 percent per year in 1985–1990 prior to the reform period to 6.5 percent during the reform period. In the Philippines, on the other hand, the growth in total CO_2 emissions was steady at around 6.0 percent per year before and during the reform period (Figure 7.2).

The driving forces for this short-term environmental performance are as follows:

- growth of fossil fuel electricity production;

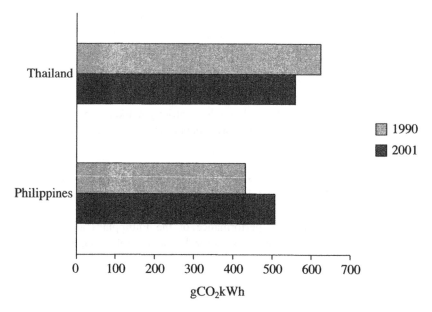

Figure 7.1   Unit CO_2 emissions

- increasing share of fossil fuels;
- decreasing share of hydropower; and
- competition between coal and gas.

Growth of Fossil Fuel Electricity Production

The big drop in the growth of CO_2 emissions in Thailand during the reform period can be immediately explained by the big drop in the growth of electricity production from fossil fuels during this period, from 15 percent per year in 1985–1990 to 8 percent per year in 1990–2001. On the other hand, the negligible decrease in the growth of CO_2 emissions in the Philippines before and during the reform is largely due to the big increase in fossil fuels electricity production, from just 2 percent per year to nearly 7 percent per year in the same periods (Figure 7.3).

Increasing Share of Fossil Fuels and Decreasing Share of Hydropower

Notwithstanding the slowdown in the increase of fossil fuel electricity production in Thailand during the reform period, the large and in fact increasing share of fossil fuels in the generation mix in the two countries partly explain the continuous growth in CO_2 emissions. In Thailand, the share of

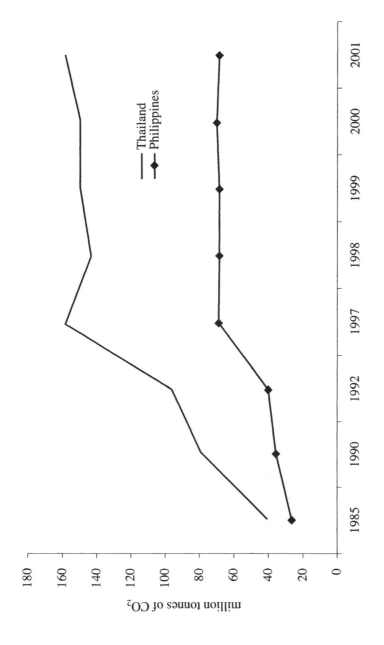

Figure 7.2   Total CO₂ emissions from fuel combustion

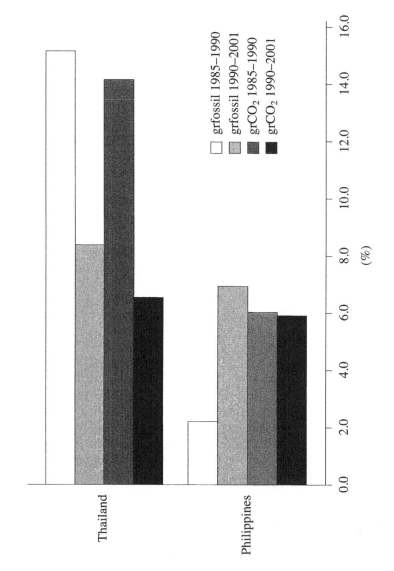

Figure 7.3   Growth of fossil fuel electricity production vs CO$_2$ emissions

fossil fuels peaked to 95 percent in 1999 from 84 percent in 1985, before settling to 92 percent in 2001. Similarly in the Philippines, electricity generation from fossil fuels peaked to 63 percent in 1995 from 54 percent in 1985 before settling to 62 percent in 2001.

The decreasing share of hydropower in the generation mix of both countries contributed further to the continuing increase in CO_2 emissions from electricity generation. In the Philippines, the share of hydropower dropped from 24 percent to 15 percent between 1985 and 2001. Similarly in Thailand, the share of hydropower fell from 16 percent to 6 percent during the same period.

Competition Between Coal and Gas

A closer examination of the structure of the fossil fuel mix in the two countries would reveal more information to explain the above-mentioned trends in CO_2 emissions, in particular the remarkable slowing down of its growth in Thailand and the almost steady growth in the Philippines. The shares of oil were decreasing in both countries, but Thailand recorded the bigger decrease, from almost 15 percent in 1985 to just barely 3 percent in 2001, compared to the Philippines' 39 percent and 21 percent, respectively. The most important factor for the slowing down of the growth in CO_2 emissions in Thailand during the reform period was the large increase in the share of natural gas, from 46 percent in 1985 to more than 70 percent in 2001. In the Philippines, the share of natural gas in the generation mix remained negligible until 2001.[12] In Thailand, the decline in the share of coal, from 23 percent to 19 percent during the same period, contributed further to the decrease in the growth of CO_2 emissions. In stark contrast, the increase in the share of coal in the Philippines, from less than 15 percent to more than 40 percent, contributed to the steady growth in CO_2 emissions.

To sum up, Thailand further increased its share of natural gas during the reform period, and the Philippines shifted to using more coal, while both countries decreased the share of oil in their generation mix (Figure 7.4).

Indeed, in parallel with deregulation of the electricity sector, the 1990s saw unprecedented increase in the use of natural gas for power generation, making it the preferred fuel, or fuel of choice. Natural gas, for one, emits 40 percent and 20 percent less CO_2 and 60 percent and 30 percent less NO_x than coal and oil, respectively. Its SO_x emission is practically zero. The choice of fuel dictates the choice of technology. Gas-fired power plants are often the particularly attractive option for IPPs because of:[13]

1. their relatively low capital construction cost;
2. the use of a well-established technology;

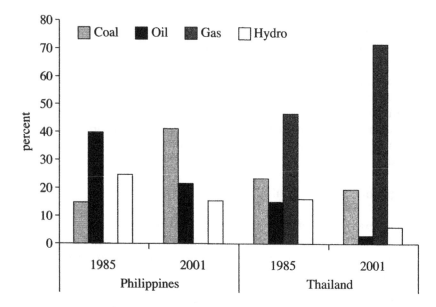

Figure 7.4   Changing fuel mix for power generation

3. their shorter construction lead times; and
4. their relatively high fuel conversion efficiency.

Privatization and deregulation of energy markets worldwide are compelling utilities and independent power producers to be more competitive. In this type of environment, there is a strong preference for equipment that has high conversion efficiency and that can be installed in months rather than in years. Gas turbine technologies feature both.

   Gas-fired technologies are also the least cost option because:[14]

*   Gas-fired power plants increase their competitiveness when using high discount rates; the levelized generation cost of gas-fired power plants is not very sensitive to load factor variation; and for gas-fired power plants, capital costs represent only a small part of total levelized costs and, therefore, increasing the economic lifetime has little influence on levelized generation costs.
*   Coal, however, remains attractive because of its abundant supply and stable and lower prices in the international market. Moreover, the availability of and continuing progress in clean coal technologies are reducing the environmental emissions from coal burning. Choosing gas-fired generation technologies is also very sensitive to natural gas price

assumptions as fuel accounts for more than 60 percent of total gas generation costs. Clean coal technologies become attractive at higher levels of natural gas prices.

- Thus, steam turbines remain popular in Asia. An old survey showed that steam turbines had accounted for 50 percent of total capacity orders in Asia from January 1994 to May 1996 (Burr 1996). Another survey, this time of independent power projects that reached financial closing in 1997 (Burr 1998), also showed that coal-fired technologies had dominated the Asian as well as the Pacific power markets for new generation capacity.

Ultimately, the choice of fuel and technology by IPPs has been driven by:[15]

- the availability of fuel;
- relative fuel prices;
- attractiveness of the corresponding generation technology, in terms of:
  - cost,
  - efficiency,
  - construction/installation lead times;
- environment compliance;
- environment considerations; and
- costs of generation.

Long-term Environmental Impacts: Implications on Renewables and Energy Efficiency

The long-term environmental impacts of power sector deregulation rest on its implications on renewables and energy efficiency.

Implications of deregulation on renewables

New and renewable energy sources have become attractive national energy options because of their environmental benefits (see Table 7.2) as well as a means of increasing energy access in areas in the developing world that could not be served by the electricity networks.[16] New and renewable energy technologies have occupied significant market shares in Asia since the early 1980s (Timilsina and Lefevre 1999). In fact, some Asian countries have implemented these technologies at an equivalent or higher level than developed Western countries. Most have already formulated policies for the development and promotion of new and renewable energy technologies or are in the process of doing so.[17]

Privatization and deregulation is posing threats on renewables by 'changing

Table 7.2 *Environmental emissions of electricity options*

Electricity generation option	GHG emissions (kt eq. CO_2/TWh)	SO_2 emissions (t SO_2/TWh)	NO_x emissions (t NO_x/TWh)	Particulate matter emissions (t/TWh)
Hydropower with reservoir	2–48	5–60	3–42	5
Diesel	555–883	84–1550	316+–12300	122–213+
Modern coal power plant: bituminous coal	790–1182	700–32321+	700–5273+	30–663+
Old coal power plant: lignite	1147–1272+	600–31941+	704–4146+	100–618
Oil thermal w/o scrubbing	686–726+	8013–9595+	1386+	
Nuclear	2–59	3–50	2–100	2
Natural gas CC	389–511	4–15000+	13+–1500	1–10+
Biomass: energy plantation	17–118	26–160	1110–2540	190–212
Wind power	7–124	21–87	14–50	5–35
Solar PV	13–731	24–490	16–340	12–190

Source: Adapted from IEA (2000), p. 8.

the rules of the game, and by reducing or eliminating traditional support mechanisms ... As markets liberalize, government's ability to intervene directly to support renewables has diminished. Price supports, mandatory purchase agreements, capital subsidies, and fixed prices contradict the fundamental premises of market liberalization' (Bess 1999). Investors in competitive electricity markets need more incentives to choose new renewables that have remained expensive options despite decreases in costs since the 1980s (see Table 7.3). Capital markets also prefer generation projects with low capital costs and short lead times, unless long-term contracting assures an adequate return on investment (Hagler Bailly 1998).

Table 7.3   Total renewable generation costs (cents/kWh, constant dollars)

	Early 1980s	1993	Projected (1995–2000)	EPRI targets (2005–2010)
Hydroelectric (new and upgrades)	1–6	1–6	1–6	n.a.
Geothermal (High-temp hydro)	7	5–7	4.7–7	6
Biomass (Landfill gas)	n.a.	5.5–7	5.5–7	n.a.
Solar PV	150	15–40	6–20	8
Solar thermal	14.2–24	8–10	8	6
Wind	25	5–9	4–5	4

Note: EPRI – Electric Power Research Institute.

Source: Lee and Darani (1995), p. 31.

Both the Philippines and Thailand have very aggressive renewable energy policies that in the Philippines are supportive of the ongoing power sector restructuring and privatization and in Thailand parallel to the introduction of competition in the generation sector.

In the Philippines, 'the DOE shall ensure that the restructured power industry will accord a preferential bias for environment friendly and renewable energy technologies and projects'.[18] Thus, DOE launched the Renewable Energy Policy Framework in August 2003. The new renewable energy policy framework aims to promote more private sector participation in renewable energy development, encourage the use of renewable energy in rural development and off-grid electrification, and prioritize renewable energy

projects through special incentives under the Board of Investment's
Investment Priorities Plan (IPP). Moreover, the new renewable energy policy
framework ambitiously targets in 2013 to (see also Table 7.4):

1. increase RE-based capacity by 100 percent, from about 4500 MW in 2002
    to more than 9000 MW in the next ten years;
2. be the No. 1 geothermal energy producer in the world by adding 1200
    MW to its current installed capacity of around 1900 MW;
3. be the No. 1 wind energy producer in SE Asia by installing 417 MW of
    wind capacity;
4. double hydro capacity from around 2500 MW in 2002;
5. be the solar cell manufacturing hub in ASEAN; and
6. increase contribution of biomass, solar and ocean by 100 MW.

Table 7.4   Philippine renewable energy targets in MW

	2002	Target additional capacity	2013
Geothermal	1931	1200	3131
Hydropower	2518	2950	5468
Wind	0	417	417
Solar, biomass, ocean	0	131	131
Total	4449	4698	9147

Source: DOE (2004).

For example, to achieve these targets for biomass, solar, and wind, the DOE
will continue to: (a) create a commercially viable environment to further
encourage public–private partnership in renewable energy development; (b)
promote optimal use of renewable energy resources particularly in off-grid
areas; and (c) enhance local manufacturing capability for renewable energy
systems. It is also looking into market options to include (a) a parallel
mechanism that will guarantee the development of renewable energy project
while maintaining security of supply; (b) various performance incentives to
increase the appeal and marketability of renewable energy power projects; and
(c) promotion and incentive for the consumers to encourage generation
companies to produce renewable energy based power.[19]
    The DOE is also pushing for a Renewable Energy bill to further promote the
development, utilization and commercialization of RE resources in view of the
government's environmental and social objectives. The bill when passed into
law would provide for a green pricing mechanism, allocate a minimum
amount of RE in power generation, promote the use of hybrid systems,

provide financial incentives and conduct a sustained information campaign on RE.

In Thailand, 1992 also saw the announcement of rules and regulations allowing the purchase of power from small power producers with capacities of not more than 60 MW that was later raised to 90 MW. Small power producers mean any private, government, and state enterprise that produces electricity from non-conventional fuels (including wind, solar, mini-hydro, waste or residues from agricultural activities or production processes, products derived from waste and residues from agriculture and production processes, municipal waste, and dendrothermal sources energy) and through cogeneration and supplies electricity to EGAT. The power purchase agreements with EGAT are labeled (a) firm contracts if it's for more than five years and includes capacity and energy payments, and (b) non-firm contract if it's less than five years and includes only energy payment. Since then and as of August 2003, 60 SPPs have closed contracts with EGAT and were selling 2098.90 MW to the grid, which represented 56 percent of total SPP installed capacity of 3767.91 MW and some 8 percent of the national installed generating capacity (including EGAT and IPP power plants). Of the 60 SPP projects, 19 are natural gas-fired cogeneration accounting for 67 percent (or 1413 MW) of the total capacity sale to EGAT.

The SPP program was conceived to promote renewable energies.[20] Renewable SPPs number 32, but account for only 18 percent (equivalent to 670 MW) of total installed capacity of SPPs and 12 percent (equivalent to 245.90 MW) of total capacity sale to EGAT. 24 (or 75 percent) of the 32 renewable SPPs use bagasse (residues from sugar mills) as fuel. But the capacity sale, equivalent to 143.20 MW, of these 24 bagasse-fired power plants represents only 28 percent of their total installed capacity, compared to 63 percent for the other renewable SPPs combined, indicating more own use electricity consumption in bagasse power plants than other biomass or renewable SPPs. After bagasse, paddy (rice) husks and wood wastes are the next most important biomass fuels used by renewable SPPs in Thailand.

In 2001 and 2002, US$70 million was allocated from the ENCON Fund[21] to provide tariff subsidies to 31 new renewable power projects with a combined capacity of more than 500 MW proposed under the SPP program. Seventeen of the 31 proposals were selected in March 2002, and 14 in May 2002 (see Table 7.5). Clearly, the objective of these subsidies is to encourage more renewable power projects in the SPP program. Thus, in two years from the time that the announcement of the subsidies was made to the submission of project proposals, the number of projects responding to the call was as many as the renewable SPPs that joined the program since 1994 or during the last ten years. Moreover, there is more generation capacity being planned for sale to the grid from the total installed capacity of these 31 projects than from the

32 projects commissioned in 1994–2003 – 60 percent compared to 37 percent. What is also striking is the number of firm contracts – 20 of the 31 projects!

Table 7.5   Renewable SPPs, 1994–2003

Year	Number of projects	Installed capacity (MW)	MW sales (firm contracts)
1994–2003	32	670.0	245.9 (4)
March 2002	17	399.8	313.0 (12)
May 2002	14	427.8	185.3 (8)

Source: EPPO.

As of May 2003, the ENCON Fund had finally approved 14 of these 31 renewable SPPs, with a combined generating capacity of 194 MW, to receive total subsidies amounting to 1116 million baht (US$28.6 million). An average subsidy of 0.17 baht/kWh (0.44 US cents/kWh) will be provided for a five-year period to the approved projects, as long as they continue to comply with environmental requirements and standards.

A number of instruments are available to make renewables an attractive option in a deregulated electricity market. In the European Union, which targets to increase the share of renewables in the generation mix to 12 percent in 2010, the approaches or instruments being considered include: (a) a network access system; (b) a tendering system; (c) internationally harmonized energy taxes on production; and (d) substitution of heat for electricity (Havskjold 1999). In the network access system, electricity generated from renewables are guaranteed access to the grid and paid a price set by the state. In the tendering system, instead of setting the price, the state decides on the site, size and type of a renewables plant, and sets a fund for the project in the form of a fixed subsidy. Electricity produced from various sources may also be taxed according to their emissions. In this case, renewables could become more attractive because of their low emissions. Lastly, some renewables (biomass, solar) are used for heating purposes to substitute for electricity. Renewables in this case can be promoted by reflecting in the tariffs the real cost of transporting electricity.

Moreover, others argue that dynamics of electricity sector reforms actually offer opportunities for new and renewable energy sources. The privatization and break up of the national electric monopoly and the unbundling of the electricity system into its different functions increase opportunities for distributed or decentralized energy systems (including cogeneration systems) that are fueled by renewables. Moreover, the increasing concern for the environment calls for internalizing the environmental costs of generation technologies. This would make renewables more competitive and increase its market value. Experience in developed countries that restructure their electricity sector indicates that a large number of consumer contract renewable electricity, or green power, from merchant power producers (generators in competitive electricity markets), despite its higher price.[22] The public awareness campaigns conducted by government and non-government organizations have been largely responsible for such consumer response.

Implications of the Reform on Energy Efficiency

Based on international experience, two observations have been made with regards to the relationship between deregulation and energy efficiency.

Structure and ownership changes in the electricity supply industry are neither necessary nor pre-conditions for enhancement of energy efficiency; but deregulation can hinder or enhance developments in energy efficiency (Clark 2001).

The Philippines and Thailand have active energy efficiency programs that have been independent of the reforms in the electricity sector.

Following the oil crises in the 1970s and 1980s, demand management had been a component of Philippine energy policy focused at achieving energy security in an environment-friendly manner. Since the mid-1990s, energy efficiency and conservation has been integrated into the key policy objective of achieving environment sustainability and recently as well as social sustainability to lessen the impact of high cost of energy and electricity. Thus, for example, the latest Philippine Energy Plan in 2004 anchors the energy efficiency policy, plans, and programs on the following objectives:

- enhance consumer understanding of energy use;
- lower consumer energy expenditure without constraining productivity;
- reduce power capacity/transmission expansion requirements; and
- reduce greenhouse gas emissions.

Specifically, the Philippines currently targets cumulative energy savings of 7.54 million barrels of fuel oil equivalent (MMBFOE), or 9.13 percent of total target cumulative energy savings by 2013, from consumer information and education campaigns, including 'Power Patrol' to increase awareness in electricity savings, 'Road Transport Patrol' to increase awareness in energy savings in transport fuel use, and Government Energy Management Program to increase awareness in energy efficiency and conservation among government agencies as well as government-owned corporations and universities. Another 26.26 MMBFOE, or 31.81 percent of total target cumulative energy savings by 2013, are expected from consumer protection programs that include energy efficiency labelling and standards on selected household, commercial, and industrial electric appliances and equipments. However, the largest contribution, equivalent to 48.76 MMBFOE or 59.06 percent, will come from technical assistance programs to improve energy efficiency in industry through energy audits, power generation through heat rate improvements in power plants, and electricity distribution through system loss reduction and demand-side management programs.

In 1992, the same time as the start of reform in the electricity sector, Thailand also promulgated the landmark Energy Conservation and Promotion Act that has been the basis of all the country's present energy efficiency policies and initiatives that are aimed mainly at curbing growth in energy demand. The Act has sought to influence final energy demand and end-use energy consumption by mandating 'designated' factories and buildings to conduct energy audits, assign energy managers and formulate energy rationalization plans, among others including setting of standards for appliance equipment and materials.

The Act gave birth to the Energy Conservation (ENCON) Program that also promotes sustainable use of natural resources, including indigenous renewable energies, and protection of the environment. The ENCON Program provides low-interest loans and grants for energy efficiency and renewable energy projects, as well as for research and development, demonstration, promotion and education.

In parallel with the ENCON Program, the government through its three electric power utilities has also launched the demand-side management (DSM) program. The first five-year phase of the DSM program started in 1993. The first phase DSM Master Plan had originally targeted a reduction of 238 MW peak demand, some 1427 GWh of electricity generation, and 1.16 million tonnes of CO_2 emissions. As of 30 September 1998, during its fifth year, the program had resulted in reductions of 468 MW of peak demand, 2194 GWh of electricity generation, and 1.64 million tons of CO_2 emission. By September 2001, the overall program had resulted in 651 MW peak demand cut and 3665 GWh energy reductions. The program has achieved more than it had targeted.The government formulated another five-year DSM Master Plan for the second phase of the DSM operation. DSM Phase II (2002–2006) consists of 13 DSM programs targeting the three major sectors of the economy: residential, commercial and industrial. The total savings targeted for the Phase 2 DSM program is 632 MW peak demand and 2508 GWh of energy. This is expected to cause a reduction of more than 1.85 million tonnes of CO_2 from accumulated energy savings at the end of 2006.

However, deregulation can enhance or hinder the implementation of energy efficiency programs, particularly utility-based demand-side management programs (DSM). In fully competitive electricity markets, the generation segment of the industry has no incentive to implement DSM programs. However, the remaining monopoly segments – transmission and distribution – could have motivations to continue DSM programs. For example, distribution utilities can continue to use DSM as customer-service programs to maintain and build market shares (Hirst *et al.* 1996).

Aside from customer service needs, DSM programs under a restructured electricity supply industry could also be motivated by operational and regulatory needs (Keating 1996). DSM can continue to be seen as a resource by utilities, with all its environmental benefits. Also because of its environmental benefits, regulators may continue to ask utilities to implement DSM programs. Finally, in the absence of utility funded DSM programs, energy service companies (ESCOs)[23] could invest in DSM programs or assist in implementing energy efficiency and conservation among energy consumers and profit from them.

The above-mentioned impacts of deregulation on DSM actually identify two possible scenarios for continuing DSM in a deregulated electricity industry: public policy-based mechanism and business-based mechanism (Rasisuddhi and Chullabodhi 2004). Rasisuddhi and Chullabodhi (2004) discuss the implementation aspects and pros and cons of the two scenarios for Thailand that are summarized in Table 7.6.

CONCLUDING REMARKS

Power sector deregulation can be beneficial or have negative impacts on the environment. The evidence from the Philippines and Thailand shows that the introduction of competition in generation through IPPs has had short-term positive environmental impacts due to choice of natural gas as the preferred fuel for power generation, not only because of the environment qualities of natural gas but also because of its availability, especially in Thailand, and competitive costs of the corresponding generation technologies. However, coal is also becoming closely competitive because of improvements in coal combustion technologies, thereby reducing further the environmental impacts of coal use in power generation, as well as its stable prices and wide availability.

The long-term environmental impacts of the power deregulation will be determined by its implications on renewable energy and energy efficiency, the main drivers of sustainable, and thus, clean energy use. Theoretically and based on evidence from developed countries that are advanced in deregulation, the environmental impacts of deregulation are mixed. This implies that to maximize positive impacts and minimize negative impacts, policy will

Table 7.6   DSM scenarios in Thailand after ESI deregulation

	Public policy-based mechanism	Business-based mechanism
Structure options	EGAT continues to manage DSM programs; EGAT enters into strategic partnerships with MEA and PEA;[a] MEA and PEA fully implement DSM	ESCOs DSM Office in EGAT spun off and privatized
Focus	Load management	Load reduction or energy saving
Financing	ENCON Fund EGAT operational funds Distribution charge (of MEA and PEA)	Private funds ENCON Fund through capital subsidies
Pros	EGAT's successful experience with DSM and credible engineering qualifications MEA and PEA have been directly linked with electricity consumers	Private sector participation More sustainable financing
Cons	DSM is second priority after EGAT's privatisation MEA and PEA have had little to do with DSM	Little experience in the private sector and of banks

Notes: [a]MEA and PEA distribute electricity to Bangkok and Thailand provinces, respectively. In a fully deregulated electricity market, MEA and PEA would have been privatized, PEA transformed into regional distribution companies, and both will continue to operate the distribution networks but also competing to with private sector to provide energy services.

Source: Rasisuddhi and Chullabodhi (2004).

continue to play an important role even in deregulated electricity markets. The evidence from the Philippines and Thailand, as well as international experience, supports this even if prior to the periods of deregulation, renewable energy and energy efficiency policies had been independent of electricity reforms. During the period of reforms, renewable energy and energy efficiency policies continue to realize not only energy security objectives but also to attain energy sustainability. Towards this end, safeguards are being put in place, particularly in the Philippines, which is continuing toward a fully competitive electricity market, to minimize the negative impacts of deregulation on renewable energy and energy efficiency. Thailand would continue its stalled deregulation, sooner or later. Notwithstanding, its active and aggressive renewable energy and energy efficiency policies should mitigate the negative impacts of deregulation on the environment.

NOTES

1. Deregulation is used here interchangeably with restructuring and reform, and includes privatization, even if strictly there are differences in the meanings of these terms.
2. For example, of the 222 private electricity projects in Asia that reached financial closure between 1990 and 1997, 193 (or 87 percent) involved the construction of new power plants by IPPs (Izaguirre 1998). This represents 67 percent of all greenfield power projects in developing countries during that period and 36 percent of all power projects with private sector participation.
3. Some cases of restructuring do proceed without immediate privatization. New Zealand is a good example.
4. Hunt and Shuttleworth (1996).
5. Ibid.
6. Ibid.
7. The electricity reform in Thailand has been stalled because the present Thai government is not convinced and attracted by the proposed privatization and restructuring plans (see Albouy and Saeed 2003). Notwithstanding, Thailand's experience in power sector deregulation, together with the parallel environmental policy and issues, remain an interesting case study. Moreover, who knows where the winds of change would blow again.
8. The EGAT Act of 1968 created EGAT.
9. The second solicitation had been interrupted by the financial crisis and was re-scheduled in 1999. However, it has not materialized.
10. Notwithstanding the strong preference for natural gas, fuel and fuel diversity had the smallest weight among the IPP evaluation criteria, accounting for only 4 percent. Price factors had 60 percent weight, level of project development 11 percent, experience and financial status of the bidder, including ability to arrange for financing, each gets 7 percent, location 6 percent, and adherence to model PPA 5 percent.
11. Albouy and Saeed (2003), p. ix.
12. The large-scale generation from natural gas started in 2002, with the commissioning of power plants with combined capacities of 2760 MW.
13. Apogee Research (1997).
14. NEA/IEA (1998).
15. CEERD (1999b).
16. Developed countries were actually the first to explore the potential of renewables but for energy security reasons, particularly in response to the oil price shock in the 1970s.
17. China and India, for example, have designed ambitious plans and programs to strengthen the contribution of these technologies to their total energy supply. Developments in renewable energy, however, have been largely as a result of direct and indirect government intervention.
18. DOE (2004), p. 17.
19. DOE (2004).
20. The current target is to increase the share of RE in the national energy mix from 19.8 percent in 2001 to 20.81 percent in 2006 and 21.21 percent in 2010 (Sailasuta 2002).
21. The Energy Conservation Promotion Fund (ENCON Fund) was established in 1995 to finance renewable energy and energy efficiency projects.
22. ADB (2000).

23. 'ESCOs are private companies that provide comprehensive energy efficiency or load reduction services to customers who own or operate facilities such as factories and buildings' Rasisuddhi and Chullabodhi (2004).

REFERENCES

Albouy, Yves and Kazim Saeed (2003) *Thailand – Why Liberalization May Stall in a Mature Power Market*, ESMAP Report 270/03, Washington, DC: World Bank, October.

Apogee Research (1997) *Environmentally Sound Infrastructure in APEC Electricity Sectors*, Singapore: APEC.

Asian Development Bank (ADB) (2000) *Energy 2000: Review of the Energy Policy of the Asian Development Bank*, Manila: ADB.

Bess, Mike (1999) 'Market Liberalization: Opportunity or Threat for Renewable Energy', *Renewable Energy World*, July, 28–33.

Boorsma, P. B. (1994) 'Privatization: Political and Economic Considerations', in Meine Pieter van Dijk and Nico G. Schulte Nordholt (eds.) *Privatization Experiences in African and Asian Countries: An Economic and Political Analysis of Institutional Transformation*, Amsterdam: SISWO.

Burr, Michael T. (1996) 'Solicitation Strategies', *Independent Energy*, Jul/Aug, 8–9.

Burr, Michael T. (1998) 'Converging Strategies', *Independent Energy*, January/February, 18–22.

Center for Energy-Environment Research and Development (CEERD) (1999a) 'Energy Sector Policy Review', a report prepared for the Asian Development Bank, May.

Center for Energy-Environment Research and Development (CEERD) (1999b) *Coal and Natural Gas Competition in APEC Economies*, Bangkok: CEERD/APEC Clean Fossil Energy Expert Group.

Chang, Youngho (2004) 'Regulatory framework of the Singapore electricity market', *Electricity Supply Industry in Transition: Issues and Prospects for Asia*, Asian Institute of Technology, 14–16 January, Bangkok.

Clark, Alix (2001) 'Making Provision for Energy Efficiency Investment in Changing Markets: an International Review,' *Energy for Sustainable Development*, 5 (2), 26–38.

Department of Energy (2004) 'Philippine Energy Plan 2004–2013: Diversified Approaches Towards a More Responsive Energy Sector', Manila.

Di Piazza, Gero (2003a), 'Consistent Policy Wins Investor', *Asian Energy Infrastructure*, August, 16, 18, 20.

Di Piazza, Gero (2003b) 'Southeast Asia: May the Power be With You', *Asian Energy Infrastructure*, September, 9 and 11.

Dubash, Navroz K. (2003) 'Revisiting Electricity Reform: the Case for a Sustainable Development Approach', *Utilities Policy*, 11, 143–54.

Dubash, Navroz K. (ed.) (2002) *Power Politics: Equity and Environment in Electricity Reform*, Washington, DC: World Resources Institute.

Eikeland, Per Ove (1998) 'Electricity Market Liberalisation and Environmental Performance: Norway and the UK', *Energy Policy*, 26 (12), 917–27.

Energy Information Administration, US Department of Energy (EIA) (1998) *Challenges of Electric Power Industry Restructuring for Fuel Suppliers*, Washington, DC: EIA, US Department of Energy.

Elauria, J. C., M. L. Y. Castro and M. M. Elauria (2002) 'Biomass Energy Technologies in the Philippines: a Barrier and Policy Analysis', *Energy for Sustainable Development*, **6** (3), 40–9.

Flavin, Christopher and Nicholas Lennsen (1994) 'Reshaping the Electric Power Industry', *Energy Policy*, **22** (12), 1029–44.

Hagler, Bailly (1998) 'Environmental Protection Under Power Sector Reform in Developing Countries', report prepared for the US Agency for International Development (USAID), March.

Havskjold, Monica (1999) 'What Role Do Renewables Play in a Deregulated Electricity Market', *Hydropower Resources Worldwide*, May, 37–9.

Hirst, Eric, Ralph Cavanagh and Peter Miller (1996) 'The Future of DSM in a Restructured US Electricity Industry', *Energy Policy*, **24** (4), 303–15.

Hunt, Sally and Graham Shuttleworth (1996) *Competition and Choice in Electricity*, Chichester: John Wiley and Sons.

Ibrahim, Hassan, Ahmad Zairin Ismail and Norasikin Ahmad Ludin (2002) 'Small Renewable Energy Power Programme for the Promotion of Renewable Energy Power Generation', paper presented at the First Regional Workshop ASEM Green IPP Network, 24–25 October, Bangkok.

International Energy Agency (IEA) (1997) *Asia Electricity Study*, Paris: OECD/IEA.

IEA (2000), 'Hydropower and the Environment: Present Context and Guidelines for Future Action', IEA Technical Report, May.

IEA (2003a) *CO₂ Emissions from Fuel Combustion Highlights 1971–2001*, Paris: OECD/IEA.

IEA (2003b) *Energy Balances of Non-OECD Countries 2000–2001*, Paris: OECD/IEA.

Izaguirre, Ada Karina (1998) 'Private Participation in the Electricity Sector – Recent Trends', *Public Policy for the Private Sector*, Note No. 154, September, Washington, DC: World Bank.

Jaafar, Mohd. Zamzam, Wong Hwee Kheng and Norhayati Kamaruddin (2003) 'Greener Energy Solutions for a Sustainable Future: Issues and Challenges for Malaysia', *Energy Policy*, **31**, 1061–72.

Keating, Kenneth M. (1996) 'What Roles for Utility Sponsored DSM in a Competitive Environment', *Energy Policy*, **24** (4), 317–21.

Kluger, Frank, Joachim Seeber and DinhCuong Tran (2004) *Power Engineering International*, January 27–9.

Lee, Henry and Nageen Darani (1995), 'Electricity Restructuring and the Environment', Discussion Paper E-95-07, Kennedy School of Government, Harvard University, December.

Lefevre, Thierry, Jessie Todoc and Govinda Timilsina (2001) 'Economic, Social, and Environmental Implications of Privatization and Deregulation of Electricity Systems – the Asian Perspective', unpublished paper prepared for the International Atomic Energy Agency.

Nuclear Energy Agency/International Energy Agency (NEA/IEA) (1998) *Projected Costs of Generating Electricity*, NEA/IEA, Paris: OECD.

Rasisuddhi, Kritika and Chullapong Chullabodhi (2004) 'Role of Demand-Side Management in Thailand after Electricity Supply Industry Reform', *Proceedings of the International Conference on Electricity Supply Industry in Transition: Issues and Prospects for Asia*, Asian Institute of Technology, 14–16 January, Bangkok.

Roseman, Elliot and Anil Malhotra (1996) 'The Dynamics of Independent Power: IPPs Seed Top-to-Bottom Reform', *Public Policy for the Private Sector*, Note No. 83,

June, Washington, DC: World Bank.

Sailasuta, Siriporn (2002), 'Opportunities in Renewable Energy and Energy Efficiency and Conservation', paper presented at the 4th ASEAN Energy Business Forum, 21–22 October 2002, Bangkok.

Schuler, Joseph (1997) 'Thirst for Natural Gas Turbines Unquenched Overseas', *Public Utilities Fortnightly*, March, 36–7.

Sheshinski, Eytan and Luis Felipe Lopez-Calva (1999) 'Privatization and Its Benefits: Theory and Evidence', Development Discussion Paper Number 698, April, Harvard Institute for International Development, Harvard University.

Tenenbaum, Bernard, Reinier Lock and Jim Barker (1992) 'Electricity Privatization: Structural, Competitive and Regulatory Options', *Energy Policy*, December, 1134–60.

Timilsina, G. and T. Lefevre (1999) 'New and Renewable Energy Technologies: Asia Overview', *Renewable Energy World*, July, 137–46.

Tjaroko, Tjarinto S., Marites I. Cabrera and Thierry Lefevre (2003) 'Policy Instruments to Promote RE Projects Interconnected to National Grids: the Case of Indonesia, Malaysia, Philippines, and Thailand', *GrIPP-Net News*, August.

8. Governance and regulation of provident and pension funds in Asia

Mukul G. Asher and Amarendu Nandy

Governance and regulation of corporations (or companies) and of provident and pension funds[1] involves managing principal-agent (or agency) relationships. These arise when principals (for example stockholders in the case of corporations, provident and pension fund beneficiaries, and taxpayers when government funding is involved) need to rely on agents (corporate managers, provident and pension fund trustees, government bureaucrats) to pursue their (principal) interests.[2]

Since the 1997 East Asian financial crisis, there has been increasing awareness of the need for good corporate governance practices in Asian countries. The progress in translating this awareness into an effective institutional and regulatory framework has predictably been slow and uneven in Asia.[3]

A parallel awareness of good governance practices and sound supervision and regulation of provident and pension schemes in Asia has however been much slower. There are several factors which may help explain this phenomenon. First, the pension sector in Asia has been dominated by the state-mandated and managed schemes. This has meant relatively low importance of occupational pension plans. The state sector has usually been reluctant to separate service delivery from supervision and regulation functions. As a result, policy formulation, oversight and its implementation are not separated. In addition, in many Asian countries (such as Singapore, China and Vietnam) even the basic socio-economic information is used as an instrument to be used tactically by the policymakers rather than as a public good. In other countries (such as Indonesia, India and Sri Lanka) effective oversight by the Parliament and state auditors over state-managed provident and pension funds has traditionally been not very effective. An instrument such as the Freedom of Information Act (FIA) may help. But unless the political environment stresses accountability and transparency throughout the system, and unless the pensions sector is brought within the purview of an independent pension regulator, sustained improvements in governance may not be possible.

Second, there has also not been a sharp demarcation between the public and

151

the private sectors in several Asian countries (for example China, Vietnam and Singapore), and the business sector is dominated by the state enterprises, and family-owned conglomerates, resulting in weak corporate governance. This is then reflected in weak governance structures for occupational pension plans.[4] Strong links between the two suggests that progress in overall corporate governance will be essential for progress in governance of occupational pension plans.[5]

Third, in several Asian countries, pension laws have been non-existent (for example Vietnam, China and Cambodia), though these countries are in the process of formally adopting such laws. In some Asian countries (for example India, Sri Lanka and Indonesia), the provident and pension fund laws were enacted nearly half a century ago and have not undergone significant modifications to reflect changes in their economic paradigm or emergence of globalization and associated technological changes. Modern pension laws[6] which are consistent with current economic paradigm are thus a pre-requisite for sound governance and regulation of provident and pension schemes.

Governance and regulation are mutually reinforcing and not independent. Thus, the regulator has a broader core objective of ensuring that the retirement income security of individuals is met through the practice of good governance of the pension funds. In addition to fulfilling this social welfare objective, proper management of pension funds through good governance practices and strong regulation also potentially leads to the evolution of financial markets; and enhancement of capital accumulation through their effect on taxes and intergenerational transfers (Carmichael and Palacios 2003). There are several public policy reasons for paying greater attention to governance and regulation issues relating to social security in Asian countries.

First, globalization has significantly increased the importance of constructing and managing social safety nets.[7] Their main role is to cushion the burden of restructuring, enhance legitimacy of reforms, and enable individuals and firms to assist in risk management strategies of the individuals. Second, Asian countries are experiencing rapid individual and population ageing[8] (Table 8.1). The challenge will be not just the level but also the pace of ageing in several Asian countries. Data in Table 8.1 clearly suggest that the number of elderly in Asia, particularly China, India and Indonesia will be large, and to provide social security for such large numbers at relatively low per capita incomes, the social security systems will have to be efficiently governed, managed, and regulated.[9] Given the large absolute numbers involved, how Asia manages its ageing challenges, will have important implications for the rest of the world as well.

Third, the Asian countries are witnessing increasing demand for public participation and better quality in delivery of governmental services, including those relating to social security, while keeping the fiscal burdens on the

Table 8.1   Demographic projections in selected Asian countries

	Population (in millions)		% of population over 65		Population over 65 (numbers in millions)		Healthy Life Expectancy (HALE)[a] at age 60 (year 2002)	
Country	2000	2030	2000	2030	2000	2030	Male	Female
China	1262	1483	7.0	16.0	88	237	13.1	14.7
India	1014	1437	4.6	9.0	47	129	10.8	11.4
Indonesia	225	313	4.5	10.9	10	34	10.7	11.5
Japan	127	117	17.0	28.3	22	33	17.5	21.7
S. Korea	47	54	7.0	19.5	3	11	12.1	13.2
Malaysia	22	35	4.1	9.4	1	3	10.9	12.0
Singapore	4	9	6.8	14.8	0	1	14.5	16.3

Note: [a] Healthy life expectancy (HALE) is based on life expectancy, but includes an adjustment for time spent in poor health. This indicator measures the equivalent number of years in full health that a newborn child can expect to live based on the current mortality rates and prevalence distribution of health states in the population.

Sources: Chakraborti (2004); World Health Organization (WHO) (2004).

population within manageable limits. This will also call for better governance and regulation.

Finally, as the importance of the private sector in the economy increases, and as a greater proportion of retirement financing is pre-funded, pension fund assets can be expected to grow from the current modest levels in most countries[10]. This requires increasing focus on governance and regulation of occupational pension funds, including their investment policies and management. Increased level of funding will also raise serious corporate governance issues if they are invested in domestic equities, particularly when investment by provident and pension funds relative to market capitalization of stock markets is high (Catalán 2004). In some cases, even large provident and pension funds will be minority shareholders. The provident and pension funds then will have an interest in how corporations treat minority shareholders.[11]

It is in the above context that this chapter examines governance and regulation issues and practices, with particular reference to Asian countries. There is considerable experience with these issues and practices in OECD countries. OECD (2002) guidelines focus on governance structure and mechanisms of pension funds. The primary objective is to encourage competition in the pension fund industry, but with strong and effective regulation.

The guidelines emphasize that the governance structure should ensure an appropriate division of operational and oversight responsibilities, and the accountability and suitability of those with such responsibilities. The guidelines on governance mechanisms are designed to ensure that pension funds have appropriate control, communication, and incentive structures that encourage good decision making, proper and timely execution, transparency and regular review and assessment.

OECD's core principles of occupational pension regulation focus on regulatory and supervision framework for private pensions (OECD 2004). They emphasize the need for appropriate legal structures and accounting systems; technical, financial and managerial criterion for setting up of pension fund companies; rules for winding up pension funds and for liability insurance; asset management; rights of members and beneficiaries; and adequacy of benefits.

While considerable energy, expertise and resources have gone into developing the above guidelines, by necessity, they remain of a general nature. The Asian countries will need to contextualize the above guidelines for their own conditions and institutional framework. The OECD guidelines should be regarded as informing the policymakers and regulators about the issues and challenges to be addressed, rather than as a blueprint.

GOVERNANCE ISSUES AND PRACTICES

Three broad institutional mechanisms can be identified through which society can ensure that provident and pension fund organizations practise good governance, violators are penalized in time, and that penalties are proportionate to the violations. These are self-regulation, competitive market structures, which will ensure that those with weak governance practices will be weeded out, and state regulation.

Provident and pension funds involve very long term and complex financial contracts; and given the importance of retirement financing, the ultimate implicit (in some cases explicit) liability is on the State. The financial industry in general and pension funds management industry in particular are oligopolistic and therefore the forces of market discipline are relatively weak[12]. International experience suggests that self-regulation has also been an inadequate instrument to ensure good governance practices even in the well-developed financial and capital markets, such as the UK and the US. Both these countries have explicit regulatory structures and laws governing pension funds. The oligopolistic nature of the financial industry also poses a systemic risk which must be managed; and self-regulation and market discipline are weak instruments for this purpose.

In well-developed financial and capital markets all financial intermediaries such as banks, insurance companies, and pension funds are therefore subjected to stringent regulations. In Asian countries, while banks and insurance companies are regulated, with few exceptions, there has been the absence of a regulatory body for provident and pension funds.

Five core functions of any provident and pension fund organization may be identified as follows (Ross 2000):

1. Reliable collection of contribution/taxes, and other receipts.
2. Payment of benefits for each of the schemes in a correct way without any side-payments. In case of pre-retirement loans, ensuring their timely repayment.
3. Secure financial management and productive investment of provident and pension funds assets.
4. Maintaining an effective communication network, including development of accurate data and record keeping mechanisms to support collection, payment and financial activities.
5. Production of timely and policy relevant financial statements and reports.

To fulfil these functions, good governance practices, including a high degree of competence in risk management, particularly in benefit administration and management of assets, are essential. Another aspect concerns minimization of administrative or compliance costs of performing these functions, that is total transactions costs (Shah 2005). These practices build upon good corporate governance principles but important differences must also be recognized (Guerard 2005). Among the major differences are the following.

First, provident and pension funds are usually distinct entities. They are neither a commercial corporation nor a state-owned enterprise.[13] Second, provident and pension funds are single purpose entities. So, usually there is no competition for customers or market share. Third, these entities are single-product entities as defined by rules or regulations to provide participants with financial security throughout retirement. Fourth, these entities do not need to seek growth to pay profits or dividends to a third party but instead they are evaluated on the basis of value addition for participants and long-term solvency. Finally, these entities limit risk by segregating their assets from assets of administrator or sponsoring entities, such as employers or governments.

We now briefly discuss selected aspects of governance practices. These involve the composition of the Board and its access to expertise; fiduciary responsibility, transparency and accountability; disclosure norms; and actuarial valuation.

The Composition of the Board and its Access to Expertise

The key objective is to obtain the services of the Board members who are both competent and independent minded. The Board should also have access to outside expertise to minimize the gap between industry developments and best practices relating to five core functions on the one hand and their adoption by the provident and pension fund organizations on the other. This needs to be accomplished through a combination of organizational structure and incentives, supervision by the regulator, and overall political economy environment.

The national provident funds in many Asian countries, such as Malaysia, Sri Lanka, Indonesia and India are publicly managed. In such countries, the typical characteristics of the Boards are:

- tripartite representation from government, employers and labor unions;
- members who are appointed by the Ministry of Labor or its equivalent without particular regard to competence or independent mindedness;
- combining service provider and regulator's role, and absence of an independent regulator; and
- no formal mechanism to access outside expertise.

Some countries such as Malaysia have a separate investment panel which does not report to the Board but to the Ministry of Finance. This has led to induction of expertise in investment management, but has also led to divided governance responsibilities and poor demarcation of oversight and managerial responsibilities (Thillainathan 2004).

The practices concerning the appointment of the Chairman of the Board tend to vary among various Asian countries. In India and Sri Lanka, it is the Minister of Labor, who acts as the Chairman of the Board. This makes the Board an overtly political body. In Malaysia, the Chairman of the Board is appointed by the Ministry of Finance; since the 1990s the Chairman is also the CEO. This tends to lessen the influence of Board of Directors as a body. In all three countries, there has been an absence of the Board members who may act as the equivalent of independent directors in private companies.

The following reform directions are suggested for publicly managed provident and pension funds.

Appointments of the Chairman and the Board members should be technocratic rather than political. This will imply that the Chairman and the members continue their appointment for a fixed period, regardless of political developments in the country. There should be unambiguous conditions under which Board members can be appointed or removed. The tripartite arrangement should be modified to add at least two Board members who are experts in macroeconomics, financial management, actuarial science and investments.

To advise the Board on policy, benefit schemes, investments, and administration, at least two standing committees should be set up. This will enable the Board to access outside expertise. If a country has a pension regulator, there should be adequate checks to ensure that the Board adheres to the regulator's guidelines.

In most Asian countries, the Board structures of occupational pension plans and of civil service schemes are even less satisfactory. Most occupational plans, as well as civil service schemes are not properly supervised or regulated and the role of the employer as a plan sponsor and its role as a trustee are not adequately separated.

In most Asian countries, the Board members and the trustees, as well as civil servants in charge of provident and pension funds themselves have a relatively low level of understanding of the intricacies of pensions. In particular, the long-term nature of a pension contract, lasting many decades, and the tyranny of small numbers (seemingly small changes in benefit formulas or investment rates could have disproportionately large impact on the viability of the pension schemes) are not well understood. Thus, any educational efforts will also need to be directed at the Board members and civil service pension administrators and policy makers.

Fiduciary Responsibility, Transparency and Accountability

In the Anglo-Saxon literature, fiduciary responsibility is usually interpreted to mean that the provident or pension fund must be managed in the sole interest of its members. In particular, investments policies should be designed to maximize risk-adjusted returns for the members. The mandate given to Canada Pension Plan (CPP) exemplifies this interpretation.[14] It states that the CPP has the fiduciary duty to manage funds 'in the best interest of the contributors and beneficiaries' and 'to invest in assets with a view to achieving a maximum rate of return, without undue risk of loss, having regard to the factors that may affect the funding of the CPP and the ability of the CPP to meet its financial obligations'. Usually it is also specified that the provident or pension fund agency once set up, should be free from government involvement in pursuing its objectives and meeting its responsibilities.

Provident and pension funds should be required to provide a statement of investment policies and procedures. These include clear statements concerning asset classes; portfolio diversification; asset mix; benchmark for anticipated return; securities lending; voting rights policies; liquidity requirements; use of derivatives; borrowing; policy review and reporting; and management control.

Broadly, the investment guidelines may adopt Prudent Person (or Portfolio)

Rule (PPR) or specified Quantitative Limits (QL) on each asset class (Galer 2002). The PPR regime leaves it to the pension fund management to allocate assets subject to broad objectives emphasizing fiduciary responsibility. However, even the PPR regimes to set some quantitative limits on self-investment in unregulated markets, in illiquid asset classes, and international investments (Galer 2002). The PPR regime requires sophisticated administrators and poses additional supervisory challenges because it addresses the entire investment management process. The QL regime is easy to understand and supervise but may be more difficult to calibrate and may leave a significant regulatory gap concerning other aspect of the investment management process and fund governance. In Asian countries, the QL regime is the most prevalent. However, in some countries even the domestic asset diversification has been extremely limited through regulation or due to limited development of capital markets (for example India, Indonesia, Sri Lanka and China) (Asher and Nandy 2005; Shah 2005; Pei 2005).

In most Asian countries, mandatory savings have been invested wholly domestically. Some countries, such as Malaysia and Thailand are considering limited international diversification as their provident and pension fund assets are too large to be productively invested domestically. But this process is expected to be very gradual.

Transparency requires full and open disclosure about the governance structure of the provident and pension funds, and about the details of investment policies and performance. Accountability should be both internal and external, and the consequences of failure to meet responsibilities should be clearly laid down. In many Asian countries, the Anglo-Saxon views on fiduciary responsibility, transparency and accountability are not fully accepted.

The mandatory savings schemes often constitute the largest pool of savings available for investment. The state-led development in such countries as Malaysia and Singapore has led to the use of such schemes for social, political and industrial policy related objectives. In other Asian countries such as Sri Lanka and India, mandatory savings have often been used to finance government expenditures, in some cases in a non-transparent manner. There is evidence to suggest that close links between the two has resulted in lower efficiency and transparency of the savings-investment process (Asher and Nandy 2005; Catalán 2004; Asher and Vasudevan 2005).

Lack of regulation and public apathy has led to a low degree of accountability for those managing the schemes. Limited development of the financial and capital markets, combined with relatively weak institutional structure and policy implementation capacity suggest that an abrupt switch to Anglo-Saxon best practices in this area may not be optimum. Instead, a more gradual and balanced transition could be more appropriate, provided it is not used as a alibi to dilute or unduly delay substantive and sustained reforms.

As a start, all provident and pension funds should be mandatorily required to publish detailed annual reports in both electronic and printed versions. The actuarial studies on which the schemes are based should also be disclosed to the public. The regulator may enforce such disclosure requirements. The accountability of the provident and pension fund trustees should also be made more explicit and enforcement made more stringent.

Disclosure Norms

There are several aspects that are relevant here. Adequate attention should be given to the internal disclosure norms for management and Board members. They should abide by the Code of Conduct (which could either be developed internally or be imposed by the regulator) and disclose any potential conflicts of interest.

For those given responsibility for investment management, whether they are internal staff or external agencies, appropriate checks for minimizing insider-trading should be put in place. The role of government in directing lending and investments should be disclosed unless there are compelling reasons to the contrary. All actual and potential liabilities of the provident and pension funds should be disclosed. Civil service pension schemes in many countries, such as Indonesia, Malaysia, India and Sri Lanka, are particularly deficient in this regard.

Actuarial Analysis

For any provident and pension fund, whether in public or the private sector, it is essential to have procedures for sound actuarial analysis, conducted at pre-determined regular intervals, and being available to the stakeholders. Such analysis can help in projecting the extent of financial or fiscal sustainability of a scheme, and in ensuring that the asset liabilities mismatch is minimized. It can also project the path of receipts and benefits over time. This is particularly important when new benefit schemes such as health schemes are part of the provident or pension fund.

In the ETF of Sri Lanka for example, health benefits are provided without any contributions. In Malaysia's EPF, death and incapacity benefits were introduced without any contributions. In both cases, actuarial analysis would reveal the extent of sustainability and opportunity costs of the scheme.

It is also important that the Board and key policy makers make every effort to understand the assumptions underlying the actuarial analysis, and how varying the assumptions will impact on the financial viability of the scheme. Having such analysis in the public domain may help in raising the quality of debate, at least in the medium term. As an example, the pension scheme (EPS) administered by India's EPFO is under-funded in large part due to the inability of its Board to fully take into account the consequences of not retaining the assumptions underlying the actuarial analysis of the scheme (Asher and Vasudevan 2005).

REGULATORY ISSUES AND PRACTICES

Governance refers to structures, processes and practices at an individual provident or pension fund organizational level. The regulator, on the other hand, is concerned with application and enforcement of good governance across all provident and pension fund organizations, and the need to balance the interests of all the stakeholders. The main purpose of the regulatory body is to set norms of operation for the pension funds, and to ensure that good governance is practised and, if there are violations, that provident and pension funds are held accountable under the existing legal system.

In addition to ensuring adherence to good governance practices and their enforcement, the regulator should also ensure that different components of a social security system are consistent with each other. The regulator should therefore ensure professionalism and take an integrated view of the social security system. In developing countries, the regulator also needs to play an important developmental role in enhancing pension economics literacy among the policymakers as well as the general public; and facilitate orderly development of the different facets of the pensions industry (Asher and Vasudevan 2005).

Unlike some other aspects of provident and pension fund management, such as investments and record-keeping, the regulatory function is unanimously regarded as the exclusive function of the state. The main policy choices concerning regulatory issues are whether to set up a special regulator (or supervisory body) or to entrust it to an existing regulator; the resources to be devoted to regulation; the source of finance for the regulator; and the governance structure of the regulator (Palacios 2003).

Choice of Regulator

The case for a specialized pensions regulator is based on the following considerations. First, pensions are a long-term financial contract of considerable complexity and risk. So a long-term perspective and specialized risk mitigation skills are needed. Second, for state mandated provident and pension plans, the contingent (or conjectural) liability is ultimately on the state. A specialized regulator is more likely to be aware of the specific standards required and of the responsibilities in this regard than a regulator with many other responsibilities.

The main shortcomings of a specialized pension regulator involve the potential higher costs as compared to regulation by a single agency or by an existing regulator[15] and the shortage of skilled personnel to effectively manage a specialized agency.

Some countries such as Australia, the UK and Singapore have set up a single regulator, covering all financial and capital market players and activities. There are pros and cons of such a move. A super regulator requires sophisticated financial and capital markets and regulatory capacity. Most Asian countries need to make considerable progress before reaching that stage. So, activity-specific regulators may be more appropriate in the initial stages of the learning curve in the pensions sector.

Resources to be Devoted to Regulation

It has been emphasized that pensions are a complex and risky long-term financial contract. Trust and confidence in the management of pension funds is therefore crucial. Sufficient resources should be devoted to ensure credibility, and avoid any financial scandal, particularly when the private sector is entrusted with managing pension assets. Thus, over-regulation which may stifle financial innovation and risk-taking may be preferred initially. Gradually, however, the regulator must permit greater flexibility, within the overall prudential norms.

Sources of Finance

It is usual for costs of regulation of provident and pension funds to be borne by the industry players and members, including those involved in backroom activities and those providing financial advice on pensions.[16] To the extent the pension industry expands, the fees collected may exceed the operating needs of the regulator. The excess receipts can be deployed in member education, activities, in developing the pensions industry, including human resources, and sharing it with the government treasury. The precise arrangements may vary from country to country.

The Governance Structure

The regulator should have a clear mandate and be judged by the extent to which it fulfils the mandate. It should have a high degree of functional autonomy and should have access to requisite professional expertise and IT support systems. Its Board should have the equivalent of independent Directors required for publicly listed companies.

Employment conditions, including compensation structures for the staff of the regulatory agency is a difficult political issue in many countries. Ideally, the regulator should have greater leeway to compensate and recruit requisite professional staff then what is usually observed in civil service systems. Attracting board members who are both competent and independent minded is essential. Broader political economy and informal norms often determine whether services of such board members are utilized.

In Asia, most of the national provident and pension funds are under the purview of a government ministry, usually Ministry of Labor or its equivalent. In some cases such as in Malaysia, the national provident fund is under the supervision of the Ministry of Finance; while in Sri Lanka the supervision responsibility is shared between the Ministry of Labor and the Central bank.

The above arrangements have meant that national provident fund organizations often act as service providers as well as regulators of those funds exempted from the mandatory scheme. India, Malaysia and Sri Lanka represent examples of countries where national provident fund organizations, contrary to good government practices, perform both these functions. In some countries (for example India and Sri Lanka), the Minister of Labor chairs the board of the national provident fund organization. This severely dilutes even the minimal role that a ministry may be able to provide in supervising the national provident fund organization. It also makes it difficult to reconcile the need for taking a long-term view of the provident and pension fund plans and short-term time horizon based on election cycles. The Ministry of Labor needs to represent all of the labour force and not just a small component of the labor force, usually covered by the national provident funds.

The civil service pension schemes are effectively unregulated. There is a particularly sharp agency problem in this case as those who are beneficiaries of the civil service pension rules are permitted to frame the relevant rules, implementing regulations, as well as supervise the schemes. As a result, most civil service pension schemes in Asia are overly generous in comparison with what is provided to the rest of the labour force; and are particularly resistant to transparency and accountability. It is therefore essential that the civil service pension schemes be brought under the purview of pensions regulator.

The occupational pension plans in Asia generally require permission from the income tax authorities as they are usually set up under the Trusts Act. The income tax authorities however have little expertise or incentive to effectively supervise these plans. Countries such as Indonesia have set up a separate pensions division in the Ministry of Finance to regulate occupational pension plans. Indonesia currently does not have a regulator for the national provident fund for civil service schemes but it is proposing to set up a single regulator for supervising the entire financial sector, including pensions. Sri Lanka is considering setting up a Superannuation Funds Regulatory Commission

(SFRC) which will regulate all provident and pension fund schemes, including those that are managed by the state.

Hong Kong has a functioning Mandatory Provident Fund Schemes Authority (MPFA) which was set up even before the MPF scheme was introduced in 2000. This is a positive example of good planning.

India has set up an interim Provident Fund Regulatory and Development Authority (PFRDA). PFRDA Bill 2005 has been introduced in the Parliament (Government of India 2005; Shah 2005). It will initially regulate the New Pension Scheme (NPS) which is a mandatory defined contribution scheme for those entering the civil service at the Centre from January 2004. Several states are expected to follow suit and the PFRDA will also regulate their schemes. The autonomous bodies and central government aided institutions as well as designated state enterprises are also mandated to join the NPS. In addition, individuals may join the NPS on a voluntary basis. It is envisaged that the current occupational schemes will also come under the purview of the PFRDA. Thus, India has opted for a specialized pension regulator.

In other Asian countries, apart from limited supervision of occupational pension plans, there has been reluctance to set up a pensions regulator which will oversee state-mandated and managed schemes, including civil service schemes. This suggests that Asia needs to make considerable progress in effective implementation of the regulatory structures.

CONCLUSION

This chapter has focused on the importance of better governance of public provident and pension schemes in which significant agency problems are inherent. While governance of these schemes is linked to corporate governance, important differences between the two should also be kept in mind. Each country needs to devise sound governance structures and mechanisms and the pace at which the desired goal of good governance of the schemes is to be achieved. There are international experiences which suggest that there is a choice of public-private mix concerning several aspects of governance, such as record-keeping and investment management.

The regulation function however is universally agreed to be the function of the state as self-regulation and competition mechanisms are less likely to be effective in this area.

In Asia, the progress in achieving good governance of provident and pension schemes is even less than the limited progress made since the 1997 East Asian financial crisis in the corporate governance. The large space taken by the state-managed schemes and the nature of the political economy which has traditionally not emphasized transparency, accountability and freedom of information have contributed to this limited progress. Moreover, the coverage of the schemes and in particular coverage of occupational pension plans has been limited. However, this sector is likely to experience growth as Asia's individual and population ageing trends become more evident and as the size of the middle class increases.

The main goals of regulation in Asia should be to ensure that each provident and pension fund scheme is professionally designed and managed as there are substantial gains which may be obtained from modernizing laws, provisions, record keeping, investment policies and regulations, and management systems; and to ensure that the different components of the pension industry are developed in an integrated manner.

Hong Kong has set up a strong regulatory regime, while India is awaiting parliamentary approval for an independent specialized pensions regulator. Indonesia has plans for a single financial regulator, including pensions; while Sri Lanka has plans to set up a pension supervisory agency. Several countries do regulate occupational pension plans either through a separate division in the Ministry of Finance or by entrusting the responsibility to the stock market regulator. But multiple regulators for the pensions sector make co-ordination difficult.

The progress in regulation however has been limited as the state organizations and the ministries which control them are reluctant to be exposed to a greater degree of transparency, accountability and fiduciary responsibility.

It must be emphasized that while formal structures and provisions are important, informal rules and practices may often result in adherence to their letter but not to their spirit. A poly-centric power-structure and public and media vigilance are often helpful in reducing the gap between the spirit and the letter of the regulation. But this requires a degree of political and societal maturity, and perhaps a cultural change. These are not easily achieved. This is the central dilemma and it also explains the often rather wide gap between goals on the one hand and actual governance and regulation practices on the other in most countries in the world, including Asia.

In conclusion, the analysis in this chapter suggests that strengthening the capacity of governance and regulation of provident and pension schemes should have much higher priority if the appropriate social safety nets in Asia are to be developed and sustained.

NOTES

1. Provident funds are essentially mandatory savings schemes, primarily for private sector employees. They are operational mainly in former British colonies such as India, Sri Lanka, Singapore, Malaysia and Hong Kong. Indonesia also has a national provident fund scheme.

Usually, such schemes do permit pre-retirement withdrawals; and provide lump sum payment (or at best withdrawal in few instalments) of accumulated balances at the withdrawal stage. They usually do not mandate annuities, and have no social risk pooling arrangements. They are thus not usually categorized as pension schemes or as social security schemes, though they are among the important instruments for financing retirement in some countries.

2. For an exposition of the agency theory, see Douma and Schreuder (2002); for application of agency theory to pension funds, see Yermo and Marossy (2001).

3. Well publicized cases of Enron, Worldcom and others suggest that even in well developed countries, corporate governance issues continue to pose challenges to regulators and policymakers.

4. In the OECD countries, serious efforts at occupational pension regulation have been in response to major episodes of fraud or mismanagement (Yermo and Marossy, 2001). Thus, in the UK, the responsibility of pension fund trustees was increased after pension plans of the Maxwell Group engaged in lending pension funds to group companies. The UK has set up Pension Protection Fund (PPF), an insurance scheme, to protect beneficiaries of occupational pension plans. Shortfalls in PPF funding needs are likely to involve state support. The ERISA law of 1974 in the US was also in response to fraud, mismanagement, and insolvency of plan sponsors.

5. While the two are inter-linked, there are important differences between the two as discussed elsewhere in the chapter.

6. Legal systems in some of the Asian countries (for example former British colonies such as India, Sri Lanka, Malaysia and Singapore) are based on common law practices. This is also the case for those countries (such as the Philippines) who have adopted legal systems from the United States. It is the Anglo-Saxon countries where fiduciary responsibility and the notion of trustees of provident and pension funds which is most prevalent. Countries influenced by French traditions (such as Indonesia and Vietnam) are known as civil code countries. In these countries, the term custodian is used instead of trustees. While the international literature on governance and regulation of provident and pension funds are heavily influenced by the Anglo-Saxon tradition, good (or bad) governance and regulation practices can be found in both traditions. This chapter uses terminology derived from the Anglo-Saxon tradition.

7. While it is recognized that there are important differences among provident and pension schemes, social security, and social safety nets, for the purpose of this chapter these are used interchangeably.

8. Individual ageing refers to longer life expectancy of individuals, while population ageing refers to an increase in the proportion of elderly in the population. Two are obviously inter-connected. But as the pension and health-financing implications of increasing life expectancy have important policy and regulatory aspects, the two are separated here.

9. For argument along these lines for China, see Pei (2005); for India, see Asher and Vasudevan (2005) and Shah (2005).

10. In some countries such as Malaysia and Singapore, national provident fund assets are already high. Thus, in 2003, Malaysia's Employees Provident Fund (EPF) balances were 60 per cent of its GDP, while the corresponding proportion for Singapore's Central Provident Fund (CPF) was 65 per cent. In most other Asian countries, the corresponding proportions range from 10 to 20 per cent (Asher and Nandy 2005; Asher and Vasudevan 2005; Pei 2005).

11. Malaysia's Employees Provident Fund (EPF) has taken the lead in forming an association to represent interests of minority shareholders in the country. Other national provident and pension funds may also consider forming similar associations in their countries.

12. This is exacerbated by the findings from the behavioural finance literature which suggests a need to 'distance ourselves from the presumption that financial markets always work well and that price changes always reflect genuine information' (Shiller 2003).

13. In some Asian countries, such as Indonesia and Sri Lanka, the national provident fund organizations are required to pay corporate income taxes just as any other business enterprise. But these are exceptions.

14. Details concerning governance and investment guidelines for Canada Pension Plan (CPP) can be found at: http://www.sdc.gc.ca/en/isp/cpp/ cpptoc.shtml
15. In some countries (such as India) insurance regulator has been advocated as compared with a specialized insurance regulator. But increased life expectancy impacts on life insurance costs and annuity costs in opposite manner, with the cost of the former declining, while the annuity cost increasing significantly. Life insurance companies are usually the annuity providers, but there are other ways to cover longevity risk (that is the risk that a person may find accumulated assets depleted before dying), and inflation risk (that is sustaining real value of the pension) in the payout phase. The scope of pension regulators is fairly broad, potentially involving hundreds of pension plan sponsors, including other governmental agencies. In contrast, the number of life insurance companies is likely to be relatively few. The debate in India has been resolved in favour of a separate pension regulator under the Pension Fund Regulatory and Development Authority (PFRDA).
16. Usually, a regulator will require those giving financial advice to pass appropriate examinations at regular intervals.

REFERENCES

Asher, M. G. and A. Nandy (2005) 'Social Security Policy in an Era of Globalisation and Competition: Challenges for Southeast Asia', paper presented at Institute of Defence and Strategic Studies (IDSS) workshop on 'Southeast Asia in the global economy: avoiding the problem of globalisation's "missing middle"', Singapore, November 10–11.

Asher, M. G. and D. Vasudevan (2005) 'Role of Pension Regulator', eSocialSciences Electronic Journal, www.esocialsciences.com.

Carmichael, M. and R. Palacios (2003) 'A Framework for Public Pension Fund Management', in A. R. Musalem and R. J. Palacios (eds) *Public Pension Fund Management: Governance, Accountability, and Investment Policies, Proceedings of the Second Public Pension Fund Management Conference, May 2003*, Washington, DC: World Bank.

Catalán, M. (2004) 'Pension Funds and Corporate Governance in Developing Countries: What do We Know and what do We Need to Know?', *Journal of Pension Economics and Finance*, 3, 197–232.

Chakraborti, R. D. (2004) *The Greying of India: Population Ageing in the Context of Asia*, New Delhi: Sage Publications.

Douma, S. and H. Schreuder (2002) *Economic Approaches to Organizations*, 3rd edition, Upper Saddle River, NJ: Prentice Hall.

Galer, R. (2002) 'Pension Fund Investment: Regulation of Pension Asset Management', OECD/INPRS/Korea Conference on Private Pensions in Asia, Seoul, 24–25 October.

Gill, I., T. Packard, and J. Yermo (2005) *Keeping the Promise of Social Security in Latin America*, Washington, DC: The World Bank.

Government of India (2005) The Pension Fund Regulatory and Development Authority Bill, 2005, Bill No. 36 of 2005.

Guerard, Y. (2005) 'Managing the Assets of Social Security Schemes', Presented at Workshop on Social Security Policies organized by Policy Implementation Assistant Project of Canada, Halong, Vietnam, 25–27 April, 2005.

Hess, D. and G. Impavido (2003) 'Governance of Public Pension Funds: Lessons from Corporate Governance and International Evidence', in A. R. Musalem and R. J. Palacios (eds), *Public Pension Fund Management: Governance, Accountability, and*

Investment Policies, Proceedings of the Second Public Pension Fund Management Conference, May 2003, Washington, DC: World Bank.

Organization for Economic Co-operation and Development (OECD) (2004) 'OECD Recommendation on Core Principles of Occupational Pension Regulation', Paris: OECD Secretariat, July.

Organization for Economic Co-operation and Development (OECD) (2002), 'Guidelines for Pension Fund Governance', Paris: OECD Secretariat, July.

Palacios, R. (2003) 'Pension Reform in Latin America: Design and Experience', in *Pension Reforms: Results and Challenges*, Santiago: International Federation of Pension Fund Administrators, pp. 13–122.

Pei, M. (2005) 'Rebuilding China's Social Safety Net: Why Governance Matters', Paper presented at the Conference on Managing Globalization: Lessons from China and India, Singapore, 4–6 April.

Ross, S. G. (2000) 'Building Pension Institutions: Administrative Issues', Paper presented at The Third APEC Regional Forum on Pension Fund Reform, Bangkok, 30–31 March.

Shah, A. (2005) 'A Sustainable and Scalable Approach to Indian Pension Reforms', Paper presented at the Conference on Managing Globalization: Lessons from China and India, Singapore, 4–6 April.

Shiller, R. J. (2003) 'From Efficient Markets Theory to Behavioral Finance', *The Journal of Economic Perspectives*, **17** (1), 83–104.

Thillainathan, R. (2004) 'Malaysia: Pension and Financial Market Reforms and Key Issues on Governance', Paper presented at International Conference on Pensions in Asia: Incentives, Compliance, and Their Role in Retirement, Tokyo, 23–24 February.

World Health Organization (2004) *The World Health Report 2004: Changing History*, Geneva: World Health Organization.

Yermo, J. and A. Marossy (2001) *Insurance and Private Pensions Compendium for Emerging Economies* (Book 2, Part 1:4 b), Paris: OECD, www.oecd.org/daf/insurance-pensions/.

9. Regulation and deregulation of the stock market in India

Ashima Goyal

INTRODUCTION

With internationalization, and the entry of new entities, government controls become ineffective. The deregulation movement of the 1980s sought to make regulatory structures for capital markets similar across emerging market economies (EMEs) in order to encourage capital movements yet minimize regulatory arbitrage. But the East Asian currency and banking crises of 1997 pointed to inadequacies in regulation.

Deregulation turns out to require reregulation or a smarter regulation that would create incentives for self-regulation. In fast moving and interlinked markets regulators do not have the information or clout to impose the earlier quantitative controls. Capital markets provide effective intermediation of savings, allocation of investment, price discovery, pricing and hedging of risk; but they are subject to information imperfections, excess volatility and market manipulation. Therefore intervention is required to protect investors, increase market transparency and reduce systemic risk. Rigid controls hamper beneficial functions of markets, but a hands-off policy makes market abuse possible. Since, even in developed markets, healthy innovation can easily shade into illegal arbitrage, regulators have a hard time keeping up. EMEs have more problems because of the dominance of insiders, of relationship lending, and a weak rule of law. There are fears of regulatory capture. Stringent investor protection is required to encourage wider retail participation in markets. Technological developments, however, offer the opportunity to create better-designed regulatory institutions and modern automated capital markets that can compensate for other weaknesses.

Successful regulation follows general principles adapted to the specific market and context; this gives it the flexibility to work with the market and respond to changing particulars. The regulator has to be something like a policeman, but a smart one, who preserves market integrity through clear and self-enforcing rules of the game while encouraging the game itself. Efficient markets with low transaction costs improve incentives and broaden participation; transparency and better monitoring makes it easier to catch deviations. Both features encourage self-regulation over detailed government intervention.

The Indian liberalization, reform of capital markets and setting up of a new regulator, Securities Exchange Board of India (Sebi), in the 1990s, illustrates this process. India had the advantage of being able to use cutting-edge technology, which facilitated rapid reform in market microstructure and in regulatory norms. Thus technology and better governance worked together. Since reregulation proceeded along with deregulation, and some protective capital controls were retained, major inter-sectoral spillovers were avoided. Problems remain – financial services are still not at the required level, market participation is shallow, large institutions dominate, and there are complaints about the consistency of punitive actions. Even so, inadequacies that are blamed on norms of behaviour were actually a response to market structure and incentives, and are changing with these. Insiders lost power as the old-style committee-based governance of stock exchanges broke down, and anonymous electronic trading systems were established.

After discussing the basic principles of regulation we extend them to the special requirements of capital markets in the context of an EME; Sebi's functioning is then used to illustrate how the principles influenced the specific types of deregulation and reregulation that occurred in the Indian capital markets.

PRINCIPLES OF REGULATION

General

Regulation can be defined as government intervention in markets to influence those decisions of private agents that would otherwise not fully consider public interest. Intervention is justified by market failure due to monopoly or market power, asymmetric or imperfect information, and the existence of externalities or of public goods (Lee 2003). All three categories of market failure occur in financial markets, and we will examine their implications one by one.

The above definitions derived from welfare economics are a subset of the public interest theory of regulation, which is broader than the concept normally used in economics. In judicial review the concern is to solve disputes according to 'certain "values" such as (a) protecting citizens from unfair treatment (e.g. due process); (b) enforcing state's police power; and (c) controlling government's power' (Hantke-Domas 2003: 187). Early reliance was on private litigation to correct social wrongs. Regulation was a later development.[1] A judicial retreat occurred since the judiciary did not want to intervene unless the regulator exceeded its mandate, although the former could still be called in to determine the public interest in case of a dispute between the regulator and the regulated.

Glaeser and Shleifer (2003) in considering protection of the public from damages due to the activities of firms, argue that whether a society chooses private litigation or regulation or a combination of the two as a law enforcement strategy, private individuals will try to subvert the processes for private gain. The vulnerability of each of these categories to subversion varies with the level of development and inequality in a society, and this can help to explain the evolution across the categories. In developing economies, where there is extreme vulnerability of law enforcement to influence, absence of legal or regulatory institutions may be more appropriate, in contrast to the standard argument for the heaviest government intervention when market failures are relatively more. Under intermediate law and order regimes, a combination of regulation of inputs and litigation may be efficient since regulation may be less vulnerable to subversion than is litigation.[2] Finally, when the system of justice is least vulnerable to subversion, a litigation regime with either a strict liability or a negligence standard would outperform regulation.

The theory of regulatory capture, where regulatory agencies come to represent special interests,[3] contrasts with the public interest theory. It makes a case for deregulation or for better-designed regulation. For example, firms may seek government regulation in order to restrain competition from technologically superior rivals. Moreover, the transaction costs of regulation may be high, or regulatory agencies may be mismanaged. Human capital or information on the public's requirements may be poor. Posner (1974) found evidence that regulation had socially undesirable effects, which benefited groups who had influenced the enactment of regulatory legislation.

Public interest is sometimes used to hide group interests
Before the 1970s, industrial regulation was influenced by the Harvard School Structure-Conduct-Performance (SCP) paradigm in which regulation aimed to prevent the high industry concentration that was thought to lead to high profits. Policy aimed at lowering concentration and preventing mergers. But the Chicago School pointed out that high profit may be due to a fall in costs, which benefits consumers. It is efficient firms, which grow larger; profits may fall over time. All firms try to make profits; perfect competition with zero profits is actually never found. The focus should therefore be on the firms' action and incentives from regulations. Making profits is acceptable as long as firms are innovating and improving efficiency. In contrast to the SCP paradigm, conduct affects structure. Regulators should aim to encourage efficiency, and only prevent price or anti-entry collusion. The transaction costs

perspective adds that the tendency towards opportunism should be minimized keeping in mind that vertical integration may be necessary to save transaction costs under asset specificity. The Austrian School emphasizes that dynamic monopoly profits may be necessary for innovation. Waves of creative destruction destroy these in time. These perspectives on preventing collusion, encouraging entry and innovation are particularly relevant for the regulation of financial markets.

In Capital Markets

The basic principles of regulation combined with the special features of capital markets, indicate the major issues for regulation in capital markets. In Asian EMEs regulation has the added task of compensating for other weaknesses. La Porta *et al*. (1998) have argued that a common law tradition is necessary for healthy equity markets. But, for example, China can set up a good regulatory institution faster than it can acquire common law.[4] And, as Glaeser and Shleifer (2002) argue, many Asian EMEs may be in the range where regulation may be more effective compared with law. Moreover, standard setting organizations such as IOSCO (International Organization of Securities Commissions), and learning from each other, can help Asian EMEs converge to best practices. IOSCO's stance is that adoption of international standards and accounting systems will help to deepen shallow debt and equity markets, changing the historical reliance on banks.[5] But special features of Asian capital markets require attention. IOSCO has an Asia Pacific Review Committee (APRC), which should take the lead in matching regulatory practices to Asian requirements. Only a small percentage of large household savings are held in stocks. The history of bank led relationship-lending leads to the dominance of insiders; there is a tendency to accommodate and adjust rather than punish behaviour on the margin of illegality. In the Chinese stock exchange there are a large number of non-traded shares mostly owned by the State, with insider trading dominating in the thin set of shares actively traded. These features imply limited protection for investors. Better investor protection can reassure households, but other positive measures are also required.

Financial regulation serves the public interest if it ensures that finance meets the needs of the real economy, through efficient intermediation of savings, price discovery, allocation of investment, and the pricing and hedging of risk. Informational imperfections are inherent in financial markets. Therefore enhancing the revelation of information and preventing the misuse of asymmetric or insider information is the most basic task of a financial regulator.

Asymmetric information, which is pervasive in financial markets, creates deep frictions and imperfections (Wilhelm 2001). For example, borrowers know more about their own credit risks than lenders do, leading to adverse selection (as borrowers select transaction terms that favour them), and under-provision of credit by lenders. Moral hazard may also occur with borrowers undertaking riskier actions than the lender had agreed to in the loan terms. Issuers of equity know more than institutional investors, each of whom has a heterogeneous information set. Retail investors have the greatest relative information disadvantage. Regulatory agencies add value by reducing these disadvantages, through measures such as transparency, disclosure of price sensitive information and conflicts of interest, and encouraging organizational forms that reduce or offer protection from these hazards.

In European jurisdictions disclosure of price sensitive information is mandated as a general principle, not as a response to specific events as was the case in the US. The Sarbanes-Oxley Act passed after the wave of corporate and securities scandals, has changed the US in this respect (Spaventa 2003). The scandals revealed regulatory gaps such as insufficient enforcement of disclosure requirements, excessive reliance on peer review for auditors, and inability to keep brokerage and investment banking activities separate. Brokerage firms took fees for offering a preferred list of firms.[6] Under diffuse shareholding and independent managers, as prevail in the US, the information asymmetries between the principal and their agent become acute and require active regulatory intervention. Under concentrated European shareholding, additional measures are required to protect minority shareholders, such as rights to appoint directors, and checks on preferential allotment and promoter holdings.

Externalities are widespread in finance because of inherent network effects, where the value to any one individual rises with the number participating, leading to effects such a rapid tipping to a particular product or institution, or a lock-in into it, so that it becomes difficult to switch products. Such externalities, where individuals follow each other rather than fundamentals also partly explain the tendency towards excess volatility, the drying up of liquidity, and wide swings in stock prices. Therefore reducing volatility, the pro-cyclicality of returns, and mitigating systematic risk, become major tasks for the regulator.

Information is costly to produce but new technology is making it cheap to reproduce. This creates an externality leading to the underproduction of information. Stock market crashes can also be understood as an externality, since wider participation or high liquidity implies that the costs of price discovery or information production are shared. But during a crisis each participant has an incentive to withdraw and let others bear the burden of price discovery. To reduce such shirking, the regulator should charge access fees that rise with each trader's demand for liquidity and are higher in times when liquidity is scarce (Wilhelm 2001).

Changes in technology have had fundamental effects on each of these aspects, on the nature of financial markets, the possibility of regulation, and the organization of stock exchanges. The latter were always subject to network effects because of liquidity – the exchange with more liquidity could tip in customers and lock them in because of lower transaction costs. In the days of floor trading the advantage went to the greatest geographical clustering of financial intermediaries. But with ICT geographically dispersed intermediaries can provide liquidity. The exchange with the best technology will be able to attract the most customers.

This also leads to a change in the governance structure of exchanges. Earlier they functioned as a no-profit club of intermediaries that through a self-regulating system of committees, rule-making processes and voting mechanisms, distributed the rent among heterogeneous members. But this does not work with dispersed membership. Internationalization intensifies the latter. Moreover, profits help in improving technology, which is now the main avenue of competition. Therefore modern exchanges are organized as for profit corporations. But the network externalities explain why some of the older exchanges have been able to prevent the full use of technology, retain some features of the earlier exclusive clubs, preserve member rents, and yet retain users (Pirrong 2003).

For example, powerful market makers in US exchanges have been able to successfully resist fully automated execution capabilities and a centralized limit order book, which they believe would lower their profitability. Because of network externalities the New York Stock Exchange (NYSE) was able to offer the lowest price deals, even though execution was slower without full automation. America's security and exchange commission's (SEC) 'best-price' stock handling rules helped NYSE lock-in users. But after the wave of trading and governance scandals at NYSE, SEC is planning to level the playing field by allowing 'fast' automated markets that execute trades automatically to bypass a better price on a 'slow' exchange within some limits. This is likely to force NYSE to automate fully. In Germany, however, a fully automated futures market (EUREX) promoted by German banks, was eventually able to tip the trading in German government bonds away from the incumbent floor-based London International Financial Futures and Options Exchange (LIFFE). When banks are the major owners and brokers, they recognize that they can supply liquidity more efficiently on an automated market.

Since with new technology liquidity comes through numbers, there is no need for the earlier exclusivity. Entry for investors and intermediaries can be made easier. Under network externalities regulators have to consider dynamic aspects. Concessions may be required to make a market initially; they are not necessarily aimed at destroying competition. Policies that improve one's product need to be distinguished from those that block a competitor.

Monopoly or anti-competitive features arise through the network effects that dominate in the industry, and the formation of various insider groups or financial cartels. New technology driven exchanges will compete through innovation and try to maximize their profits in the typical ways of a network. There is a tension for the regulator between discouraging size and encouraging the innovation it sometimes makes more feasible.

Technology also allows improved real time but non-invasive monitoring. Laffont (2005) argues that poor monitoring in developing countries limits the power of incentives that regulators of public services can give service providers. But technology is changing this quickly, especially in stock markets, making it possible to give market participants more economic incentives in EMEs.

In financial services, technology allows the diffusion of information to be increasingly mechanized and taken over by large firms, while human capital is released for innovation. But although the ease of flow of information has increased, the governance structures that maintained an incentive for its flow have yet to change. Earlier exclusive yet transient groups such as investment bankers managing an issue served to reduce free riding, make reputations, and create and share rents. Differential information is also a source of trade in markets. But the areas in which such groups survive are shrinking, as technology takes over mechanized functions. Book building for a new issue continues to be one such area. Since the speed of diffusion of new ideas is much faster, new ways of profiting from them have to be discovered. Among these are financial patents and buying equity into implementations of new ideas (Wilhelm 2001). For example, in 1993 AMEX developed the idea of an exchange traded fund which tracked the value of a specified portfolio, but it was imitated so quickly that AMEX got low returns on the resources it had expended in developing the concept. In 1998 a US federal court upheld a patent on an accounting system; business-method patents came to be accepted leading to a flood of such patents.

In general, superior sales and service, lead-time and secrecy are more important to appropriate returns from innovation. Patents are used more for blocking and defensive purposes, except in pharmaceuticals (Hall 2002). Moreover, for a rise in competitive pressure to increase the speed of technological progress high knowledge-diffusion is required, because the follower has a higher incentive to innovate. With low diffusion, competition may even decrease innovation and growth (Encaoua and Hollander 2002). Therefore patents should be granted only when costs of development are very high compared with the cost of adoption; they then spur creativity. But patents should be avoided when many small sequential innovations lead to an invention; they would then raise legal and licensing fees too high and discourage creativity (Shiller 2003). And the regulator should encourage competitive pressures. There are sometimes simple measures available that encourage innovation. For example, reimbursement of costly medical procedures through health insurance encouraged their development and adoption (Jones 2003).

Regulatory arbitrage and financial innovations occur and are copied with such speed that the regulator often does not have enough information to act, or to discriminate between fine issues of legality.[7] The regulator should, therefore, ensure market integrity, set and implement strict norms, encourage disclosure and revelation of information, prevent conflicts of interest, and then avoid micromanaging.

SPECIAL FEATURES OF REGULATION IN THE INDIAN CONTEXT

Since the rate of financial innovation is high regulatory practices should retain flexibility, even at the cost of some regulatory uncertainty, as long as they satisfy general principles. Then they would be able to encourage market functions, while moderating market flaws. Regulatory practices also need to be attuned to country specific features. We turn next to see how far the Indian regulatory structure satisfies these conditions.[8]

SEBI: History, Objectives, Powers

Latecomers have the advantage of adopting best practices, but this is easiest done when a new institution is created. Changing old established institutions is difficult.

The Capital Issues (Control) Act 1947, administered by the Controller of Capital Issues (CCI), governed capital issues in India. As part of liberalizing reforms CCI was abolished and Sebi, set up in 1988, was made a statutory body in 1992. Its objectives, in line with public interest, are to protect the interests of investors, ensure the fairness, integrity and transparency of the securities market, and reach best international regulatory practices.[9] Sebi's tasks and powers, expanded over time, are to regulate stock and other securities markets, register and regulate all intermediaries associated with securities markets. Under the Sebi (Amendment) Bill 2002 its powers were expanded to cover all transactions associated with the securities market. In 2003 it was empowered to impose enhanced monetary penalties.

This flexibility was required to respond to market arbitrage, and to emerging requirements in the Indian context. There has been a constant attempt to improve regulatory practices and contribute to the ongoing capital market reforms. Once the policy decision had been taken to open out, reach

and exceed international standards and practices, the direction of change was
clear and Sebi contributed to progress along it. Continuous reregulation has
followed the initial deregulation.

Even so, these regulatory and market microstructure reforms were unable to
revive the stock markets over an extended period (see Table 9.1) from the mid-
1990s. Among the reasons were the periodic financial scams that deepened the
lack of confidence in the effectiveness of the regulator's monitoring,
surveillance and implementation of the new world class rules, the industrial
slowdown that persisted over 1997–2000, and shallow markets with a relative
neglect of the retail investor and domestic requirements. Even as market
capitalisation and stock indices revived with growth from 2003–2004 the
contribution to fresh private investment and savings was not commensurate.

No major insider scandal has occurred since the Ketan Parikh scam in
March, 2001. The Joint Parliamentary Committee (JPC) set up after the scam

Table 9.1　Capital market indicators

Year	Market capitalisation BSE, as percentage of GDP at market prices	New capital issues of non-government public limited companies as a percentage of GDP at market prices	BSE sensitive index, annual average	Shares and debentures as a percentage of household financial savings
1990–1	16.0	0.8	1049.5	8.4
1991–2	49.5	0.9	1879.5	10.0
1992–3	25.1	2.6	2895.7	10.3
1993–4	42.8	2.2	2898.7	9.2
1994–5	43.0	2.6	3974.9	9.3
1995–6	44.3	1.3	3288.7	7.1
1996–7	33.9	0.8	3469.3	4.2
1997–8	36.8	0.8	3812.9	2.6
1998–9	31.3	0.2	3294.8	2.5
1999–2000	47.1	0.3	4658.6	7.7
2000–01	27.4	0.3	4269.7	4.1
2001–2	26.8	0.3	3331.9	2.7
2002–3	23.2	0.3	3206.3	1.6
2003–4	43.3	0.1	4492.2	1.4

Source:　RBI Handbook of Indian Statistics and Annual Report (2004).

indicted the management of markets. In 2002 G. N. Bajpai took over as the new regulator and set a clear agenda to improve transparency, and corporate governance. Structural changes were introduced to shorten the settlement cycle, and improve margining and surveillance systems in accordance with the JPC recommendations. His predecessor, D. R. Mehta had moved slowly to allow market participants to learn and adapt,[10] but his regime was widely regarded as being too soft. Sharp 200–300 basis points swings in the Sensex, however, continue to occur after events such as budgets, regulatory announcements, PSU IPOs, elections. But these reverse quickly suggesting that only vestiges of insider manipulation remain, although markets are still shallow.

In the sections to follow we compare the major measures Sebi has undertaken to the regulatory principles identified.

Information, Externality, Excess Volatility, Incentives

Asymmetries and imperfections of information leave investors susceptible to cheating. They also cause participants to follow each other in swings that create excess volatility and externalities. So improving transparency of markets is a top regulatory priority. Moreover, better corporate governance can reduce asymmetries of information between management and shareholders, improve incentives for complying with rules, and reduce conflicts of interest.

Disclosure
Strict norms regarding disclosure of price sensitive information, and conflicts of interest, contribute to reducing asymmetries of information and aid the markets in price discovery. Companies issuing capital in the primary market are required to disclose the facts and specific risk factors associated with their projects; they should also give information on the procedure for the calculation of premium, but they can fix the premium. Sebi permitted companies to determine the par value of shares issued by them, and allowed issues of Initial Public Offers (IPOs) to go for 'Book-Building', that is get bids within an announced band to help discover market demands and price. Measures continue to be taken to improve transparency in markets. In 2003 the National Stock Exchange (NSE) prohibited any cash transaction. In 2004 Sebi asked brokers to reveal details of transactions involving more than 0.5 per cent of the listed shares of a company, and banned them from trading with each other on the same exchange.

Volatility
Price bands, complex value at risk (VaR) margining systems, circuit filters, exposure limits and suspension are all used to curb volatility. These allow

adjustment for risk to be individually specific and therefore less inefficient than a common margin, while achieving the desired result of putting concave boundaries on convex returns, thus reducing one-way price movements. Margins that vary with liquidity are required in response to the externalities that follow from herd behaviour in capital markets. Moreover, such margins reduce deposit requirements and therefore lower costs of trade. A daily mark-to-market margin system prevents large risks from building up, and lowers the possibility of a payments crisis.

Margin requirements were adjusted in response to episodes of volatility, implementation of the VaR based systems, and of rolling settlement. An index based market wide circuit breaker system can be applied at three stages of the index movement either way at 10 per cent, 15 per cent, 20 per cent, to bring about a co-ordinated trading halt to nationwide equity and equity derivative markets. These are required since VaR cannot cover systemic shocks; such a shock can force margin sales that intensify index movements.

Technology allows instant registration of price sensitive information and of financial results. Exchanges quickly check market rumours with company compliance officers. Market surveillance system and risk containment measures were set up in 1997–1998. There is an electronic stock watch system functional in most exchanges. In times of excess volatility, surveillance systems are put on high alert. Other measures are possible like shifting stocks to trade-for-trade category. Margin trading and stock lending and borrowing systems are to be introduced, as part of continuous market development, to make possible the physical settlement of derivative trades.

Since market participants earn fees from transactions the current system is biased towards high trading volumes. Physical settlement, which is the norm in international markets, is yet to be introduced for stock futures. Therefore a large share of the trading volume is not delivery based and raises volatility of share prices (Gupta 2005).

Corporate governance

Corporate governance (CG) is being tightened, and gradually extended to all companies. In 2000 Sebi specified principles of CG and introduced a new clause in the listing agreement of the stock exchanges. Statutory requirements now call for one-third of directors to be independent. They have to periodically review legal compliance reports and steps taken for any correction, and to reveal any non-fee-based pecuniary connection with the company, although the latter does not as yet automatically disqualify them as independent directors.

CG practices protect minority shareholder rights. In 2003 the Bombay High Court ruled that majority shareholders cannot ease out minority shareholders by paying them the value of their shares. Controlling shareholders are a threat to minority shareholders when ownership is concentrated. Divestment and higher floating stock will improve their position. But full disclosure and reserving seats on boards and audit committees for directors representing minority shareholders also protect their interest. These issues resonate in India because of the closely held PSUs, IT and family-based business houses.

Brancato (2002) lists measures adopted in Singapore and that could be emulated in India. Among these are nomination and remuneration committees for board members, so that they are fully independent of management; frequent board meetings and remuneration for work done to inform and motivate the board, and reliance on technical sub-committees for technical matters.

Conflicts of interest

In 2003 Sebi planned for new model bylaws for governance of stock exchanges. A separate entity would manage the surveillance and investigation functions of the stock exchanges or else the functions would be outsourced. The agency would be responsible for any misuse of the system. Stock exchanges would be empowered to impose penalties for failure to comply with any of the provisions of the listing agreement, subject to a limit of Rs 0.5 million for a specific violation and an overall limit of Rs 5 million in a financial year. These steps were expected to improve self-regulation of stock exchanges, define responsibility more clearly, remove conflicts of interest in policing members, and encourage clearer contracts, without deliberate or sloppy ambiguity.

Technology and Transactions Costs

Automation made many of the above improvements possible. Insiders lost power not only due to more transparency but also as the old club-style governance structure of the stock exchange changed. India used new technology effectively to reach and sometimes exceeded international benchmarks in disclosure norms, trading volume, settlement cycle and low transaction costs. In the order driven system, each investor can access the same market and order book, at the same price and cost, irrespective of location. Dematerialization of securities had been introduced to reduce bad paper risk. Settlement of trades in the depository is compulsory except for sales by small investors.

Political economy and governance

The rapid dominance of the Indian for-profit, fully automated NSE promoted by leading banks and financial institutions (mainly public sector), over the powerful traditional Bombay Stock Exchange (BSE), which was also forced to automate, and the collapse of all other small stock exchanges throughout the country, demonstrates the tipping equilibria discussed in section 3. The government ability to sponsor a new technology had a powerful effect in an industry with network effects. Moreover, technology affects the governance structure chosen. NSE is a company incorporated under the Companies Act (1956), and makes a profit. Unlike the other broker run exchanges the management is independent of the broker members. The official view is that this allows a fair, equitable and efficient market to develop, free of the conflict of interest experienced in broker run exchanges (NSE 2003), but our analysis suggests that governance structure follows from technology.

Insider groups generate rents as well an incentive to trade. There were arguments made against anonymity, that it was important to know the counterparty among heterogeneous participants. But these arguments lost force as technology made a tight system of deposits and margins feasible, and a clearing corporation, NSCCL, was created to absorb counterparty risk[11] and guarantee trades.

Badla, the old system of carry forward trade without delivery that was popular with brokers, was another contentious issue. Those for badla said that removing this would seriously hurt liquidity, those against that it was responsible for excess volatility and scams. But replacing it by modern forward and future derivatives was quite smooth. A phased programme of T+5 rolling settlement introduced in 2000, for eligible compulsorily dematerialized scrips with a daily turnover of above 1 crore, was expanded to cover more scrips having the facility of ALBM/BLESS (automated lending and borrowing mechanism) or MCFS (modified carry forward system) in any stock exchange. The settlement cycle was shortened smoothly to reach T+1 in 2004. Trading in future contracts based on BSE Sensex index and on S&PCNX nifty index began in June 2000, and exchange traded interest rate and currency derivative contracts were to follow.

FIIs

With new technology liquidity comes through numbers, barriers to entry can fall. Liberalization has encouraged entry not only from within the country but also from abroad. There has been constant procedural simplification to facilitate entry and exit of foreign institutional investors (FIIs) to the Indian capital market. FIIs have contributed to improved market analysis and volumes. FII Investment is allowed in any instrument, including commercial paper, subject to 70 per cent of their portfolio being in securities, with a limit of 5 per cent in the equity of any one company. The registration fee was reduced to $5000 and $1000 for a sub-account in 1995. Investments on behalf of other parties through sub-accounts are allowed provided the name of the investor is disclosed to the board, and the entity is regulated somewhere. In

2002 FIIs were allowed to hedge their entire exposure in Indian equities compared to the earlier level of 15 per cent. They could trade in derivatives subject to the prescribed position limit. By 2003 the number of FIIs exceeded 500, with over 1500 sub-accounts. Because of FII interest the Rupees 100 billion ONGC IPO in March 2004 was oversubscribed in 10 minutes.

Flexibility

A principles-based stance gives flexibility to adjust to emerging trends. An example is Sebi tightening the norms for private placement in 2003, after many firms began to use these, since the stock markets were in the doldrums. But the resulting absence of disclosure increased risk. Apart from the stick Sebi also offered the carrot of reduction in the cost of open offers. In 2004 all listed companies were required to have a minimum 25 per cent non-promoter holding, but since earlier companies had been allowed to list with less, they were given time to adjust. In 2005, following complaints that Sebi norms for public issues were too time consuming, steps were taken to simplify norms for follow on issues, and for companies with a good track record on disclosures. Other examples of flexibility in action are:

Exemptions
In 1998, Sebi exempted infrastructure firms from certain norms while floating public issue, since infrastructure is a public good. The minimum application size and the proportion of each issue allowed for assured allotment to institutions were raised when IPOs were doing poorly. Margin requirements were decreased before major PSU disinvestments in order to release funds for investment. Allocation to FIIs and high net worth individuals (HNIs) were decreased when it was feared that they were hammering down prices before the IPOs. Following complaints regarding high discretionary allotment to QIBs (qualified institutional buyers) in 2004 IPOs, Sebi was looking to reduce the discretionary power of issuers in public issues; preferential issues were available for those looking for quality investors.

Participatory notes
At the end of January 2004 the Sensex fell by nearly 500 points in three trading sessions after Sebi started seeking details of parties that had been investing through participatory notes (PNs) on the FII account. Under this route brokers buy and sell on behalf of a foreign client, often hedge funds, but instead of giving the shares issue PNs. In August 2003 FIIs had been asked to file fortnightly information on PNs, following the general principle of increasing transparency. Markets stabilized after Sebi clarified at the end of January that only 'regulated entities' could be issued PNs. Hedge funds were

allowed as long as they were regulated abroad,[12] and the identity of the actual investor revealed to the regulator in a know-your-client mapping process. If hedge funds came in through sub-accounts of FIIs they could be under Sebi's regulations. Hedge funds, which account for about 35 per cent of global flows, make money by moving quickly to benefit from arbitrage opportunities across markets. They hedge against market risk by going long on undervalued stocks and short on overvalued, and then use leverage to pick individual stocks and raise returns. Sebi wanted to ensure that Indian operators did not use NRIs and Overseas Corporate Bodies (OCBs) investments to manipulate the market. Ketan Parekh had used the Mauritius route and it had been banned after the stock market scam in 2001, but different categories of investors are welcome.

After the technology and principle related successes of regulation we turn to areas, such as building more confidence and attracting more participation, where performance could have been better and improvements are still required.

Retail Investors

Indian capital markets differ in that the retail investor has an independent role. In most countries the small investors come in only through mutual funds. In the late 1970s a large retail investor base was created when multinationals had to issue shares to Indian investors as part of the FERA dilution of share holdings. But small investors incurred losses due to fluctuations and scams in stock markets. Household investor surveys show that the retail investor base has been shrinking[13] since 1997, due to fear of insiders. Thus even the 2003 boom in stock markets was largely driven by FIIs and many domestic investors used the opportunity to liquidate their holdings and exit the stock markets. Mutual funds have also not been able to attract small investors. Table 9.1 shows the drastic fall in household savings going into the stock markets.

But huge potential numbers make a low margin–high volume a viable business model in India. Attracting retail investors would also lend stability to the markets since they tend to follow a buy and hold strategy. Therefore measures to build up investor confidence are required, systemic features that discourage them have to be removed, and positive incentives offered. A positive feature is the appreciable growth in depository accounts even in small towns and rural areas.

The Maruti IPO in June 2003 showed that the retail investor was still interested in good companies. The issue was oversubscribed 13 times and 3 lakh retail investors responded to it even though the share price was decided by bidding. All three stakeholders gained from the process and by January the share price had appreciated to Rs 380 compared with the issue price later fixed at Rs 125. Sale in 70 cities, with help from Maruti dealers in the sales of shares, contributed to the success of the issue. Large public sector undertakings (PSUs) IPOs of Rs 160 billion that followed in March 2004 were also oversubscribed by retail investors alone, even though they were given only a small discount.

But the allotment to the retail investor was small, partly because the discretionary quota allowed to merchant bankers went to large investors. The rationale for this discretion was to allow selection of quality investors who would contribute to making markets. After complaints, Sebi discontinued the discretion in favour of proportionate allotment. This continued its steady reforms to make markets more accessible for the retail investor. It had earlier hiked the small investor quota from 25 per cent to 35 per cent. The definition of the small investor was changed from those applying for up to Rs 50 000 worth of shares compared to the earlier one of 1000 shares. Exchanges were allowed to lower the number of shares in the market lot for derivative trade in order to bring the contract size down to Rs 2 lakh. Price appreciation had raised the value of the minimum contract far above that for some companies and made margins unaffordable for the small player. Sebi recommended in January 2004, that the small investor should not be charged demat account maintenance and dematerialization of shares; instead an *ad valorem* charge could be put on each transaction. They should not be charged on moving their demat account from one depository participant (DPs) to another but only on going out of the demat environment. Excessive charges DPs levy on various heads should be rationalized. These added up to high overheads that had discouraged the small investor's participation in share markets.

Part of the problem was that companies were not investing; they were cash-rich, and able to borrow abroad at low interest rates. As share markets boomed, and investment rose, there was a rise in IPOs over 2004 and 2005. The stringent norms Sebi had painstakingly put in place over the years facilitated these, but it was clear that primary markets had to be further improved.[14]

Monitoring and Surveillance

Deregulation or moving away from government controls on allocation decisions and giving more economic incentives to market participants depends on strong non-invasive monitoring, surveillance and punitive actions to prevent deviations from the rules of the game. Technology has allowed great improvements in surveillance so that Laffont's (2005) argument that monitoring is poor in developing countries does not hold for the stock market, but implementing of rules is still perceived to be imperfect and inconsistent.[15] Primary responsibility for implementation lies with the exchanges, with oversight by Sebi. Retail investors are still concerned about management frauds and lack of transparency, price manipulation and volatility (NSE 2003), although Sebi's reforms in 2001 have improved matters. Insider dominance and market manipulation becomes less feasible as the number of constituents and their geographical dispersion increases, and structural improvements reduce the power of remaining groups.

Implementation of regulations

Consistency in punitive actions is essential for effective regulation. This stick has to be fairly used, along with the carrot of more efficiency and incentives. Actions Sebi takes are largely under Regulation 11, Prohibition of Fraudulent and Unfair Trade Practices Relating to Securities Markets, and Regulation 13 (4) Procedure for Holding Enquiry and Imposing Penalties. An enquiry officer is appointed after investigations, adjudication proceedings are initiated against those against whom evidence is found, then a show cause notice is issued and order passed, which can be appealed at the Securities Appellate Tribunal (SAT), set up in 1997. It has taken up to two years to settle a case, and the conviction rate is poor;[16] some of Sebi's orders have been struck down or diluted by SAT. The award of the Tribunal can be challenged in higher courts under section 15Z of the Sebi Act if rights of the parties are affected, and in the Supreme Court only if matters of law are involved.

After the report of the JPC, the number of cases taken up shows a sharp jump in 2001–2002, and completion of cases shows a similar jump the next year (Table 9.2). Prosecutions launched against collective investment schemes over 2001–2003 were 250 compared with only two in the earlier years. Actions taken against brokers and others also jump up the same year (Table 9.3 and 9.4).[17] For example, in 1997–8, out of 9000 brokers registered only 157 were inspected. Out of 65 enquiries ordered, 52 were only warned and eight were suspended. There is public disclosure of actions taken against brokers. Sebi's record in grievances-redressal improved after 1998 (Table 9.5). It became much more aggressive.

The fines Sebi used to charge were very small compared with the amounts involved. In general penalties were to be proportional to the damage inflicted. The Bhagwati Committee on takeovers (1997) had argued strongly for stringent and speedy penalties as effective deterrents and recommended that the 'Sebi Act be amended to expand the scope of adjudication and levy of monetary penalties; increase the amount of monetary penalties to make the penalties meaningful'. To reduce delays, Sebi was exploring, in 2005, the possibility of having bands of punishment for different offences, to allow entities to pay a fine to settle cases without admitting guilt. Plea-bargaining was being considered.

An amendment in 2003 did enhance penalties. An adjudicating officer can now impose stiff penalties ranging from Rs 5000 daily to a total amount of Rs 10 lakhs, to be credited to the Consolidated Fund of India. The Sebi penalty of

Table 9.2 Investigations by Sebi

Particulars	1992–3	1993–4	1994–5	1995–6	1996–7	1997–8	1998–9	1999–2000	2000–2001	2001–2	2002–3	Total
Cases taken up for investigation	2	3	2	60	122	53	55	56	68	111*	125	657
Cases completed	2	3	2	18	55	46	60	57	46	21	106	424

Note: * of these 111 cases 86 involved market manipulation and price rigging, 16 insider trading.

Source: Sebi (2003) Table 2.71.

Table 9.3 Actions taken by Sebi

Particulars	No. of cases 1997–8	1998–9	1999–2000	2000–2001	2001–2	2002–3
Cancellation	2		4	1	1	11
Suspension	39	16	30	4	8	42
Warning issued	9	17	28	9	36	62
Prohibitive directions issued under section 11B of Sebi act	10	62	58	21	98	140
Issues refunded/options given	3		1	4		2
Impound of auction/close out proceeds (Rs.6 crore)	12					
Total	75	97	121	39	143	257

Source: Sebi (2003) Tables 2.48, 2.49, 2.52, 2.76, Table 11.20 in Annual Report 1997–8, other reports.

Table 9.4   Actions taken against brokers and sub-brokers

	2002–3	2001–2	2000–2001	1999–2000	1998–99	1997–8
Cases where Enquiry Officer has been appointed						
Brokers	158	136	21	39	65	34
Sub-brokers	13	13	1	1	–	–
Cases where enquiry proceedings have been completed						
Brokers	41	80	12	65	7	76
Sub-brokers	5	8	–	–	–	–

Source: Sebi (2003) Tables 2.50, 2.51, 2.74, 2.75, other reports.

Table 9.5   Sebi: redressal of grievances

Financial year	Grievances (received)	Grievances (resolved)	Redressal rate (per cent)
End March			
1991–2	18 794	4061	21.61
1992–3	129 111	27 007	20.92
1993–4	713 773	366 524	51.35
1994–5	1 229 853	718 366	58.41
1995–6	1 606 331	1 034 018	64.37
1996–7	1 823 725	1 465 883	80.38
1997–8	2 335 232	2 142 438	91.74
1998–9	2 434 364	2 269 665	93.24
1999–2000	2 532 969	2 416 218	95.39
2000–2001	2 629 882	2 501 801	95.13
2001–2	2 711 482	2 572 129	94.86
2002–3	2 748 916	2 611 101	94.99

Source: Sebi (2003).

up to three times the profit made, fines and up to three years in prison compares with the stiffer fines and prison sentences of up to 21 years in Singapore and Malaysia. Nageshwaran and Krithivasan (2004) argue that only Singapore, Hong Kong and India are effective in enforcement among Asian countries. Indeed Sebi's current record compares well with Malaysia where in 2002 out of a total of 775 cases (including backlogged) 165 were completed and disciplinary action taken against only 16 (see Tables 9.4 and 9.5). The number of future cases may actually fall if penalties are effective deterrents.

Stiffer penalties, together with the rise in cases initiated and completed, can curb insiders' malpractices if regulators are upright. Penalties work better than bans which either cause extreme hardship or can be avoided using some other participant as a front. A combination of non-discretionary regulation of inputs such as in the automatic computer generated deduction of margin violations from deposits with stiff penalties plus an appeal structure in more complicated cases, where judgment is involved, should both serve as a deterrent and prevent abuse of power.[18]

In order to prevent corrupt regulators from harassing an innocent participant court fees should remain much lower than the fines imposed. Prior to the recent changes, fees to be paid for an appeal to SAT against a penalty were Rs 500 if the penalty was less than Rs 10000, and were Rs 1200 for a penalty above 10000 and less than Rs 100000. If a corrupt enquiry officer threatens a law abiding participant, and the penalty is below the appeal fee plus the time cost of appealing, the participant would prefer to pay a bribe. Thus innocent participants could be harassed and corruption set in. Court fees set an upper limit to such harassment threats. Of course, it is possible that even the appellate judiciary is corruptible because of large inequalities and wealthy market players.

Effective checks are required to prevent regulatory abuse, neglect of public interest, and capture. Haldea (2004) argues for an overarching law to regulate all regulators. A continuing problem is the low government salaries paid to regulators and the non-transparent government appointments, based on political favour. Payment should be adjusted to skills and not past salaries, in order to attract skills, retain them against competition from the higher private sector salaries, and reduce corruptibility. Kane (2002) suggests incentive-based deferred compensation to align regulators' incentives and maximize long-run net social benefits. He argues that a forfeitable fund together with provisions for measuring, verifying, and rewarding multi-period performance would make top regulators accountable. In Glaeser and Shleifer's (2003) framework, a rise in the regulators' skills and pay will reduce the likelihood of subversion, since its cost would rise.

Finally, there is the third case of regulatory capture, where the regulator and the insider are both corrupt and collude. Ways to counter this are transparency, investor, press and public activism. There is a transparent reporting of the cases on the Sebi website, and India's democratic economic press is active, but investor activism needs to be further developed.

Investor activism
Investor awareness and activism can be effective to ensure regulatory effort and uprightness. The Securities Investor Association of Singapore (SIAS) set up in 1999 actively pushes for market improvements. In India the Investor

Education and Protection Fund was set up in October 2001, but funds available are not actively utilized. There is scope for learning from other countries.

Innovations and Other Improvements

Depth of markets, width of instruments and participation rates should improve as growth firms up and capital markets revive. But space has to be actively made for the small investor in order to help bring household savings back to the securities markets (see Table 9.1). There is disappointment that mutual funds have not delivered on this, and they are being pushed to innovate more. Allocation of market funds to small firms has to improve for more effective intermediation of savings; measures such as encouraging analyst research on small firms, venture capital for initial financing and enabling its exit through over-the-counter exchanges (OTCEI) are required (Nageswaran and Krithivasan 2004). The OTCEI, which is not automated, offers more customized products and works through market makers, is yet to take off in a big way. Most innovations have been technology based and have been initiated by the government. Although there is a beginning in private innovations,[19] considering the depth of human capital available in this sector in India, much more should be done. Business method patents, in cases where products are not inputs in other products, may help.

A continuing problem is the unclear demarcation of responsibility between regulators. Although all publicly traded market instruments come under Sebi's jurisdiction, the Department of Company Affairs is also responsible for debentures after the Companies (Amendment) Act instituted a number of tighter provisions. Implementation suffers because of poor co-ordination among regulators. Some regulatory consolidation is required.

In order to prevent regulatory arbitrage, and facilitate ease of movement of capital it is important that Asian countries learn from each other. Sebi had signed an MOU on mutual co-operation, consultation and provision of technical assistance with the US SEC in 1998 and the monetary authority of Singapore on 14 October 2000. Asian EMEs can benefit from India's experience in implementing new technologies, and India can learn effective organizational structures, for example effective corporate governance structures.

CONCLUSION

The chapter has enumerated the plusses and minuses of regulation in the context of capital market development in India – the many achievements and further potential improvements. Principal based capital market regulation has been able to flexibly evolve with markets in India. Deregulation of government controls was accompanied by continuous reregulation, which allowed more economic freedoms and incentives but enforced strict rules and more transparency. Scams occurred in the transition period, but since some controls were retained, the scams did not spill over into other sectors. For example, capital controls helped Indian markets escape contagion from the 1997 East Asian crises.

With respect to technology, automation, disclosure, risk containment and reduction in transaction costs, Indian bourses have outperformed those in developed countries. Lacunae arose perhaps because the initial focus on international standards led to a neglect of the special features of Asian markets. More participation, depth in instruments, and financial innovation is required. Innovations are necessary to draw in the retail investor, the small firm and start-ups. This should happen with a revival of growth, better implementation of regulations, and adjustment in procedures to encourage the small investor. Principle based flexibility has allowed Sebi to respond not only to financial arbitrage but also to local requirements.

The chapter brings out gaps between perception and reality. Because of a history of speculation in thin markets, there is a misperception that insider dominance is a feature of Indian capital markets. But it turns out to be a feature of open outcry and geographically concentrated capital markets. Technology and the geographical dispersion it brings about decreases their power. The latter has happened in India while it is still resisted in more developed countries. Once the government decided to back new technology these forces tipped trade in favour of modern systems. A rapid change became possible in Indian securities markets, without a change in the general level of legal and institutional development.

Imperfections in monitoring and surveillance were also due not so much to insider collusion as to imperfections in the structure of incentives and penalties. Design improvements are possible and are ongoing, as they are elsewhere in the world. The 'miasma of corruption' from which markets are said to suffer is system specific and not inevitable. As growth revives and markets become more active, the tight norms established and the deep steady capital market reforms, to which Sebi has contributed, seem to be paying off.

ACKNOWLEDGEMENTS

The chapter gained from presentations at the Regulation Conference of the Public Policy Programme, National University of Singapore, March 2004, and at Claremont McKenna College, USA. I thank the audience especially M. Ramesh for comments, and also D. R Mehta, R. H. Patil, Anupam Rastogi, Ajay Shah, Susan Thomas and other participants of the annual Money and Finance Conference at IGIDR for discussions on Indian capital markets that contributed to my interest in this topic. Ankita Agarwal provided cheerful research assistance and T. S. Ananthi excellent secretarial assistance.

NOTES

1. In the US, reformers established state regulatory agencies in the progressive era (between 1887 and 1917).
2. In the progressive era of the US courts could not stand up to the large corporations or 'robber barons'. When law and order is weak, and inequality is high, private litigation based pure liability regimes, which entail large payments with small probability, are more vulnerable to ex-post subversion than is the regulation of inputs. This explains the evolution of regulation.
3. Public interest can also be subverted if the judiciary itself is corruptible or lacks a clear understanding of economic principles.
4. See www.csrc.gov.cn, the website of the Chinese Securities Regulatory Commission. The slogan the CSRC has adopted is 'Investor protection is our top priority'.
5. See its website at www.iosco.org
6. There were a series of scandals involving the US mutual-fund industry. For example, Morgan Stanley had failed to inform investors of the compensation it received for selling certain funds. As a result the SEC has proposed reforms forcing the disclosure of fees, expenses and any conflicts of interest to investors, and filing of quarterly reports. It also wants financial intermediaries to place trading orders before the stock market closes, more independent fund boards and clearer statements of funds' policies on other disputed trading practices.
7. Miller (1986) points out that tax laws have often functioned as the bit of sand in the oyster producing the pearl of financial innovation.
8. The sections below draw upon Sebi annual reports, NSE capital markets reviews, Sebi press releases available at www.Sebi.gov.in., press reports and conversations with participants. Shah and Thomas (1997) survey the early phase of Indian capital market reforms.
9. Sebi's vision statement put up on its website is for 'Sebi to be the most dynamic and respected regulator globally'. It is a member of IOSCO and committed to reaching compliance standards for different markets, disclosure norms and capital adequacy.
10. This remark was made at the inaugural lecture at the IGIDR Money and Finance Conference in 2000. M. Damodaran who followed Bajpai announced that his priorities were to improve transactional efficiency, simplify regulations, improve participation, and reduce inactive scrips.
11. The dominant view is that NSE took Indian capital markets kicking and screaming into the modern age. But it was technology, and the policy decision to adopt the most modern technology, that did so. After the initial protests markets realised its advantages quite rapidly. R. H. Patil, the founder director of NSE, recounted, at a 2004 IGIDR dinner talk, the exciting story of how a clear vision to implement a virtual market won out.
12. US SEC had released proposed rules for hedge funds in September 2003, after corporate and financial scandals. Fund managers now have to register with SEC and funds must allow scrutiny of their books. But there is still no unanimity on hedge fund regulation.
13. The Sebi-NCAER survey shows a decline in the number of individual shareholders from 23 million in 1998–9 to 19.5 million in 2000–2001 and would have fallen further (comments by L. C. Gupta and Prithvi Haldea in the *Economic Times* Debate, 6 January 2004).

14. The Securities Market Infrastructure Leveraging Expert (SMILE) task force made recommendations to improve the functioning of primary markets and suggested solutions to a number of problems on process flows.
15. A survey response from 367 investors on potential measures to improve confidence in Indian primary markets gave the highest weight to improvements in regulation (Santi Swarup 2003).
16. As of 2003, 136 appeals had been filed before SAT, 26 allowed, 26 dismissed and 78 were pending (Sebi 2003).
17. An investigation may lead to actions against other indicted intermediaries, and a number of people are affected in any one case.
18. The Indian business press has for long accused Sebi of being too soft and not punishing the guilty. Harshad Mehta, prime accused in the 1992 stock market rigging case, was first convicted 10 years after the fraud had been busted, and he had been dead for a year. But when Sebi accused Samir Arora, ex chief investment officer of Alliance Capital Mutual Fund, of insider trading in August 2003, and served a ban order on him in less than a year, the press was sympathetic. There were rumours of victimisation. In Indian mythology Shiva sets strict laws, but Vishnu finds the loopholes when they start to threaten humanity. SAT is essential to preserve the spirit and not the letter of the law.
19. Mutual funds have begun to innovate and offer customised products, but much more can be done to attract more savings. Private banks have formed productive partnerships with self-help groups in Andhra to deliver effective rural credit; securitization of NGOs' microfinance loans has begun.

REFERENCES

Brancato, C. K. (2002) *Singapore Corporate and Investor Confidence*, The Conference Board Research Reports, PricewaterCoopers.

Encaoua, D. and A. Hollander (2002) 'Competition Policy and Innovation', *Oxford Review of Economic Policy*, **18**, 63–79.

Glaeser E. L. and A. Shleifer (2003) 'The Rise of the Regulatory State', *Journal of Economic Literature*, **XLI**, 401–25.

Gupta, L. C. (2005) 'Contribution to the *Economic Times* Debate on "Primary Issues: Fool's gold for retail investors?"', Mumbai Edition, 16 August.

Haldea, G. (2004) 'Crisis of Credibility: Laws must Regulate the Regulator', *Times of India*, Mumbai Edition, 22 January.

Hall, B. (2002) 'The Assessment: Technology Policy', *Oxford Review of Economic Policy*, **18**, 1–9.

Hantke-Domas, M. (2003) 'The Public Interest Theory of Regulation: Non-existence or Misinterpretation?', *European Journal of Law and Economics*, **15**, 165–94.

Jones, D. C. (ed.) (2003) *New Economy Handbook*, San Diego, USA and London, UK: Academic Press, Elsevier.

Kane, E. J. (2002) 'Using Deferred Compensation to Strengthen the Ethics of Financial Regulation', *Journal of Banking and Finance*, **26**(9), 1919–33.

Laffont, J.-J. (2005) *Regulation and Development*, Frederico Caffe Lectures, New York, USA and Cambridge, UK: Cambridge University Press.

La Porta, R., F. Lopez de Silanes, A. Shleifer, and R. W. Vishny (1998) 'Law and Finance', *Journal of Political Economy*, **106**, 1113–55.

Lee, B.-C. (2003) 'Regulation and the New Economy', in D. C. Jones (ed.), *New Economy Handbook*, San Diego, USA and London, UK: Academic Press, Elsevier, pp. 890–909.

Miller, M. (1986) 'Financial Innovation: The last twenty years and the next', *Journal of Financial and Quantitative Analysis*, **21**, 459–71.

Nageswaran V. A. and S. Krithivasan (2004) 'Capital Market Reforms in India and ASEAN: avenues for co-operation', paper presented at the 1st ASEAN-India Roundtable, 9–10 February, Singapore.

NSE (National Stock Exchange) (2003), *Indian Security Markets: A Review*, and earlier issues, available at www.nse-india.com.

Pirrong, C. (2003) 'The New Economy: Implications for the Organization and Structure of Securities Markets', in D. C. Jones (ed.) *New Economy Handbook*, San Diego, USA and London, UK: Academic Press, Elsevier, pp. 372–86.

Posner, R. (1974) 'Theories of Economic Regulation', *Bell Journal of Economics and Management Science*, **5**(2), 335–58.

RBI (Reserve Bank of India) (2004) *Handbook of Statistics on the Indian Economy, and Annual Report*, Mumbai: RBI.

Santi Swarup, K. (2003) 'Measures for Improving Common Investor Confidence in Indian Primary Market: a Survey', NSE Research Initiative, Working Paper No. 28, December.

Sebi (Securities and Exchange Board of India) (2003) *Annual Report 2002-03*, and earlier reports, http://www.Sebi.gov.in/Index.jsp?contentDisp=SubSection&sec_id=41&sub_sec_id=41, 25 June.

Shah, A. and S. Thomas (1997) 'Securities Markets: Towards Greater Efficiency', in Kirit S. Parikh (ed.) *India Development Report 1997*, New Delhi: IGIDR and Oxford University Press, pp. 167–92.

Shiller, R. (2003) 'Nurturing Creative Roots of Growth', *Economic Times*, Mumbai Edition, http://economictimes.indiatimes.com/articleshow/378235.cms, 22 May.

Spaventa, L. (2003) 'Incorporating a Scam-free Europe', *Economic Times*, Mumbai Edition, http://economictimes.indiatimes.com/articleshow/47092757.cms, 22 May.

Wilhelm, W. J. (2001) 'The Internet and Financial Market Structure', *Oxford Review of Economic Policy*, **17**(2), 235–47.

PART III

Policy design principles for regulatory reform

10. Design principles for smart regulations

Neil Gunningham and Darren Sinclair

Over the last decade, considerable thinking has gone into the issue of how to design more efficient and effective regulation. Much of this has been in the field of social regulation, and that of environmental regulation, in particular. While not all the innovations that have emerged from a radical re-conception of the roles of environmental regulation have broad application to other fields of regulation, nevertheless many of them do. This chapter draws from our previous work on this area and seeks to identify some broad themes and insights based around the theme of 'smart regulation'.[1] We use this term to include an emerging form of regulatory pluralism that embraces flexible, imaginative and innovative forms of social control which seek to harness not just governments, but also business and other third parties. For example, we are concerned with self-regulation and co-regulation, with utilising both commercial interests and non-government organisations, and with finding surrogates for direct government regulation, as well as with improving the effectiveness and efficiency of more conventional forms of direct government regulation.

TOWARDS PRINCIPLE-BASED REGULATORY DESIGN

Because threats to the environment take many forms, the appropriate strategies to address environmental degradation are likely to be context-specific (Opschoor and Turner 1994). What sorts of policies work will be highly dependent upon the characteristics of the environmental issue under consideration. The strategies most effective in addressing point-source pollution from manufacturing are likely to be very different from those most suited to remedying land degradation or overfishing, as are the likely array of available instruments and institutional actors, and the political and economic contexts in which policy mixes must be designed. As a result, it would be futile to attempt to construct a single optimal regulatory solution that would be applicable to a wide variety of circumstances.

Does this mean that nothing of value can be said at a general and abstract level and that the most we can ever do is focus on solutions to particular types of problems (point-source pollution, land-clearing, soil degradation, and so on) with little hope of learning any wider lessons or of extrapolating from one policy area to another? We believe that such a conclusion is too bleak, and that, notwithstanding the context-specific nature of most environmental problems, it is possible to build a principle based framework for designing environmental regulation in any given circumstances. By this we mean an approach which, while falling short of providing determinative regulatory solutions, leads policymakers to assess their decisions against a set of design criteria which form the basis of reaching preferred policy outcomes.

REGULATORY DESIGN PRINCIPLES

We identify the core principles which should underpin regulatory design. Although these do not purport to prescribe specific solutions to specific environmental threats, these principles provide the guidelines and roadmaps which will enable policymakers to arrive at those solutions. The five principles described below are intended to be addressed sequentially.

Principle 1: Prefer Policy Mixes Incorporating Instrument and Institutional Combinations

There are very few circumstances where a single regulatory instrument is likely to be the most efficient or effective means of addressing a particular environmental problem. Certainly such circumstances exist. For example, a ban on the manufacture of certain highly toxic substances may be a highly effective way of preventing their use, without the need to invoke additional instruments. In the majority of circumstances, however, individual instruments have both strengths and weaknesses and none are sufficiently flexible and resilient to be able to successfully address all environmental problems in all contexts.

Command and control regulation has the virtues of high dependability and predicability (if adequately enforced), but commonly proves to be inflexible and inefficient. In contrast, economic instruments tend to be efficient but, in most cases, not dependable. Information-based strategies, voluntarism and self-regulation have the virtues of being non-coercive, unintrusive and (in most cases) cost-effective, but also have low reliability when used in isolation. Their success also depends heavily on the extent of the gap between the public and private interest.

Our general conclusion is that the best means of overcoming the deficiencies of individual instruments, while taking advantage of their strengths, is through the design of combinations of instruments. Similar arguments for regulatory pluralism apply with regard to regulatory participants. In most jurisdictions, the regulatory process has been restricted to government and industry. This reinforces outmoded notions of government as an omnipotent source of regulatory authority. A greater range of actors, including commercial (such as banks, insurers, consumers, suppliers and environmental consultants) and non-commercial third parties can assist in taking the weight off government intervention. Thus government can redirect its limited resources to those companies which are genuinely recalcitrant, and increasingly assume the mantle of facilitator and broker of third party participation in the regulatory process.

If one accepts this general approach of using combinations of instruments and participants, then there may be a temptation to succumb to a 'kitchen sink' approach to policy design (Hahn 1993: 1719), throwing in every conceivable policy combination on the assumption that the severity of the environmental problems we confront justify almost any level of resource input. However, this approach is not desirable for a variety of reasons. First, there are practical limits to the capacity of industry to comply with a large range of regulatory and quasi-regulatory requirements – regulatory overload is now a well recognised phenomenon (Osborne and Gaebler 1992). Second, the imposition on the public purse and the demand on public resources would also be excessive. Third, not all combinations of instruments or institutions are likely to be complementary.

Principle 2: Prefer Less Interventionist Measures

Intervention has two principal components: prescription and coercion. Prescription refers to the extent to which external parties determine the level, type and method of environmental improvement. Coercion, on the other hand, refers to the extent to which external parties or instruments place negative pressure on a firm to improve its performance. By way of example, it may be argued that industry self-regulation is higher in terms of its prescriptiveness than its coercion. That is, firms may be required to address specific issues and adopt certain behaviours, but there is little external enforcement to ensure that their obligations are met.

In contrast, some economic instruments such as taxes and charges are high on coercion and low on prescription. That is, coercion is exercised through a price signal, which firms by and large cannot avoid. How they respond to that price signal, however, is independent of outside influence – they may choose to pay the higher tax or change their behaviour so as to limit its impact. If they choose the latter, then they also have total control over the type of remediation implemented. Ranking instrument categories according to the level of intervention therefore requires a balancing or assessment of the respective contributions of the two constituent components, prescription and coercion.

There are a variety of reasons why less interventionist approaches should be preferred to more interventionist ones. In terms of efficiency, highly coercive instruments usually require substantial administrative resources for monitoring and policing, without which they are likely to be ineffective. Highly prescriptive instruments lack flexibility and do not facilitate least cost solutions. They may also result in the unnecessary deployment of resources to policing those who would be quite willing to comply voluntarily under less interventionist options. Good performers may be inhibited from going beyond compliance with such regulation.

High intervention is unlikely to be as effective as alternative approaches essentially because conscripts generally respond less favourably than volunteers. Highly coercive measures may cause resentment and resistance from those who regard them as an unjustifiable and intrusive intervention in their affairs. Unsurprisingly, high intervention also tends to score badly in terms of political acceptability. This is particularly the case in sectors with a history of independence from, and a strong resentment of, government regulatory intervention.

In contrast to the problems of high interventionism described above, low interventionist options have the considerable advantages of providing greater flexibility to enterprises in their response, greater ownership of solutions which they are directly involved in creating, less resistance, greater legitimacy, greater speed of decision making, sensitivity to market circumstances and lower costs (Sigler and Murphy 1989). From a regulator's perspective, a focus on less interventionist approaches also has the attraction of freeing up scarce resources which may be redeployed against those who are unwilling or unable to respond to such measures and against whom there is no viable alternative to the deployment of highly intrusive instruments.

Implicit in this principle of 'starting with the least interventionist policy measure' is the assumption that the measure actually works. That is, the instrument must be capable of delivering the identified environmental outcomes. In some cases, this will mean that 'what works' requires a relatively high level of intervention, but even in such cases it should still be possible to apply the principle.

In applying the principle of least intervention, policymakers should bear in mind the capacity to raise the level of intervention, if and when required, with various instruments and/or instrument combinations. That is, it is not necessarily a matter of choosing one instrument in preference to another in a static sense, but rather that of invoking a temporal sequence of instruments, as described in the next principle below. Alternatively, firms may be segregated into different streams of regulatory intervention, for example, one might introduce a 'green track' of low intervention regulation for leading edge environmental performers, while retaining a more interventionist track for those firms which are merely complying with minimum standards or are recalcitrant.

Principle 3: Escalate up an Instrument Pyramid to the Extent Necessary to Achieve Policy Goals

We asserted in the previous principle that preference should be given to the least interventionist measure(s) that will work. However, it is not always apparent to policy designers whether a particular measure they contemplate using will work or not, principally for two reasons. First, a given instrument may be effective in influencing the behaviour of some, but not of others. Second, a particular instrument which, prior to its introduction, seemed likely to be viable in its entirety, may in the light of practical experience, prove not to be so (suggesting the need for instrument sequencing to increase dependability).

A window into solving the first problem is provided by John Braithwaite, whose 'enforcement pyramid' conceives of responsive regulation in which regulators signal to industry their commitment to escalate their enforcement response whenever lower levels of intervention fail (Ayres and Braithwaite 1992). Under this model, regulators begin by assuming virtue, but if their expectations are disappointed, they respond with progressively coercive strategies to achieve compliance.

Central to Braithwaite's model is the capacity for gradual escalation from low to high intervention, culminating in a regulatory peak which, if activated, will be sufficiently powerful to deter even the most egregious offender. It is possible to reconceptualise and extend this enforcement pyramid in two important ways. First, beyond the state and business, it is possible for third parties to act as quasi-regulators. Similarly, second parties in the form of business may themselves perform a (self) regulatory role. In our expanded model, escalation would be also possible by using non-government actors. For example, the developing Forest Stewardship Council (FSC) is a global environmental standards setting system for forest products. Its success depends very largely on influencing consumer demand. While government involvement, for example through formal endorsement or though government procurement policies which supported the FSC would be valuable, the scheme is essentially a free standing one: from base to peak (consumer sanctions and boycotts) the scheme is entirely third party based. In this way, a 'new institutional system for global environmental standard setting' will come about, entirely independent of government (Meidinger 1996).

Second, Braithwaite's pyramid utilises a single instrument category, specifically, state regulation, rather than a range of instruments and parties. In contrast, our pyramid conceives of the possibility of regulation using a number of different instruments implemented by across a number of parties. It also conceives of escalation to higher levels of coerciveness not only within a single instrument category, but also across several different instruments and actors.

A graphic illustration of exactly how this can indeed occur, is provided by Joe Rees's analysis of the highly sophisticated self-regulatory program of the Institute of Nuclear Power Operators (INPO), which, post-Three Mile Island, is probably amongst the most impressive and effective such schemes worldwide (Rees 1994). However, even INPO is incapable of working effectively in isolation. There are, inevitably, industry laggards, who do not respond to education, persuasion, peer group pressure, gradual nagging from INPO, shaming, or other instruments at its disposal. INPO's ultimate response, after five years of frustration, was to turn to the government regulator, the Nuclear Regulatory Commission (NRC). That is, the effective functioning of the lower levels of the pyramid may depend upon invoking the peak, which in this case, only government could do. As Rees puts it: 'INPO's climb to power has been accomplished on the shoulders of the NRC'.

This case also shows the importance of integration between the different levels of the pyramid. The NRC did not just happen to stumble across, or threaten action against recalcitrants, rather there was considerable communication between INPO and the NRC which facilitated what was, in effect, a tiered response of education and information, escalating through peer group pressure and a series of increasingly threatening letters, ultimately to the threat of criminal penalties and incapacitation, the latter being penalties government alone could impose. Thus, even in the case of one of the most successful schemes of self-regulation ever documented, it was the presence of the 'regulatory gorilla in the closet' that secured its ultimate success.

We do not wish to give the impression, however, that a co-ordinated escalation up our instrument pyramid is practicable in all cases. On the contrary, controlled escalation is only possible where the instruments in question lend themselves to a graduated, responsive and interactive enforcement strategy. The two instruments which are most amenable to such a strategy (because they are readily manipulated) are command and control and self-regulation. Thus it is no coincidence that our first example of how to shift from one actor to another as one escalates the pyramid was taken from precisely this instrument combination. However, there are other instruments which are at least partially amenable to such a response. A combination of government mandated information (a modestly interventionist strategy) in conjunction with third party pressure (at the higher levels of the pyramid) might also be a viable option. For example, government might require business to disclose information about its levels of emissions under a Toxic Release Inventory (Gunningham and Cornwall 1994), leaving it to financial markets and insurers and environmental groups to use that information in a variety of ways to bring pressure on poor environmental performers (Hamilton 1995).

In the case of certain other instruments, the capacity for responsive regulation is lacking either because an individual instrument is not designed to facilitate responsive regulation, or because there is no potential for co-ordinated interaction between instruments. For example, some economic instruments have both these characteristics. An environmental tax, for example, cannot be imposed depending upon whether or not an enterprise has responded positively to less intrusive instruments, but rather, is intended as a uniform price signal which will apply to all members of the target group equally, irrespective of their past behaviour. By the same token, there are significant limits to the extent to which broad based economic instruments, such as pollution taxes and tradeable emission permits, can be designed to interact in a co-ordinated and complementary fashion with other instruments, except by means of temporal sequencing as described below.

Another limitation for those aspiring to a co-ordinated and gradual escalation of instruments and coerciveness, is the possibility that in some circumstances, escalation may only be possible to the middle levels of the pyramid, with no alternative instrument or party having the capacity to deliver higher levels of coerciveness. Or a particular instrument or instrument combination may facilitate action at the bottom of the pyramid and at the top, but not in the middle levels, with the result that there is no capacity for gradual escalation. For example, lender liability gives banks and other financial institutions a considerable incentive to scrutinise the environmental credentials of their clients very closely before lending them money, and at this stage they may counsel a client towards improved environmental performance. However, subsequent to providing the loan, the only available sanction may be to foreclose, without credible intermediate options. In these circumstances, our proposed instrument pyramid still has some value but it will operate in a less than complete fashion. In the substantial range of circumstances when co-ordinated escalation is not readily achievable, a critical role of government will be to fill the gaps between the different levels of the pyramid, either through direct intervention or, preferably, by facilitating other actors.

Finally, there are two general circumstances where it is inappropriate to invoke the pyramid response. First, where there is serious risk of irreversible loss or catastrophic damage: the endangered species may have become extinct, or the nuclear plant may have exploded, before the regulator has determined how high up the pyramid it is necessary to escalate. In these circumstances a horizontal rather than a vertical approach may be preferable: imposing a range of instruments, including the underpinning of a regulatory safety net, simultaneously rather than sequentially (Gunningham and Young 1997). Second, a graduated response is only appropriate where the parties have continuing interactions. In contrast, where there is only one chance to influence the behaviour in question (for example because small employers can only very rarely be inspected), then a more interventionist first response may be justified, particularly if the risk involved is a high one.

Instrument sequencing to increase dependability

In the event that an instrument (or instrument combination) that seems viable in its entirety turns out not to be so, our proposed solution is to introduce instrument sequencing: enabling escalation from the preferred least interventionist option, if it fails, to increasingly more interventionist alternatives. For example, a particular industry sector may be allowed to conduct a voluntary self-regulation scheme on the proviso that if it fails to meet the agreed objectives, mandatory sanctions will be introduced. Such a solution is not only consistent with design principle 3 above, it also avoids a slide into 'smorgasbordism': rather than using all instruments and participants simultaneously, it is only when the least interventionist (viable) instrument(s) have demonstrably failed that one escalates up the pyramid and invokes a broader range of instruments and parties, and even then, only to the extent necessary to achieve the desired goal.

The precise nature of sequencing arrangements will be determined by the level of discretion that is associated with their implementation. That is, some sequencing arrangements will entail the automatic application of more interventionist measures if and when earlier measures fail, thus reducing the level of discretion, while others will require some further action by first, second, or third parties prior to their implementation, thus increasing the level of discretion. Minimising the amount of discretion, once certain defined parameters have been breached, sends a powerful message to industry to deliver on less interventionist forms of regulation. Of course this does not preclude lobbying by business, but this is less likely to succeed if government has already publicly committed itself to a specified course of action.

Triggers, buffer zones and circuit breakers

The proposed methods of sequencing are dependent on triggers to warn the authorities when less interventionist measures have failed. For example, under a scheme of self-regulation, the industry itself may invite government intervention. Alternatively, government and industry may agree to defined performance benchmarks. A failure to comply with these benchmarks would automatically trigger tougher regulations. Or it may be that public interest groups are able to identify serious breaches which would warrant intervention from governments or other third parties.

In order to increase the dependability of sequencing provisions, several possible triggers would be preferable, though precisely which ones are most appropriate will depend upon the particular context. In broad terms, appropriate triggers might include: random government inspections; independent auditors; mechanisms for industry association reporting; in-house whistle blowers; community oversight; and compulsory firm reporting. In relying on triggers to invoke sequencing, it is important that the triggers pre-empt unacceptable levels of environmental harm. That is, there needs to be a buffer zone between the point at which a trigger is set off and the level of environmental harm that is being monitored.

A related strategy is the use of circuit breakers. This is an instrument which is introduced as a short term measure (and ultimately withdrawn), the purpose of which is to pre-empt the anticipated failure of another instrument. Circuit breakers tend to be low intervention instruments introduced in anticipation that certain high intervention instruments, introduced in isolation, have a high chance of failure. For example, a ban on land clearing in South Australia was regarded as essential to halt widespread environmental degradation, but was also politically unacceptable and largely unenforceable in the absence of some complementary positive inducement. Compensation was introduced for those who were refused a permit to clear, in order to overcome both these problems and to facilitate the cultural change that was needed in the long term (that is from a belief that all landowners had an unencumbered right to clear, to a sustainable land use). Once this had been achieved, the right to compensation was withdrawn (Gunningham and Young 1997).

Principle 4: Empower Participants which are in the Best Position to act as Surrogate Regulators

We argued earlier that there are a range of second and third parties, both commercial and non-commercial, which may play valuable roles in the regulatory process, acting as quasi-regulators. These range from industry associations (administering self-regulatory programmes) through financial institutions to environmental and other pressure groups. All too often, however, policymakers have avoided or ignored the potential contributions of such parties, treating government as the sole regulatory provider. Yet by expanding the regulatory 'tool box' to encompass additional players, many of the most serious shortcomings of traditional regulatory approaches may be overcome.

There are several reasons why the recruitment of additional parties to the regulatory process may provide for improved outcomes. First, in some instances quasi-regulation may be far more potent than government intervention. For example, the threat of a bank to foreclose a loan to a firm with low levels of liquidity is likely to have a far greater impact than any existing government instrument. Second, it may be perceived as more legitimate. For example, farmers are far more accepting of commercial imperatives to reduce chemical use. Similarly, participation by non-commercial third parties, in particular, may well be crucial in terms of political acceptability. Third, government resources are necessarily limited. Accordingly, it makes sense for government to reserve its resources for situations where there is no viable alternative but direct regulation. The potential for Responsible Care to supplement government regulation of the chemical industry is a case in point (Gunningham 1995). Finally, even if resources were more readily available, governments are not omnipotent. There are many areas of commercial activity which impact on the environmental performance of industry where direct government influence is impractical. For example, where there are a myriad of small players, such that it is impossible even for government to identify, let alone regulate all of them.

Applying the principle of empowerment

The participation of quasi-regulators is unlikely to arise spontaneously, except in a very limited range of circumstances where public and private interests substantially coincide (Gunningham and Rees 1997). Such parties may have little existing interest in environmental performance, lack the necessary information even if they did, or indeed may have a commercial interest in maintaining or accelerating environmental degradation. For example, banks are unlikely to promote the conservation of remnant vegetation on farms where they perceive the clearing of land to provide increased earnings, nor are they likely to oppose the running of extra stock where this increases the ability to repay loans. There remains, therefore, a significant role for government in facilitating and commandeering the participation of quasi-regulators.

One powerful illustration of this principle can be drawn from Mitchell's work on pollution by oil tankers at sea (Mitchell 1994). Mitchell demonstrates how the imposition by the state of penalties for intentional oil spills (pursuant to an international treaty) was almost wholly ineffective, due in no small part to difficulties of monitoring, and, in some cases, to a lack of either enforcement resources or political will. Nor, in the absence of government intervention, did third parties have incentives to contribute significantly to the reduction of oil spills. However, all this changed when a new regime was introduced, requiring tankers to be equipped with segregated ballast tanks. Despite the increased cost of the new equipment, this regime has been extremely successful, a fact owed substantially to the role played by a range of powerful third parties. First, the new regime facilitated coerced compliance by three powerful third parties, namely non-state classification societies, ship insurers, and ship builders. As Mitchell demonstrates, none of these parties had any interest in avoiding the new regime yet shipowners were critically dependent upon each of them (Mitchell 1994, ch. 8). Together, and in conjunction with state action, they achieved far more than state action alone was ever likely to.

There are a variety of mechanisms through which government may seek to engage quasi-regulators. Most of these will require government to seek out lateral means of extending its reach through innovative market orderings. An obvious starting point is the provision of adequate information. Without reliable data on the performance of industrial firms, those actors which may be in a position to exert influence, for example in the commercial sphere, will be unable to make objective judgements about preferred company profiles. For example, it was only when government mandated collation and disclosure of toxic releases that financial markets were able to factor this information into share prices, thereby rewarding good environmental performers and disadvantaging the worst performers (Hamilton 1995).

Some strategies for empowering quasi-regulators will be specific to particular target groups. For example, government may facilitate the activities of environmental organisations through the provision of funding support, the enactment of community-right-to-know legislation, and the provision of legal standing. In seeking to target banks, government might increase lender liability for a range of environmentally destructive behaviours. Insurers may be invoked by making insurance a condition of licence, or a condition of authorisation to engage in activities which have a high environmental risk.

Governments could also harness the very considerable power of supply chain pressure. For example, governments may make it a condition of regulatory flexibility that firms over a certain size not only adopt environmental management systems (a form of process based regulation) but also ensure that their major suppliers also conform to a simplified version of the system. Alternatively, such a condition could be included in an industry wide self-regulation programme, as is already the case under the Product Stewardship code of practice of the chemical industry's Responsible Care initiative (Gunningham 1995). Thus the use of supply chain pressure by large firms to improve the environmental performance of smaller firms may be enhanced by a complementary combination with process based regulation or self-regulation.

Consistent with our design principles, the preferred role for government is to create the necessary preconditions for second or third parties to assume a greater share of the regulatory burden rather than engaging in direct intervention. This will also reduce the drain on scarce regulatory resources and provide greater ownership of environmental issues by industry and the wider community. In this way, government acts principally as a catalyst or facilitator. In particular, it can play a crucial role in enabling a co-ordinated and gradual escalation up an instrument pyramid (described in principle 3), filling any gaps that may exist in that pyramid and facilitating links between its different layers.

This role can be illustrated by example. Insurance has the potential to be a useful instrument in the middle layers of the pyramid. Insurers have the capacity to conduct site visits, engage independent auditors, vary the size of premiums, and if necessary, withdraw their services altogether. Insurers are, however, dependent on the availability of reliable information on which to make their initial and subsequent assessments of firm performance, but commonly have great difficulty obtaining relevant information over and beyond that required to be disclosed by their clients (Freeman and Kunreather 1996). As a consequence, there is a necessary role for government (at the bottom layers of the pyramid) to ensure that this information is accessible, for example, through the provision of compulsory pollutant inventory reporting by industry. It may also be that that insurers lack the necessary muscle at the top of the pyramid to deal with unrepentant recalcitrants. In such circumstances, insurers may advise government regulators of a firm's transgression and invite the full force of the law to be applied.

Principle 5: Maximise Opportunities for Win/win Outcomes

Two major criticisms of conventional regulation are the lack of incentives for firms to continuously improve their environmental performance, and the failure to encourage firms to adopt pollution prevention measures over end-of-pipe solutions. Such opportunities will be considerably enhanced to the extent that firms can achieve higher levels of environmental performance at the same time as increasing productivity and/or profits: the classic win/win scenario. A key challenge for policymakers, therefore, is to ensure that regulatory solutions maximise the opportunity for win/win outcomes by facilitating and rewarding firms for going 'beyond compliance', while also maintaining a statutory baseline.

Will firms voluntarily go beyond compliance?
It is increasingly argued that it is in a business's own self-interest to move beyond compliance with existing legislative requirements and adopt a 'proactive' stance on the environment, voluntarily exceeding mandated minimum performance standards. According to its proponents, firms going down this path may (in addition to improving profitability) enhance their

corporate image, position themselves to realise new environment-related market opportunities, generally improve efficiency and quality, foster a greater consumer acceptance of their company and products, and reduce potential legal liability. They may also develop new environmental technologies which can be sold into the rapidly growing and lucrative global market for environmental goods and services (Gunningham 1994 and references therein). And yet, despite these apparent benefits, the large majority of firms have taken very few steps to position themselves as environmental leaders. Assuming that considerable win/win opportunities do indeed exist (that is, even if proponents of this position may overstate the benefits, their basic position is sound), why have the majority of enterprises adopted a position which is, on the face of it, irrational? The most plausible answers are an emphasis on short-term profits and bounded rationality.

The former is probably the single largest impediment to improved environmental performance (Rappaport and Flaherty 1991). Crucially, most environmental investments will only pay-off in the medium to long term, while the up-front investment is primarily short term. Because corporations are judged by markets, investors and others principally focusing on short-term performance, if they cannot demonstrate tangible economic success in the here and now, there may be no long term to look forward to.

Bounded rationality assumes not that people are irrational (although they sometimes are) but rather that they have neither the knowledge nor the powers of calculation to allow them 'to achieve the high level of optimal adaptation of means to ends that is posited by economics' (Simon 1992, p. 3). For example, it is widely accepted that there are substantial energy efficiency improvements which industry could profitably adopt. And yet, most firms fail to take advantage of them. Only where energy is a large component of business input costs have substantial investments in energy efficiency been made. In the least energy efficient industries where energy costs are only a minor component of overall business costs, energy efficiencies have been almost entirely ignored. This is bounded rationality at work: management focuses on core business functions and ignores lesser costs, even though these costs could be reduced through environmentally beneficial behaviour.

The role of government
Based on this analysis, the market, unaided, cannot be relied upon to deliver win/win outcomes. Arguably, there is a role for government intervention to increase the uptake within firms of existing economically rational environmental improvements: in effect, seeking to compensate for both the inadequacy of markets (unaided) and of business rationality in order to maximise both the public (environmental) and private (economic) benefits.

But what form should this intervention take? Of course, government could simply mandate improved levels of business environmental performance. However, because there is a coincidence between self-interest and environmental improvement, other less interventionist measures should have a high chance of success, rendering prescriptive forms of intervention unnecessary or even counterproductive (see principle 2 above). Accordingly, the most appropriate role for governmental regulation lies in nudging firms at the margin towards cleaner production, heightening their awareness of environmental issues, and encouraging the re-ordering of corporate priorities in order to reap the benefits of improved environmental performance.

One way of increasing the chances of win/win outcomes is through the provision of information (for example cleaner production demonstration projects, technical support, databases and clearinghouses). A related strategy would be to encourage full cost accounting, on the assumption that unless business knows the costs and benefits, in environmental terms, of its current practices, it is unlikely to change them. Such strategies may be particularly important in addressing bounded rationality. Not only can government provide information to industry, but other non-government sources of information can also be harnessed and, in some cases, may be more effective. Sometimes, because of institutional inertia, even when firms are made aware of potential cost savings they still will not exploit win/win opportunities. In such cases information alone is not enough, but is a necessary prerequisite. Here, information strategies can be supplemented by other voluntary promotional schemes which attempt to elicit a commitment to cost-effective environmental improvement.

Governments might also consider some form of financial inducements to 'nudge' firms in the right direction (for example, subsidising the cost of environmental audits). Again, once firms become aware of how to achieve win/win outcomes, and can easily access the consulting expertise and internal systems necessary to achieve them, they are far more likely to take action. Smaller firms may also require some assistance to cover up front costs and to more easily access capital.

However, it makes sense to target any financial inducements at those firms which are genuinely achieving beyond compliance rather than those firms that merely intend to comply with minimum standards. One way of achieving this is via a 'two-track' regulatory system that provides incentives to those firms committed to higher levels of environmental performance which go substantially beyond compliance – increased flexibility, autonomy and public relations benefits less demanding administrative requirements, reduced licence fees, preferential purchasing, and so on. The intention is to attract as many firms as possible to the 'green track', but to maintain the conventional track as a fall back mechanism.

Moving the goal posts: turning win/lose into win/win

It is inevitable that even the most progressive firms will eventually reach a point at which win/win is no longer a viable option, and where any further spending on environmental protection will directly threaten corporate profits (Walley and Whitehead 1994). At this point, two strategies are available to government. The first is to recognise the tension between environment protection and corporate profit, and to design policy instruments and enforcement responses accordingly. Here we simply restate the importance of a escalating pyramidal enforcement response such as we advocated at principle three above. Critically, at the peak of the pyramid will be a deterrence-orientated approach that makes it no longer economically rational for firms to avoid their environmental responsibilities.

A second strategy is for government to push back the point at which win/win becomes win/lose (Jacobs 1991: 157). Michael Porter suggests that countries that have the most rigorous environmental requirements often lead in exports of affected products (Porter 1991). While such markets may evolve in the absence of government intervention, their scope and success can be influenced by such action. For example, Germany has had perhaps the world's tightest regulations in stationary air pollution control, and German companies appear to hold a wide lead in patenting – and exporting – air pollution and other environmental technologies. However, Porter is at pains to emphasise that not all standards will lead to desirable trade outcomes, and that we need regulations that aim at outcomes rather than methods (that is, performance based rather than technology based standards), that are flexible and cost effective and which encourage companies to advance beyond their existing control technology. It must also be acknowledged that Porter's views have been strongly challenged from a variety of sources (Walley and Whitehead 1994), and that empirical support for his position is somewhat tenuous (Robinson 1995: 388).

We agree that there is much that governments can and should do to encourage firms to develop environmental technologies and to harness environmental services markets. However, we disagree that more stringent regulation is necessarily the only or indeed the best means of achieving this outcome. Take, for example, the issue of pollution from the chemical industry. While it would certainly be viable, following Porter, to mandate tough standards, it would also be possible to adopt a self-regulatory scheme, as is the case with Responsible Care (with a proviso that if the scheme was not demonstrably achieving certain performance outcomes within a given period, government would intervene more directly). Such a scheme might be coupled with external audit, and government might itself require disclosure of results, enabling commercial third parties and to a lesser extent consumers and public interest groups to bring pressure on those who were achieving poorest results.

Besides being less interventionist than the Porter solution, co-regulation has additional advantages of providing greater flexibility, giving industry ownership of the solution, and of avoiding much of the culture of resistance that may accompany government regulation.

CONCLUSION

We have argued that successful regulatory design depends crucially upon adhering to a number of regulatory design principles which have hitherto not featured prominently on the policy agenda. In particular, we advocate that policymakers should not only prefer combinations of instruments to 'stand alone' instrument strategies, but also stress the importance of preferring the least interventionist measures that will work. We also introduced the heuristic device of a three dimensional pyramid, as a means of escalating regulatory responses, and consistent with the pursuit of pluralistic regulatory policy, argued the importance of harnessing quasi-regulatory actors outside the public sector. We further addressed the extent to which it is possible to design environmental policy in such a way as to encourage and facilitate industry in going 'beyond compliance' with existing regulatory requirements. Such an approach, we believe, will assist policymakers to introduce various forms of 'smart regulation'.

NOTES

1. This was first developed in N. Gunningham and P. Grabosky, *Smart Regulation: Designing Environmental Policy*, OUP, UK, 1998. See further N. Gunningham and D. Sinclair *Leaders and Laggards: Next Generation Environmental Regulation*, Greenleaf, UK, 2002.

REFERENCES

Ayres, I. and Braithwaite, J. (1992) *Responsive Regulation*, New York: Oxford University Press.

Freeman, P. and Kunreather, H. (1996) 'The Roles of Insurance and Well Specified Standards in Dealing With Environmental Risk', *Risk Management and Decision Economics*, **17**, 513–30.

Gunningham, N. (1994) 'Beyond Compliance: management of environmental risk', in B. W. Boer, R. Fowler and N. Gunningham (eds) *Environmental Outlook: Law and Policy*, Canberra: ACEL, Federation Press.

Gunningham, N. (1995) 'Environment, Self-Regulation, and the Chemical Industry: Assessing Responsible Care', *Law and Policy*, **17**(1), 58–109.

Gunningham, N. and Cornwall, A. (1994) 'Legislating the Right to Know', *Environmental and Planning Law Journal*, **11**, 274–88.

Gunningham, N. and Rees, J. (1997) 'Industry Self-regulation', *Law and Policy*, **19**(4), 363–414.

Gunningham, N. and Young, M. D. (1997) 'Towards Optimal Environmental Policy: The Case of Biodiversity Conservation', *Ecology Law Quarterly*, **24**, 243–98.

Gunningham, N. and Grabosky, P. (1998) *Smart Regulation: Designing Environmental Policy*, Oxford: Oxford University Press.

Gunningham, N. and Sinclair, D. (2002) *Leaders and Laggards: Next Generation Environmental Regulation*, Sheffield: Greenleaf, UK.

Hahn, R. (1993) 'Towards a New Environmental Paradigm', *Yale Law Journal*, **102**(7), 1719–62.

Hamilton, J. T. (1995) 'Pollution as News: Media and Stockmarket Reactions to the Capital Toxic Release Inventory Data', *Journal of Environmental Economics and Management*, **28**(1), 98–113.

Jacobs, M. (1991) *The Green Economy*, London: Pluto Press.

Meidinger, E. (1996) 'Look Who's Making the Rules: The Roles of the Forest Stewardship Council and International Standards Organisation in Environmental Policy Making', a paper presented to Colloquium on Emerging Environmental Policy: Winners and Losers, Oregon State University, Corvellis, Oregon, 23 September.

Mitchell, R. (1994) *International Oil Pollution at Sea: Environmental Policy and Treaty Compliance*, Cambridge, MA: MIT Press.

Opschoor, J. B. and Turner, R. K. (eds) (1994) *Economic Incentives and Environmental Policies: Principles and Practice*, Dordrecht: Kluwer Academic Publishers.

Osborne, D. and Gaebler, E. (1992) *Reinventing Government*, Reading, PA: Addison Wesley.

Porter, M. (1991) 'America's Green Strategy', *Scientific American*, **262**(4), 168.

Rappaport, A. and Flaherty, M. (1991) 'Multinational Corporation and the Environment', Massachusetts: Center for Environmental Management, Tufts University.

Rees, J. V. (1994) *Hostages of Each Other: The Transformation of Nuclear Safety Since Three Mile Island*, Chicago, IL: University of Chicago Press.

Robinson, J. C. (1995) 'The Impact of Environmental and Occupational Health Regulation on Productivity Growth in US Manufacturing', *Yale Journal on Regulation*, **12**(2), 387–434.

Sigler, J. A. and Murphy, J. E. (1989) *Interactive Corporate Compliance: An Alternative to Regulatory Compulsion*, New York: Quorum Books.

Simon, H. (1992) *Economics, Bounded Rationality and the Cognitive Revolution*, Brookfield, VT, USA and Cheltenham, UK: Edward Elgar, UK.

Walley, N. and Whitehead, B. (1994) 'It's Not Easy Being Green', *Harvard Business Review*, **72**(3), 46–52.

11. Universal service, and the transition from state control to state-monitored competition[1]

Jon M. Peha

A critical objective in any national telecommunications policy is advancing universal service: making telecommunications services available and affordable to a greater fraction of the population. Similar issues can arise with other services that a government wishes to make widely available, such as electric power, broadcast radio or TV, or health clinics. Universal service is easy when services are provided by a government agency or government-controlled monopoly. Government can decide where to build and what to charge customers irrespective of actual costs, provided that total revenues (plus any government subsidies) are sufficient to cover total costs. However, in country after country, experience in the telecommunications sector has shown that competing profit-seeking carriers are more willing than government ministries to minimize costs, expand the infrastructure and customer base, lower prices, and improve quality of service. This provides strong motivation for privatization and deregulation. But will profit-seeking carriers advance universal service? The problem is particularly acute in developing countries, where there are often large regions with little or no basic telephone infrastructure. Developed nations may face similar issues with newer and more expensive services, like broadband Internet. This chapter proposes a novel universal service policy for countries (a) with entire regions that lack adequate infrastructure for the desired service, and (b) where multiple private-sector firms are capable of providing this service. The policy is invoked when dispensing cash, licences, or resources to the private sector. This occurs during privatization, the introduction of competition, the release of spectrum, or the allocation of significant cash subsidies for universal service. While telecommunications is the focus of this work, the concept can apply to other sectors.

Some argue that competition and the expansion of telecommunications infrastructure are incompatible, so deregulation is undesirable. The concern is based on a genuine problem. Unregulated profit-seeking companies will not serve individuals who cannot pay the costs of providing a service, and they will not serve entire regions when collective demand is insufficient to cover regional costs. Due to economies of scale, serving a small number of users in a region is prohibitively expensive. Thus, regions with low population densities, many low-income households, or difficult terrain can be unprofitable. Explicit policies are needed that motivate commercial carriers to serve these regions.

This chapter proposes a policy of tradable universal service obligations to foster the expansion of infrastructure into unserved regions. Although the policy can be employed at any time, privatization, the introduction of competition, and the release of large spectrum blocks often mark the beginning of a transitional phase conducive to infrastructure expansion. This policy is designed to maximize (useful) expansion and minimize cost during this phase by giving private-sector providers the appropriate incentives. The policy remains consistent with the principles of open competition, and thus most effective plans for deregulation.

Ironically, if this or another universal service policy is adopted early, it is typically viewed as part of deregulation. On the other hand, if it is adopted later, or employed a second time, it is incorrectly labelled as re-regulation. This allows opponents to falsely claim the banner of the free market. In reality, if done well, the imposition of a universal service policy is not a reversal to the old days of regulation; it is the next step forward towards a competitive policy that serves all of society.

There is a considerable literature on universal service policies for basic telephone service in wealthier nations (e.g. Tyler *et al.* 1995). However, such policies do not address this issue, and are therefore a poor model to emulate. The wealthier nations did not introduce competition until infrastructure was sufficiently widespread that service was available to almost everyone, although it is not always affordable to everyone. Thus, the monthly charges to individuals with low incomes or who live in costly regions must be partially subsidized (implicitly or explicitly). These policies may also be of use when availability is not pervasive, but they are not sufficient. Effective universal service policies must also spur significant capital investments in infrastructure expansion, not just reduce prices for monthly service where needed.

The second section defines more specifically the objectives of a good universal service policy. The principal models typically used in developing countries are described in the third section. The fourth section describes the proposed policy. The chapter is summarized in the final section.

UNIVERSAL SERVICE POLICY OBJECTIVES

This section describes the three primary objectives of a transitional universal service policy to expand infrastructure, plus a fourth which applies in some nations due to political constraints.

Expand Telecommunications Access such that Social Benefits are Maximized

The universal service policy should cause infrastructure to be deployed in those regions of greatest social value. This may mean all areas that are currently unserved, or areas may be targeted specifically because they contain health care facilities, manufacturing plants, universities, or other important institutions. Infrastructure must also be expanded into targeted regions at a reasonable pace, as demarcated by appropriate intermediate milestones.

Minimize Costs and Minimize Subsidies

An efficient policy will minimize the costs of infrastructure expansion. Governments also wish to minimize subsidies. (These are closely related, but occasionally in conflict, since companies seek to increase subsidy minus costs.) We adopt four tenets of an efficient policy.

First, wherever possible, infrastructure expansion should be the responsibility of competing commercial entities, or at least regulated commercial monopolies, rather than a government agency. Commercial entities have every incentive to maximize efficiency.

Second, policies should influence results, but not technical means. There is an extraordinary variety of technical approaches to expanding infrastructure. Should the medium be a fibreoptic backbone, a wireless local loop, or a satellite link? Should it employ circuit switching (as in traditional telephone networks), or IP (Internet protocol)? Should there be separate telephone, Internet and television networks, or should there be integrated-services networks carrying diverse traffic types? The best answer will vary from region to region, and year to year. An efficient policy must be technology-neutral.

Third, the regions served by any given entity should be selected to exploit economies of scope and scale. There may be economies due to geographic proximity. For example, for cellular service, efficiency might be maximized when all of the areas surrounding a particular hill are served by one entity. With the break-up of AT&T in the Untied States, some of these economies were lost when one company gained the right to provide cellular service in New York City, and another gained the right to provide service for the New York City suburbs in the neighbouring State of New Jersey. Economies are not limited to geographic proximity. For example, a satellite service is most efficient (relative to terrestrial) at reaching remote users, even when those users are far apart.

It is equally important that the services offered by a carrier benefit from economies of scope (Peha and Tewari 1998). In some cases, there are great efficiency gains in combining two kinds of traffic on a single packet-switched network, such as high-definition television and e-mail. In other cases, such combinations actually reduce efficiency. Traffic mix profoundly influences prices (Peha and Tewari 1998, Wang *et al*. 1997).

Fourth, the costs associated with administering a universal service policy should be minimized by reducing government involvement and oversight where possible.

Logical Transition to Steady-state Universal Service Policies

This universal service policy addresses a transitional phase of infrastructure expansion, but it coexists with other policies that will continue thereafter. The policy should remain coherent at all phases, and should not require drastic regulatory shifts.

Use No General Funds

In some nations, it is not possible to mix universal service funds with general funds. The primary reasons are political. After a long history of implicitly using telecommunications revenues to subsidize universal service, it may not be politically acceptable to use general funds for this purpose. Moreover, when funds supposedly for universal service flow from telecommunications providers and users into general coffers, they are often diverted to other national needs, effectively becoming just another tax on telecommunications.

TYPICAL UNIVERSAL SERVICE POLICIES

This section describes the three primary policies that are currently used to motivate infrastructure expansion into unserved areas: build-out requirements, universal service funds, and targeted implicit subsidy obligations. In each case, a success story is described. Although quantitative assessment is notoriously difficult, we will qualitatively discuss the advantages and disadvantages of each approach.

Build-Out Requirements

The most common approach is to require a newly privatized telecommunications carrier, or a newly licensed competitor, to meet specific requirements with respect to infrastructure expansion. These build-out requirements are bundled with one or more items of value: the infrastructure of the government carrier, permission to operate (a licence), access to spectrum, and freedom from regulation for some fixed period. Attaching obligations to these assets reduces what buyers will pay for the asset. In effect, subsidies are provided to meet universal service obligations without the problems and inefficiencies of actually collecting and distributing those subsidies. Governments need only monitor progress, and impose sanctions when requirements are not met (as occurred in Argentina, Mexico, Peru and elsewhere).

For example, Ghana's 1996 National Communications Authority Act called for the privatization of the state's monopoly, and the introduction of competition. A licence was later sold that would allow a new company to provide a competing telephone service nationwide. The new licence-holder would be required to serve 50 000 new customers. The private company that purchased a managing (30 per cent) interest in the state telecommunications monopoly would face similar obligations. Thus, the government could be certain of some infrastructure expansion. The number of new subscribers for both providers increased dramatically as a result of this policy, greatly exceeding expectations.

In the case of Ghana, carriers were allowed to serve those new subscribers anywhere, so there was little motivation to expand access outside the triangle formed by Ghana's three largest cities, where profits are greatest. This did not help rural Northern Ghana, which before the new policy was accepted had 40 per cent of Ghana's population and only 7.8 per cent of its phone lines (Ghana Ministry of Transport and Communications 1994). In general, build-out requirements may be more specific with respect to geography, technology and type of service (such as fixed telephone, mobile telephone, Internet, paging, or payphones).

There are disadvantages to the build-out-requirement approach. As the Ghanaian example above demonstrates, commercial companies may not expand infrastructure into unserved areas unless the build-out requirements specifically require it. But how can the government determine what specific build-out requirements can be implemented efficiently? Ghana could have required the incumbent monopoly to extend access to a specific set of regions, and the new competitor to extend access to another set. As described in the second section, it is important to do this in a manner that would allow each carrier to exploit economies of scale and scope. To do this effectively, the government would need detailed knowledge of the technology each company would use, and their deployment strategy, before the companies were ever selected. Even if a government could somehow gather this information before privatization, demand and technology can change considerably in the years before those build-out requirements must be met. Thus, there are inherent inefficiencies in this approach.

Ghana also had a power company with significant telecommunications capacity, and three cellular providers, who could possibly expand the telecommunications infrastructure in a cost effective manner. They were not affected by this universal service policy. If the government were to try, the inherent inefficiencies of central planning grow when build-out requirements must be divided among an even greater number of firms.

Universal Service Funds for Explicit Subsidies

A number of countries have created a government-managed universal service fund. These funds are to be spent in the manner that best advances universal service objectives. Because subsidies are explicit, it is easier to determine whether the benefits justify the costs.

Funds can come from annual taxes on the telecommunications sector (as in Peru, Ghana and the United States) or from general tax funds (as in El Salvador and Chile). Universal service funds can also come from the one-time sale of resources, as occurs when a carrier is privatized. For example, Guatemala auctions spectrum licences, which can be renewed indefinitely without cost. Proceeds of this one-time auction go into a universal service fund.

Universal service funds can be used to subsidize a commercial provider's expansion into unserved areas. In 1994, Chile established a temporary fund (through 1998) to extend access to rural and low-income regions through a series of auctions. Regulators select a set of regions for which the ratio of estimated social value to estimated cost is greatest for the next auction. For each selected region, regulators specify a number of localities where public payphones should be placed, a maximum price for phone calls, and a maximum subsidy deemed commensurate with costs. Firms then bid on the smallest subsidy (below the stated maximum) that they will accept to serve a given region. Winners must offer reliable payphone service for ten years. Because of economies of scale, once those first phone lines have been installed, the firm is likely to provide more.

This approach effectively harnesses the private sector to expand infrastructure, targets subsidies to high-value regions, and is technology neutral – all important advantages. Proponents also argue that competitive bidding always minimizes subsidies, minimizes infrastructure costs, and maximizes social benefits, as the auction will continue until bids to serve targeted regions approach actual costs. This is not the case, for a variety of reasons. Among them, when the value of two auctioned items is not simply the sum of their individual values, then auctions do not necessarily lead to the most efficient result (Milgrom 1997). As described in the second section, there are often economies of scale and scope when serving multiple regions, in which case the value of auction items is not simply the sum of individual values.

Under the Chilean approach, one might expect that every region would receive a subsidy greater than 0 and less than the listed maximum. Chile's first auction brought service to 1100 new localities. Forty-six regions were auctioned simultaneously, with an average of 28 localities per region. There was little competitive bidding. Nine per cent of the regions received no bids. Thirty-five per cent went for the maximum allowable subsidy, because there was only one bidder. Perhaps most surprisingly, 39 per cent went for no subsidy whatsoever, even though the bidders had not been willing to serve these regions in the past without a subsidy. Economies of scope are a reasonable explanation (Wellenius 1997).

With such economies, simultaneous auctions do not maximize efficiency, that is assign those obligations being auctioned to the firms that can meet them at minimum cost, nor do the auctions minimize subsidies to meet the selected obligations. Consider the following simple example of the problem. Regions 1, 2 and 3 may be subsidized. The maximum subsidy for any region is 100. Any firm would require a subsidy of 120 to serve any one region. However, serving both regions 1 and 2, or both regions 2 and 3, would require a subsidy of only 140 for firms A and B, because they use a wireless technology that yields an economy of scope. Firm A bids 100 each for regions 1 and 2. If successful, Firm A would receive a subsidy of 200 when 140 would suffice. Firm B bids 100 for region 3 and 95 for region 2. This too would be highly profitable if successful, but now firm A stands to receive a subsidy of 100 where 120 is needed. The only way for firm A to avoid loss is to bid again on region 2, causing firm B to lose money. If the bidding war continues, both firms will lose money, possibly leading to bankruptcies rather than infrastructure expansion. On the other hand, cautious firms that are aware of this danger may be unwilling to accept a subsidy of less than 120 when subsidies are set through such an auction. This caution can prevent the firm that can develop the infrastructure at minimum cost from ever bidding, thereby increasing infrastructure costs. This also increases the subsidies the government must pay. It has been argued that this phenomenon undermined the 1998 Personal Communications Services (PCS) spectrum auctions in the Netherlands (Milgrom 1998).

Another serious problem with this approach is in the selection of obligations for the next auction. The cost of serving a given area and the potential revenues change over time, so correctly timing the imposition of a particular obligation can dramatically affect both the deployment cost and the subsidy required. This makes it difficult for a government to determine the auction in which a given service obligation should be auctioned.

The problem is considerably more complex (and severe) since entire sets of obligations are selected for auction, some of which may have economies of scope. For example, consider the case where there are 10 regions. Each region i: $1 \le i \le 10$ requires a subsidy of 120 to serve alone, but a subsidy of 20 is sufficient if the same firm has already deployed infrastructure in region $i-1$ or $i+1$. All ten regions could be served for 210, but if only even-numbered regions are auctioned, it would require a subsidy of 600 to serve just five regions. This is a disadvantage of distributing obligations through a series of auctions.

Targeted Implicit Subsidy Obligations

Another approach is to emulate the implicit subsidies typically used by monopoly carriers. In the context of a competitive industry structure, a licence to offer a profitable service like cellular telephony or international toll service is coupled with the obligation to serve an unprofitable region. This approach has been adopted by the Philippines. In 1993, two executive orders in the Philippines mandated interconnection among all carriers and declared universal service provisions. These were reinforced by the Telecommunications Policy Act of 1995 which paved the way for privatization. Thanks to these reforms and a growing economy, the number of telephone lines increased remarkably from 1.2 per 100 people in 1993 to 9.1 per 100 people in 1998 (Cabarios and Rubio 1998).

As with the other approaches, these implicit subsidies succeed in motivating commercial carriers to meet the needs of unserved areas, and the obligations are technology neutral. However, the system depends on the regulator's ability to match profitable and unprofitable regions in an optimal way, much like the build-out requirement approach described earlier in the chapter. Worse yet, even if optimal decisions are made when licences are granted, circumstances change. Regions can become more or less profitable over time, possibly driving some firms to bankruptcy and giving others a tremendous competitive advantage. If the policy remains fixed, this is a risky proposition for potential bidders. There is no obvious way for the policy to evolve to steady-state policies without major disruptions.

A similar proposal was planned for India. Regions were categorized as having high, intermediate, or low market potential. Firms serving the former must also serve the latter. The approach was abandoned after strong protests from potential bidders, provoking concerns that few would bid (Petrazzini 1996; Sinha 1996). The final policy was less restrictive, requiring firms to deploy 10 per cent of their lines in rural areas.

PROPOSED POLICY

Overview

The third section shows technology-neutral policies that induce commercial carriers to expand infrastructure. Each policy has advantages, but there is a recurrent theme in the disadvantages: a lack of flexibility. To minimize costs, the right firms must be given the right set of universal service obligations to be fulfilled at the right time, and advance central planning by a government regulator is unlikely to produce that result. The solution is for government to set overall requirements, and give private firms greater flexibility to determine dynamically how to meet those requirements. This can be achieved through tradable universal service obligations.

An analogous approach has been used to limit air pollution in the United States and elsewhere. A permit allows a company to emit a given amount of pollutants into the atmosphere. By controlling the number of permits in circulation, the government can limit the total annual pollution rate. Permits can be sold and traded. Thus, a factory that can reduce its pollution levels inexpensively will sell its permits to a factory that cannot, thereby minimizing the costs of pollution reduction. In this section, we describe a universal service policy that builds upon this simple concept.

There are two aspects of the proposed universal service policy that make matters more complicated than the emissions policy described above. First, firms are trading obligations rather than permits. Second, because the objective of the proposed policy is to motivate the initial deployment of infrastructure, the universal service obligations are transient, and optimal timing is an important issue. Both these differences must be addressed.

Flexible Obligations

There are two components to an obligation: what must be done, and when it must be completed. Thus, a universal service obligation consists of two components: a milestone to achieve, and a commitment to meet a specific deadline.

Beginning with the former, milestones may take many forms. All of these forms should refer to the availability of services, and thereby remain technology neutral. A successful infrastructure expansion in Chile may be the installation of payphones in selected localities of importance within a region. India would like to see at least one phone in every village of a given size. Ghana seeks to increase the number of subscribers to reach a specific teledensity. In the Untied States, a more likely definition of successful infrastructure expansion is that anyone in a region willing to pay the given rate for a specified service should be able to get it. A milestone might even be so flexible that it does not specify whether the firm has to make phone service or Internet service available (at least in nations like Guinea and Haiti where those are offered through separate infrastructure (Peha 1999)). Whatever the form, a set of N_r clear milestones ($N_r \geq 1$) must be defined for each region r. The N_rth milestone meets the objective for expansion in region r. There are a total of $\Sigma_{8r} N_r$ milestones to achieve.

A typical build-out requirement might mandate that milestone i in every region must be competed by time T_i, but greater flexibility would improve efficiency. Investment could take place more quickly in some regions than others to maximize economies of scope and scale. Furthermore, there is strong financial incentive to time an infrastructure upgrade appropriately when equipment costs and demand are changing, and it is difficult for a regulator to motivate efficient timing with typical regulatory tools like price regulation (Wang and Peha 1997). The national interest is served as long as telecommunications carriers are making progress towards their assigned objectives at a reasonable rate. Thus, we might require that industry meet a specific number of milestones each year, without specifying which ones will be met. There should therefore be up to $\Sigma_{8r} N_r$ commitments outstanding, where a commitment requires that some milestone be met by the associated deadline. This deadline may differ from one commitment to another. If the number of outstanding milestones exceeds the number of outstanding commitments, then the government is implicitly allowing industry to achieve the milestones that cost the least.

Consider a firm with seven milestones, and five commitments. The firm is free to match each commitment with a milestone in any way that the firm chooses, corresponding to its strategy for infrastructure expansion. When a commitment is due, if the firm has not successfully met the requirements of any milestone that it currently holds, then that firm will be fined. Commitments are therefore liabilities, as they obligate a firm to either pay fines or invest capital to avoid those fines. Milestones are assets, as one needs a milestone in order to avoid paying a fine.

Firms are free to buy, sell, and trade milestones and commitments, alone or in combination. Thus, a firm that cannot meet the deadline associated with a given commitment may pay another firm to take that commitment. This exchange could bring capital to another firm that has a more aggressive expansion plan. For example, a low earth orbit (LEO) satellite provider that is still several years from operation might seek out later commitments, while firms that are expanding aggressively accept the earlier commitments, for a price. Firms would also be free to exchange milestones, allowing each to put together a portfolio of obligations that can be met efficiently. Where there is an economy of scope, a firm will seek to either obtain or divest of all complementary obligations.

If industry is free to select which milestones to meet at a given commitment deadline, the milestones should be of comparable social benefit. If this is not the case, a weight $w(r,i)$ might reflect the estimated social value of the ith milestone in region r. Commitments would also have weights, indicating how much must be accomplished by the given deadline. The sum of the weights of all milestones should equal or exceed the sum of the weights of all commitments.

What if the regional boundaries are not conducive to minimizing cost? With regulator approval, a firm might divide a milestone into two pieces such that the sum of the weights is less than or equal to that of the original milestone. The regulator will ensure that the relative weights assigned to each piece are reasonable. Commitments can also be divided, although regulator scrutiny is unnecessary in that case, provided that the total weight does not change.

Efficiency of Tradable Obligations

Tradable obligations allow industry to come close to minimizing the long-term costs of meeting commitments. Let k_c be the cost of meeting commitment cs deadline for the milestone associated under the current configuration of obligations, where cost is the net present value of infrastructure deployment and operating expenses minus revenues. $K = \Sigma_{8c}\, k_c$ is the total cost under current obligation assignments, and K' is the minimum cost of meeting current commitments under an optimal assignment. T is the maximum transaction costs of a trade, which includes identifying and negotiating a profitable trade. If $K > K' + T$, then there exists a trade that would reduce costs and benefit all parties involved. As long as transaction cost T is small, this approach is efficient.

In some markets, transaction cost T can be fairly large, especially when the number of firms grows large. However, in this case, T is probably small, for several reasons. First, the number of firms in a developing country is generally small. Second, firms can typically easily identify obligations that complement their own. Third, the government can and should require the registry of who possesses which milestone or commitment to be public, making it easy to find useful trading partners. Fourth, because each firm knows the obligations held by its trading partners, it has some idea which obligations others might value and how much.

Who Can Accept Obligations?

Because firms are trading obligations (liabilities) rather than permits (assets), there is a danger that a firm with many outstanding obligations could go bankrupt. Indeed, in the absence of some protection, this is a tempting strategy for borrowing money; a pharmaceutical company could raise money by accepting many universal service commitments, with no intention of building telecommunications infrastructure. The company would later either 'repay' the money by paying a telecommunications carrier to accept the commitments, or it would simply declare bankruptcy. A simple requirement that a firm must have at least as many milestones as commitments might curb the most flagrant abuses.

One way to further reduce the likelihood of this is to regulate who can accept universal service obligations. A firm need not have any telecommunications expertise, any more than a stock broker who sells agricultural futures must know how to run a farm. However, a firm must have the financial resources to be held accountable if obligations are not met. Firms that wish to own commitments could first prove their solvency to a regulator, and perhaps declare collateral.

The other approach is to require that when a firm goes bankrupt, its commitments for universal service revert back to the previous owner. The regulator could then auction the milestones of a bankrupt carrier to those firms who were forced to take back its commitments, or the milestones could be auctioned to all interested bidders. This approach will discourage firms from giving universal service commitments to unstable companies. In effect, small companies and co-operatives can accept universal service obligations, while the larger firms that have demonstrated solvency to the state provide bankruptcy insurance.

The First Years after Deployment

It is not sufficient to simply lay cable in a costly region; firms must provide services for a specified period of years to avoid fines. That period can begin once the commitment has officially been met.

Achieving the commitment may trigger other regulatory responses as well. Normally, if a telecommunications monopoly emerges in a given region, that monopoly should be price regulated. However, limiting a company's profits right after it makes a large capital investment is not the best way to encourage expansion. The regulator can grant a predefined period of relative freedom from price regulation that begins when the commitment is met, or if a company fails to meet its commitments on time, when the fines begin.

Initial Distribution of Obligations

Previous sections discuss how universal service obligations can be met, or traded. Before any of this can happen, they must somehow be distributed. Since the trading phase will tend to minimize costs, the principal objective in the distribution of obligations is to minimize subsidies. This can be achieved in an open and competitive environment through use of an auction.

Designing an auction to minimize subsidies when there are potential economies of scope is nontrivial. With a small number of items to auction N, one possibility is to ask firms to bid on each of the 2^N-1 possible combinations of these items, as in a generalized Vickrey auction (Clarke 1971; Groves and Loeb 1975; Vickrey 1961). However, N would generally be too large to use this approach for universal service obligations. (Recall that Chile covered 46 regions and over 1300 localities in their first auction alone.) This is an open and active research area (Kelly and Steinberg 1998).

A great deal can be achieved with a simple ascending simultaneous auction in which firms bid on each individual item until there are no more bids on any item, and the firm with the largest bid for a given item gets it. Combining sets of obligations into appropriate packages is the key to reducing subsidies. Obviously, if two obligations complement each other, that is the value of the combination exceeds the sum of their individual values, they should be bundled together.

Even when there are no such economies of scope, bundling helps considerably (Cameron *et al.* 1997; Milgrom 1997; Palfrey 1983), especially when there are a limited number of bidders. For example, Firm A can serve region 1 for a subsidy of 50, and region 2 for 100. Conversely, Firm B can serve region 1 for 100, and region 2 for 50. When regions are auctioned separately, Firm A will get region 1 the first time it bids 100 or less. The same occurs for Firm B with region 2, so the total subsidy is roughly 200. If the regions were bundled, bidding would continue until one firm accepted a subsidy ≤ 150. (The winner would then promptly trade away one of the regions. This again demonstrates the value of tradable obligations; they make tolerable the inevitable tradeoff in auction design (Milgrom 1997) between minimizing subsidies and minimizing infrastructure expansion costs.) Bundling often reduces subsidies, especially when there are only a handful of bidders. Indeed, when there are only two interested bidders and minimum bid increments are small, bundling always reduces subsidies.[2]

When a package of universal service obligations (both commitments and milestones) is auctioned alone, the auction determines the government's cash subsidy, similar to the Chilean approach described earlier. It is also possible to bundle these obligations with a resource of value, as with build-out requirements. Universal service obligations may be bundled with a state-owned carrier that is being privatized, with a spectrum licence, or simply a licence to operate. Licences can be exclusive or non-exclusive, and may or may not leave the licence-holder subject to regulation in the initial years.

When bundling obligations and resources, there is no administrative overhead and no risk that money will be sidetracked, as opposed to cases where revenues are collected during privatization and then disseminated through auctions. Note that the valuable resources should also be tradable. In the case of spectrum, rules must be established on the flexibility that licence-holders have to use spectrum for applications other than telecommunications, which influence both the value and the economies of scope; there are many tradeoffs in this decision (Peha 1998; Peha and Panichpapiboon 2004; Peha 2005).

The bidding itself can take different forms, depending on the national objectives. At one extreme, the assets, milestones, and commitments are fixed, and are given to whoever will pay the most for them. At the other extreme, the price might be fixed, where the winner is the one that will accept the most or earliest commitments. Intermediate forms are also possible.

SUMMARY

This chapter has presented a highly flexible policy of tradable obligations to advance universal service in the context of competing private-sector carriers. Firms receive tradable universal service obligations in the form of milestones that must be met, and commitments to meet deadlines.

Tradable obligations motivate private firms to bring given services to areas where these services have not been available. The approach could be used to improve the availability of telephone lines, Internet points of presence, broadcast radio stations, electric power, or even toll roads. Developing countries may adopt the approach to expand basic telephone infrastructure, especially when privatizing or introducing competition. At these times, obligations can be distributed along with the incumbent's assets or permission to compete. Obligations could also be distributed with other resources, such as spectrum (as in Guatemala) or cash subsidies (as in Chile).

Tradable obligations are technology neutral. Like build-out requirements, this approach allows private sector firms to accept obligations at subsidies that are determined through a market mechanism (an auction) without requiring the government to collect and distribute funds. Like the Chilean universal service fund approach, tradable obligations allow a government to prioritize needs and target subsidies based on cost-benefit ratios.

A tradable-obligations policy is the only approach that allows each carrier to determine which set of milestones and which deadlines it can meet most cost-effectively, while still insuring continual progress towards the desired final state. Exchange of milestones and commitments does not diminish the obligations that must be met by industry as a whole, insuring the timely expansion of infrastructure in a manner that meets social objectives. By exchanging its commitments, a firm can increase or decrease the rate at which it must expand infrastructure. By exchanging milestones, a firm can change where it must expand infrastructure. Making milestones and commitments independent and fully tradable allows each firm to develop the most cost effective business plan possible. Indeed, tradable obligations allow firms to change their strategies dynamically as technology and demand evolve. This is impossible with build-out requirements, where the regulator acts as central planner, determining everything in advance. With the universal service fund approach, obligations are determined via auction. This also yields less cost effective results when there are economies of scope among the items being auctioned.

Unlike a system of targeted implicit subsidies, a policy of tradable universal service obligations will transition easily to a regulatory environment in which areas with monopolies are regulated, areas with competition are not regulated, and no (uncompensated) accident of history will leave one player with a greater universal service burden than another.

NOTES

1. This chapter is derivative of Peha, Jon M. (1999), 'Tradable Universal Service Obligations,' *Telecommunications Policy*, **23**(5), 363–74.
2. When regions are auctioned, the firm offering to accept the smaller subsidy wins, but the winner's subsidy is roughly what the other firm would accept. X_r and Y_r are the subsidies firms A and B will accept for region r, respectively. When regions are auctioned separately, the total subsidy is $\Sigma_{\theta r} \max(X_r, Y_r)$. When both regions are auctioned as a package, the total subsidy is $\max(\Sigma_{\theta r} X_r, \Sigma_{\theta r} Y_r)$, which is $\leq \Sigma_{\theta r} \max(X_r, Y_r)$.

REFERENCES

Cabarios, Edgardo V. and Aurora A. Rubio (1998) 'Rates Regulation in the Philippines,' *Regulators Workshop*, February.
Cameron, Lisa, Peter Cramton and Robert Wilson (1997) 'Using Auctions to Divest Generating Assets,' *The Electricity Journal*, **10**(10), 22–31.
Clarke, E. (1971) 'Multipart Pricing of Public Goods,' *Public Choice*, **8**, 19–33.
Ghana Ministry of Transport and Communications (1994) Telecom-munications Policy for an Accelerated Development Programme.
Groves, Theodore and M. Loeb (1975) 'Incentives and Public Inputs,' *Journal of Public Economics*, **4**, 311–26.
Kelly, Frank and Richard Steinberg (1998) 'A Combinatorial Auction with Multiple Winners for Universal Service,' www.statslab.cam.ac.uk/~frank/ AUCTION, June.
Milgrom, Paul (1997) 'Putting Auction Theory To Work: The Simultaneous Ascending Auction,' www-econ.stanford.edu/econ/workp/swp98002.pdf.
Milgrom, Paul (1998) 'Combination Bidding in Spectrum Auctions,' *Proceedings of the Telecommunications Policy Research Conference*, October, Section 13, 34–8.

Palfrey, Thomas (1983) 'Bundling Decisions by a Multiproduct Monopolist with Incomplete Information,' *Econometrica*, **51**, 463–83.

Peha, Jon M. (1998) 'Spectrum Management Policy Options,' *IEEE Communications Surveys*, **1**(1), also at www.ece.cmu.edu/~peha/ papers.html.

Peha, Jon M. (1999a) 'Haiti's Wireless Path to Internet Growth,' *Communications of the ACM*, **42**(6), 67–72, also at www.ece.cmu.edu/~ peha/papers.html

Peha, Jon M. (1999b) 'Tradable Universal Service Obligations,' *Telecommunications Policy*, **23**(5), 363–74.

Peha, Jon M. (2005) 'Approaches to Spectrum Sharing,' *IEEE Communications*, **43**(2), 10–12, also at www.ece.cmu.edu/~peha/ papers.html.

Peha, Jon M. and Sooksan Panichpapiboon (2004) 'Real-Time Secondary Markets for Spectrum,' *Telecommunications Policy*, **28**(7–8), 603–18, also at www.ece.cmu.edu/~peha/papers.html.

Peha, Jon M. and Saurabh Tewari (1998) 'The Results of Competition Between Integrated-Services Telecommunications Carriers,' *Information Economics and Policy*, **10**(1), 127–55, also at www.ece.cmu.edu/~peha/ papers.html.

Petrazzini, Ben A. (1996) 'Telecommunications Policy in India: The Political Underpinnings of Reform,' *Telecommunications Policy*, **20**(1), 39–51.

Sinha, Nikhail (1996) 'The Political Economy of India's Telecommunication Reform,' *Telecommunications Policy*, **20**(1), 23–38.

Tyler, Michael , William Letwin and Christopher Roe (1995), 'Universal Service and Innovation in Telecommunication Services,' *Telecommunications Policy*, **19**(1), 3–20.

Vickrey, William (1961) 'Counterspeculation, Auctions, and Competitive Sealed Tenders,' *Journal of Finance*, **16**, 8–37.

Wang, Qiong, Jon M. Peha, and Marvin Sirbu (1997) 'Optimal Pricing for Integrated-Services Networks,' in Joseph Bailey and Lee McKnight (eds) *Internet Economics*, Cambridge, MA: MIT Press, pp. 353–76, also at www.ece.cmu.edu/~peha/papers.html.

Wang, Qiong and Jon M. Peha (1997) 'Proactive Price Regulation for Upgrading Telecommunications Infrastructure,' *Information Economics and Policy*, **9**(2), 161–76, also at www.ece.cmu.edu/~peha/papers.html.

Wellenius, Bjorn (1997) 'Extending Telecommunications Services to Rural Areas – The Chilean Experience,' *Viewpoint*, The World Bank Group, Note No. 105.

12. Conclusion: the de/reregulatory cycle: learning and spill-over effects in regulatory policy-making

Michael Howlett

The chapters in this book show that as in North America and Europe, regulatory regimes in the Asia Pacific region have evolved gradually, emerging in response to the turbulence caused by industrialization and the growth of unfettered market capitalism (Eisner 1993, 1994a and 1994b). Its development, in fact, is co-terminus with that of the enhancement of the bureaucratic capacity of the modern state (Hodgetts 1964; Skowronek 1982). As an inexpensive and plentiful source of government control, it was often invoked by governments eager to reduce their direct government agency-level involvement in ongoing monitoring and enforcement of government policies.

Although regulation was often opposed by industry and many professional economists as promoting inefficiency, it was generally accepted in mainstream policy circles as essential for addressing market imperfections and dealing with the uncertainties of modern economic and social life. It is only recently that a broad body of opinion emerged which regards regulations as often inefficient and burdensome for the state itself (Cheung 2005). Subscribers to this point of view particularly dwell on the pervasive impact of globalization which they believe has not only undermined the need for regulations due to overwhelming market pressures but also eroded governments' capacity to enforce them against increasingly mobile capital (for a review of this literature, see Kahler 2004). Lack of convincing empirical evidence to support this view has not weakened subscription to it or its acceptance in policy circles.

The chapters in this volume, however, show that the expansion of reservations and even antipathy towards regulations can lead to two quite distinct movements: towards, on the one hand, 'regulatory reform' and, on the other, 'deregulation'. These two movements are quite different and represent two separate approaches to resolving 'the regulatory dilemma' (Birch 1984).

REGULATORY REFORM VERSUS DEREGULATION AS POLICY PROCESSES

As Eisner has pointed out, deregulatory activities and regulatory reforms, or streamlining, are often juxtaposed (Eisner 1994a and 1994b). However, while regulatory reform has involved activities such as the mandating of cost-benefit analyses before the enactment of any new rules, deregulation involves wholesale roll back and even abolition of existing rules (McGarity 1991).

Understanding why deregulation occurs has proven to be a challenge to regulatory theorists, since many of the imperatives regarded as the source of regulation – such as industry collusion and the desire to retain market share through the erection of barriers to entry to new firms – continue to be vital in the deregulatory context (Crew and Rowley 1986). Some analysts have therefore searched for exogenous causes – such as foreign or technical pressures for regulatory harmonization (Lazer and Mayer-Schonberger 2002; Garcia-Murillo 2005) or the penetration of new ideas into existing regulatory regimes – in order to understand deregulation. Although insightful, these suggestions are equally incompatible with earlier theories of regulation, since they involve granting a great deal more autonomy to the state in responding to, or leading, change than is usually assumed by regulatory theorists (Derthick and Quirk 1985; Quirk 1988).

As Libecap has argued, ultimately:

> Five conjectures regarding the forces underlying deregulation are offered: i) dissatisfied incumbent firms join with consumers in lobbying for deregulation and seek to capture quasi-rents during the transition to a more competitive environment; ii) stockholders, dismayed at poor firm performance, pressure management to jettison regulation; iii) management chafes at government restrictions; iv) regulators lose enthusiasm for regulatory controls, and v) exogenous forces, such as changes in regulatory policies in other jurisdictions force adoption of more competitive arrangements. (Libecap 1986, p. 72)

These arguments, of course, do not explain why these actors act this way, or why this activity should have occurred when it did. A suitable explanation, however, is one which argues that these events occurred as the social and/or economic basis of the previous regulatory status quo was undermined by evolving technological and economic changes, spurring state, economic and social actors to search for a new arrangement (Torres 2004). Deregulation, in this sense, is simply a different set of regulatory arrangements developed by the same sets of actors, pursuing the same sets of motivations, that led to the development of regulation in the first place. That is, it is not a different process but a different result emerging from the same 'regulatory imperative' which, under different conditions, led to the creation or establishment of an initial regulatory regime or framework. Regulation and deregulation are two different phases in the same cycle of government activity and can therefore be understood by utilizing the same analytical concepts and methods.

THE DEREGULATORY IMPERATIVE: CAUSES AND CONSEQUENCES

What are the conditions and circumstances, then, which lead to transitions between phases in the regulatory cycle? The cases presented in this volume highlight the importance of changes in social, economic or technological conditions which undermine the economic or social basis of the previous stage. Hence, as in North America and Europe where the development of large-scale enterprises and corporate trusts undermined earlier regimes based on competitive market conditions, fed public discontent, and led to the regulatory compromise between capital and the state in many counties in the late nineteenth and early twentieth centuries (Eisner 1993, 1994a and 1994b), so similar movements led to reform efforts in the Asia Pacific and Latin America in the 1990s and later (Cheung 2005; Hira *et al.* 2005). Similarly in the case of deregulation, the economic and technological processes associated with globalisation undermined many elements of the regulatory compromise and led both firms and governments to seek arrangements allowing regulated industries to compete more effectively on the world stage (Garcia-Murillo 2005).

This is an example of the oft-noted tendency for 'systemic perturbations' – a formal term provided to describe the external crises which upset established policy routines – to affect policy dynamics (Meyer 1982). In East Asia, the most pronounced manifestation of systemic perturbations was the economic recession of the mid-1980s and the late 1990s. The former was widely interpreted as significantly a result of excessive government meddling in the economy which needed to be rolled back if the economies were to regain their international competitiveness. This was followed by a wave of privatization and deregulation and the advocates of these measures felt vindicated as the economies in the region began to grow at even a faster rate than in pre-recession days. The economic contagion that erupted in 1997, in contrast to its predecessor, was blamed on the lack of an appropriate and strong regulatory framework to take contemporary economic imperatives, especially capital mobility, into account. This realization was followed by a spate of new regulations and tightening of existing regulations with the objective of providing a stable framework for market competition.

Deregulation was, of course, driven by other forces as well, notably the 'ratchet' or 'imitation' effect of new arrangements. Once some industries achieve a measure of protection from their competitors, the allure of this to other businesses is evident and results in agitation and pressure for similar treatment in different sectors. Similarly, when some firms escape from regulatory regimes which threaten their survival in the face of new sources of competition, the demand for deregulation also enjoys a 'ratchet'-like effect (Hammond and Knott 1988).

This, again, is an example of a more general process of policy change – policy learning – whereby policy-makers and participants adjust their behaviour based on their knowledge of their own and others' experience with similar policies (Heclo 1974). What is learned is often the experiences of other jurisdictions, but can also involve reflection on experiences originating within the confines of a subsystems' existing boundaries (Rose 1991 and 1993; Olsen and Peters 1996). This behaviour can result in a variety of feedback-like policy learning processes (Pierson 1993; Knoepfel and Kissling-Naf 1998) which include instances ranging from those in which policy actors in one country investigate and report on activities in another, to situations in which administrators attempt to emulate 'best practices' in service delivery. While some types of learning are limited to reflections on existing practices, other types are much more far-reaching and can affect a wide range of policy elements (Bennett and Howlett 1992; May 1992; Torres 2004). Chapters in the book capture numerous instances of such policy emulation and learning. Asher and Nandy refer to emulation of international best practices in pension management while Goyal does the same for regulation of capital markets in India. Lampietti *et al.*, Skoufa, Todac, and Wu and Sulistiyanto in their respective chapters in the book refer to different levels and types of deregulation of the electricity sector in the Asia Pacific region which followed similar prior efforts in other countries.

A similar, third, process affecting policy change is 're-framing' and its associated institutional counterpart 'venue shifting'. In this scenario, policy change occurs as a result of an alteration in the strategies policy actors follow to pursue their interests (Schattschneider 1960). This usually involves members of policy communities attempting to redefine policy issues in order to facilitate the alteration of the location in which policy formulation occurs (Baumgartner and Jones 1993). In this case, it involves actors lobbying judicial or legislative actors to break-up established administrative arrangements. Skoufa and Todac in their chapters allude to such efforts to reframe the understanding of deregulation in the power sector in the Asia Pacific region.

A fourth very important process involves the impact that previous phases of the regulatory cycle have on the next, a form of what Paul Pierson terms 'policy feedback' (Pierson 1992 and 1993). That is, some authors see deregulation occurring as an unintended consequence of the previous stage of regulation. Some see this as simply an inevitable consequence of imperfect governments trying to create perfect regulatory arrangements (Roots 2004), but others see more specific mechanisms at work. As David Dery has suggested, crowded 'policy spaces' or 'tightly coupled systems' involve plentiful external effects as changes made in one sector or issue-area spill-over into another:

> Given a high degree of inter-relatedness in public policy, it is reasonable to look for some of the crucial independent variables of policy success and failure not only in the attributes of a given policy, or those of the problem addressed, or in the politics that surround public policy making or in implementation apparatuses, but also in what other policies impose on it ... policy-makers wish to make policy [...] but inevitably end up adjusting to neighboring policies. (Dery 1999, p. 164)

A very important source of policy feedback in the Asia-Pacific region has been subsystem spill-overs which occur in situations in which activities in otherwise distinct subsystems transcend old policy boundaries and affect the structure or behaviour of other subsystems (Haas 1958; Keohane and Hoffman 1991). Instances such as those which have occurred as Internet-based computing collided with existing telecommunications regimes, or when long-established natural resource policy actors find it necessary to deal with Aboriginal land claims issues, are examples of this phenomenon. Spill-overs can occur on specific issues without any permanent change in subsystem membership – subsystem intersection – or they can be more long-term in nature – subsystem convergence (Grant and MacNamara 1995; Hoberg and Morawaski 1997). The chapter by Lampietti *et al.* provides a comprehensive account of the numerous spill-over effects found in the reform of electricity regulations in Central Asia and Eastern Europe.

REREGULATION AS A THIRD STAGE IN THE REGULATORY POLICY CYCLE

Does this same logic apply to the third phase of the regulatory cycle, 'reregulation'? While we are still at the early stages of understanding the reregulated environment in the Asia-Pacific region, the case studies in this volume suggest a positive answer. In terms of systemic perturbations, we have the settling down or 'solidification' of globalization, as the first wave of changes brought about by internationalization were consolidated (Howlett and Ramesh 2002). With the elements of the new status quo visible, firms and publics can once again demand regulatory regularization of new relationships (Lodge 2003; Pollitt 2001a and 2001b). This was evident in the aftermath of the Asian Financial Crises which saw the institution of new and tighter regulations in a variety of sectors, notably capital markets.

With respect to policy learning, as Eisner pointed out as early as the late 1980s, once the effects of deregulation become known, then their evaluation can take place:

> The growing concentration in the airline industry and the instability in commercial finance have stimulated debates concerning the need for reregulation. As existing regulations and the effects of deregulation are subjected to critical scrutiny and efforts are initiated to adjust the regulatory system, one can expect the goals to change once again to reflect contemporary problems and concerns. (Eisner 1994b, p. 113)

And, with respect to venue shifting and other kinds of strategic actions undertaken by key policy actors, Grantham, for example, has noted how deregulatory activity, like the regulatory activity which preceded it, can alter the network of actors and interests involved in policy promotion and defence of the status quo – leading to a reregulatory imperative (Grantham 2001; Wilks and Battle 2003). In the Asia-Pacific region, this is evident in areas as disparate as telecommunications, banking, and of course, the environment.

All of this is made much more complicated by the kinds of spill-overs and externalities that exist in increasingly dense policy spaces (Milner and Keohane 1996). As nations and international policies intersect, the potential for spill-overs greatly increases, often driving the reregulatory agenda. The chapters on electricity and capital markets sectors in this volume point to the many unanticipated consequences of deregulation which have had to be, or need to be, addressed through new regulations.

CONCLUSION: DE/REREGULATION AS MATCHED PROCESSES

The de/reregulatory cycle found in the Asia-Pacific region is a good example of these general regulatory dynamics and its study helps shed light not only on developments in the region, but also, more generally on the little studied deregulatory and reregulatory aspects of the regulatory cycle.

The chapters in this book make it clear that a key to understanding the regulatory/deregulatory/reregulatory cycle is to think of regulation as only one part, or link, in an overall governance system (Elkin 1986; Minogue 2002). These systems vary in terms of the nature of the linkages they contain, especially in terms of the number of linkages and the 'tightness' of their links (Perrow 1984). As Dery has argued, the nature of the linkages that exist in governance systems is critical for policy-making: 'Public policy making is

[…] a precarious venture: Externalities and unanticipated consequences are as likely to follow as intended outcomes' (Dery 1999, p. 164).

Designing policies to take into account these externalities is very difficult and helps to explain why 'unanticipated consequences' have been prevalent in regulatory rearrangements (Wenig 2004). That is, not only do changes in the external environment affect the nature of the 'policy space' and hence the kinds of interactions which occur in the policies found within it, but alterations within one system also upset arrangements made in other sectors and areas (Dietzenbacher 2000). Nevertheless, conceiving of de-reregulatory processes as a cycle of inter-linked activity helps to make sense of these policy phenomena, not only in the Asia Pacific region, but wherever they occur.

REFERENCES

Baumgartner, Frank R. and Bryan D. Jones (1993) *Agendas and Instability in American Politics,* Chicago, IL: University of Chicago Press.

Bennett, Colin J. and Michael Howlett (1992) 'The Lessons of Learning: Reconciling Theories of Policy Learning and Policy Change,' *Policy Sciences,* **25**(3), 275–94.

Birch, A. H. (1984) 'Overload, Ungovernability and Delegitimization: The Theories and the British Case,' *British Journal of Political Science,* **14**, 136–60.

Cheung, Anthony B. L. (2005) 'The Politics of Administrative Reforms in Asia: Paradigms and Legacies, Paths and Diversities,' *Governance,* **18**(2), 257–82.

Crew, Michael A. and Charles K. Rowley (1986) 'Deregulation as an Instrument in Industrial Policy,' *Journal of Institutional and Theoretical Economics,* **142**, 52–70.

Derthick, Martha and Paul J. Quirk (1985) *The Politics of Deregulation,* Washington, DC: Brookings Institute.

Dery, David (1999) 'Policy by the Way: When Policy is Incidental to Making Other Policies,' *Journal of Public Policy,* **18**(2), 163–176.

Dietzenbacher, Erik (2000) 'Spillovers of Innovation Effects,' *Journal of Policy Modeling,* **22**(1), 27–42.

Eisner, Marc Allen (1993) *Regulatory Politics in Transition,* Baltimore, MD: Johns Hopkins University Press.

Eisner, Marc Allen (1994a) 'Discovering Patterns in Regulatory History: Continuity, Change and Regulatory Regimes,' *Journal of Policy History,* **6**(2), 157–87.

Eisner, Marc Allen (1994b) 'Economic Regulatory Policies: Regulation and Deregulation in Historical Context,' in D. H. Rosenbloom and R. D. Schwartz (eds), *Handbook of Regulation and Administrative Law,* New York: Marcel Dekker, pp. 91–116.

Elkin, Stephen L. (1986) 'Regulation and Regime: A Comparative Analysis,' *Journal of Public Policy,* **6**(1), 49–72.

Garcia-Murillo, Martha (2005) 'Regulatory Responses to Convergence; Experience from Four Countries,' *Info – The Journal of Policy, Regulation and Strategy for Telecommunications,* **7**(1), 20–40.

Grant, Wyn and Anne MacNamara (1995) 'When Policy Communities Intersect: The Cases of Agriculture and Banking,' *Political Studies,* **43**, 509–15.

Grantham, Andrew (2001) 'How Networks Explain Unintended Policy Implementation Outcomes: the Case of UK Rail Privatization,' *Public Administration*, **79**(4), 851–70.

Haas, Ernst B. (1958) *The Uniting of Europe: Political, Social and Economical Forces 1950–1957*, London: Stevens and Sons.

Hammond, Thomas H. and Jack H. Knott (1988) 'The Deregulatory Snowball: Explaining Deregulation in the Financial Industry,' *Journal of Politics*, **50**(1), 3–30.

Heclo, Hugh Modern (1974) *Social Politics in Britain and Sweden: From Relief to Income Maintenance*, New Haven, CT: Yale University Press.

Hira, Anil, David Huxtable and Alexandre Leger (2005) 'Deregulation and Participation: An international Survey of Participation in Electricity Regulation,' *Governance*, **18**(1), 53–88.

Hoberg, G. and E. Morawaski (1997) 'Policy Change Through Sector Intersection: Forest and Aboriginal Policy in Clayoquot Sound,' *Canadian Public Administration*, **40**(3), 387–414.

Hodgetts, J. E. (1964) 'Challenge and Response: A Retrospective View of the Public Service of Canada,' *Canadian Public Administration*, 7(4), 409–21.

Howlett, Michael and M. Ramesh (2002) 'The Policy Effects of Internationalization: A Subsystem Adjustment Analysis of Policy Change,' *Journal of Comparative Policy Analysis*, **4**(3), 31–50.

Kahler, Miles (2004) *Modeling Races to the Bottom*, unpublished paper http://irpshome.ucsd.edu/faculty/mkahler/RaceBott.pdf.

Keohane, Robert O. and Stanley Hoffman (1991) 'Institutional Change in Europe in the 1980s,' in Robert O. Keohane and Stanley Hoffman (eds), *The New European Community: Decision-Making and Institutional Change*, Boulder, CO: Westview, pp. 1–40.

Knoepfel, Peter and Ingrid Kissling-Naf (1998) 'Social Learning in Policy Networks,' *Policy and Politics*, **26**(3), 343–67.

Lazer, David and Viktor Mayer-Schonberger (2002) 'Governing Networks: Telecommunication Deregulation in Europe and the United States,' *Brooklyn Journal of International Law*, 3, 820–51.

Libecap, Gary D. (1986) 'Deregulation as an Instrument in Industrial Policy: Comment,' *Journal of Institutional and Theoretical Economics*, **142**, 70–74.

Lodge, Martin (2003) 'Institutional Choice and Policy Transfer: Reforming British and German Railway Regulation,' *Governance*, **16**(2), 159–78.

Marion, Russ (1999) *The Edge of Organization: Chaos and Complexity Theories of Formal Social Systems*, London: Sage.

May, Peter J. (1992) 'Policy Learning And Failure,' *Journal Of Public Policy*, **12**(4), 331–54.

McGarity, Thomas O. (1991) *Reinventing Rationality: The Role of Regulatory Analysis in the Federal Bureaucracy*, New York: Cambridge University Press.

Merton, Robert K. (1936) 'The Unanticipated Consequences of Purposive Social Action,' *American Sociological Review*, **6**, 1894–904.

Meyer, Alan D. (1982) 'Adapting to Environmental Jolts,' *Administrative Science Quarterly*, **27**, 515–37.

Milner, Helen V. and Robert O. Keohane (1996) 'Internationalization and Domestic Politics: A Conclusion,' in R. O. Keohane and H. V. Milner (eds), *Internationalization and Domestic Politics*, Cambridge: Cambridge University Press, pp. 243–58.

Minogue, M. (2002) 'Governance-Based Analysis of Regulation,' *Annals of Public and Cooperative Economics*, **73**(4), 649–66.

Olsen, Johan P. and B. Guy Peters (eds) (1996) *Lessons From Experience: Experiential Learning in Administrative Reforms in Eight Democracies*, Oslo: Scandinavian University Press.

Perrow, Charles (1984) *Normal Accidents: Living with High Risk Technologies*, New York: Basic Books.

Pierson, Paul (1992) '"Policy Feedbacks" and Political Change: Contrasting Reagan and Thatcher's Pension Reform Initiatives,' *Studies in American Political Development*, **6**(2), 361–92.

Pierson, Paul (1993) 'When Effect Becomes Cause: Policy Feedback and Political Change,' *World Politics*, **45**, 595–628.

Pollitt, C. (2001a) 'Convergence: the Useful Myth?,' *Public Administration*, **79**(4), 933–47.

Pollitt, Christopher (2001b) 'Clarifying Convergence: Striking Similarities and Durable Differences in Public Management Reform,' *Public Management Review*, **4**(1), 471–92.

Quirk, Paul J. (1988) 'In Defense of the Politics of Ideas,' *The Journal of Politics*, **50**, 31–45.

Roots, Roger I. (2004) 'When Laws Backfire: Unintended Consequences of Public Policy,' *American Behavioral Scientist*, **47**(11), 1376–94.

Rose, Richard (1991) 'What is Lesson-Drawing,' *Journal of Public Policy*, **11**(1), 3–30.

Rose, Richard (1993) *Lesson-Drawing in Public Policy: A Guide to Learning Across Time and Space,* Chatham: Chatham House Publishing.

Schattschneider, E. E. (1960) *The Semisovereign People; A Realist's View of Democracy in America*, New York: Holt, Rinehart and Winston.

Skowronek, Stephen (1982) *Building a New American State: The Expansion of National Administrative Capacities 1877–1920*, Cambridge: Cambridge University Press.

Torres, Lourdes (2004) 'Trajectories in Public Administration Reforms in European Continental Countries,' *Australian Journal of Public Administration*, **63**(3), 99–112.

Wenig, Michael M. and Patricia Sutherland (2004) 'Considering the Upstream/Downstream Effects of the Mackenzie Pipeline: Rough Paddling for the National Energy Board,' *Resources*, **86**, 1–8.

Wilks, Stephen and Ian Battle (2003) 'The Unanticipated Consequences of Creating Independent Competition Agencies,' in M. Thatcher and A. Stone Sweet (eds), *The Politics of Delegation*, London: Frank Cass, pp. 148–72.

Index

9/11 attack 30

abatement technologies 70
Abbott, J. 30
ACCC 82, 97, 98, 99, 100
accountability 151, 154, 158–9, 160,
 162, 163, 164, 187, 223
acid deposition 125
actuarial analysis 159–60
ADB 147
adverse selection 172
AEMC 98
AER 98
ageing population 152, 153
agency problem 88, 151, 162, 172
air pollution 3, 53, 68–72, 85–7, 124,
 125, 131–7, 138, 209, 220
 see also carbon dioxide emissions;
  CFCs; nitrogen oxide emissions;
  particulate matter; sulphur
  dioxide emissions
air transportation 15, 40
Airbus 21
Akerlof, G. 15
Albony, Y. 116
Albouy, Y. 147
Almaty 69, 71
Amendola, V. 82
AMEX 174
Amsden, A. 17
Anderson, Arthur 5, 32
Andrews, R. 5
Angus, W.H. 1
annual reports 159
anti-dumping procedures 21
anti-trust regulations 14, 16, 21
Antons, C. 20
Apogee Research 147
APRC 171
Armenia
 education expenditure in 51

electricity sector in 49, 51, 52, 54, 56,
 57, 58, 60, 61, 62, 64, 66, 70
gas consumption in 66, 70
income transfers in 68
indoor air pollution in 72
non-network energy use in 55, 70
Armstrong, D. 30
Armstrong, M. 94
arrears 60, 66, 67
Arvis, J.-F. 19
Asher, M.G. 158, 160, 165
Asia Pacific Review Committee (APRC)
 171
Asian Development Bank (ADB) 147
Asian Financial Crisis (AFC) 13, 36,
 151, 163, 168, 189, 230, 232–3
 and developmental state 18–21
 and IPPs 109, 110, 117–19, 126
asymmetric information 5, 15, 31, 83,
 169, 171–2, 177
AT&T 214
auctions *see* competitive bidding
Aussie Power 97
Australia
 electricity sector in 81, 85–8, 90–94,
  97–101, 102
 provident and pension funds in 161
Australian Competition and Consumer
 Commission (ACCC) 82, 97, 98,
 99, 100
Australian Energy Market Commission
 (AEMC) 98
Australian Energy Regulator (AER)
 98
Austrian School 171
autonomous regulatory agencies 35
Ayres, I. 199
Azerbaijan
 electricity sector in 49, 52, 53, 56, 70
 health and education expenditure in 51
 indoor air pollution in 72

Printed and bound by CPI Group (UK) Ltd, Croydon, CR0 4YY

23/04/2025

14660988-0003